bistronomy

—

NOUN
French casual fine dining: refined and inventive food,
relaxed attitude, scaled-down prices

ETYMOLOGY
Blend of bistro and gastronomy

bistro

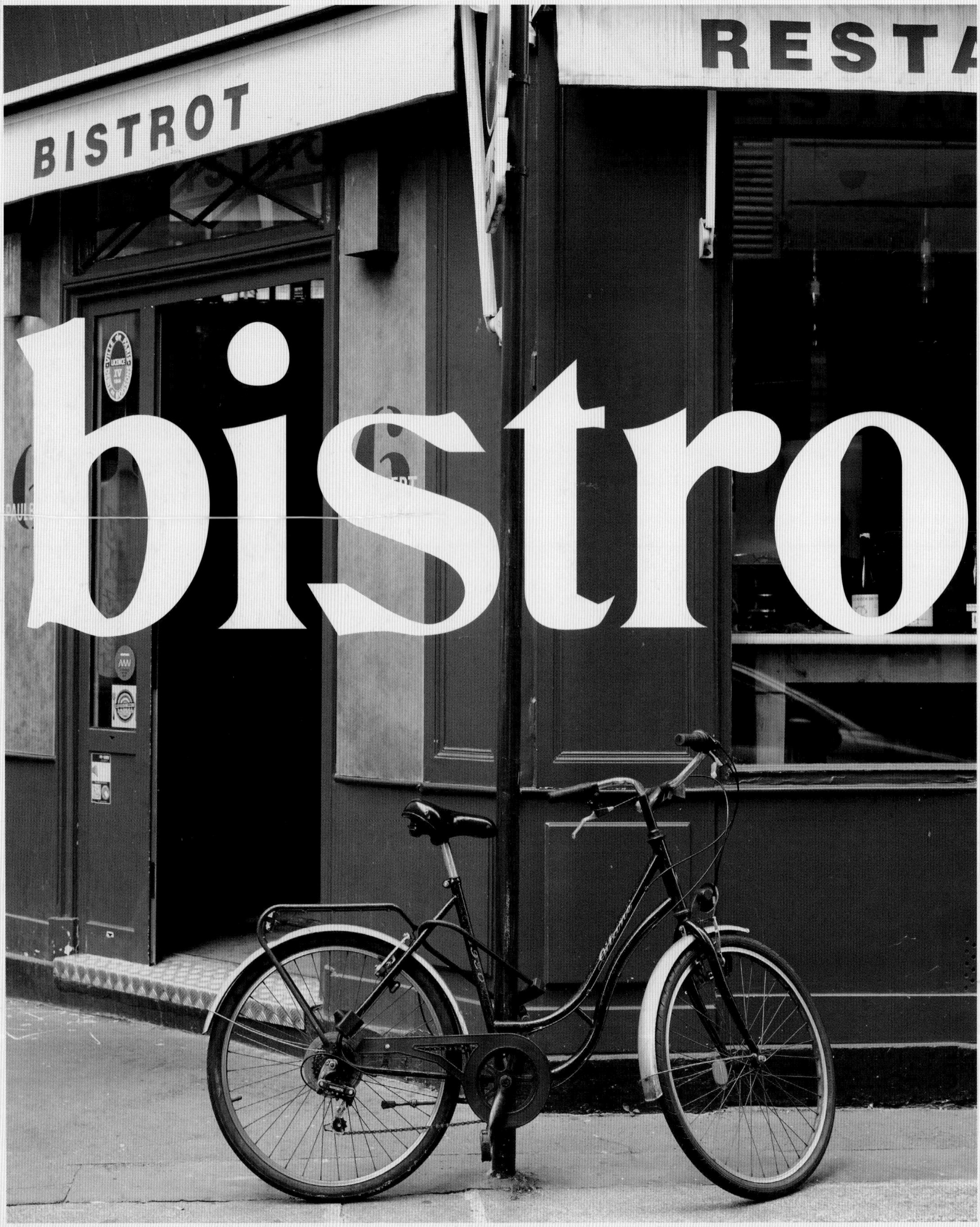

RIZZOLI
NEW YORK
New York · Paris · London · Milan

nomy

Recipes from the Best New Paris Bistros

Jane Sigal

Photographs by Fredrika Stjärne

Contents

foreword

I can't think of anyone more qualified to report on and write about the ever-changing Paris bistro scene than Jane Sigal. >

She not only has her fingers on what's evolving in the city's contemporary food scene, but also has a remarkable pedigree and font of knowledge about the French culinary world.

Jane was my assistant for many years (mostly as we drove unmarked dirt roads and highways throughout France, visiting farmers and cheesemakers, chefs and bakers, touring markets, and scoping out the best of the nation while researching *The Food Lover's Guide to France* in the mid 1980s). And, of course, now she is also a great friend and colleague. I admire her reporting skills and her knowledge of food history, as well as her intense and detailed understanding of how to cook, how to write a recipe, and how to follow a chef's thoughts. Jane is adept at taking a handful of ingredients that a chef may verbally toss to her, then miraculously transforming them into recipes that will work for the home cook.

The two of us—sometimes together, sometimes separately—have followed and reported on the Paris food scene for nearly four decades, noting the 1970s birth of the revolutionary and minimalist nouvelle cuisine, as well as the creation of Paris's "baby" bistros in 1987. At that time, Guy Savoy and Michel Rostang went "off piste" and began satellite bistros using their classical knowledge and cadre of chefs to augment their Michelin-three-starred endeavors with simpler restaurants that appealed to a younger, less-monied crowd. (Today it is hard to believe that there was a time when a star chef had only one restaurant!) We also catalogued the "retirement" of famed chef Joël Robuchon, who then went on to create his own line of baby bistros under the name of L'Atelier de Joël Robuchon.

What Jane has created here is a modern history of not just Parisian food but world food. It's a movement that has many roots. The birth of Internet food bloggers made it possible for restaurateurs to become overnight sensations and fill a whole dining room for months—something that could not have happened when diners waited for an annual guide, a monthly magazine report, a weekly notice, or even a daily newspaper review to fill them in on the restaurant scene.

At the same time, in Paris, the geographic expansion of where people are now willing to go to dine has dramatically improved the bistronomy movement. As Jane notes, chefs no longer need to invest in white linens, expansive bouquets of flowers, fine china, or waiters in formal costume, but can quite literally, "scrape the paint off the wall," open the door, and do business in once-faraway neighborhoods, such as the tenth, eleventh, twelfth, eighteenth, and nineteenth arrondissements.

As ever, Jane did her footwork and her homework. She didn't just sit in the dining room, enjoy the meal, and sip a glass of Chardonnay. She jumped into the tiny kitchens, notebook in hand, and in her impeccable French, got into chefs' hearts and minds, leaving with a treasure trove of thoughts, concepts, theories, recipes, and wonderful quotes!

My favorite comes from American chef Daniel Rose at Spring: "Food is twenty percent about cooking, fifty percent about buying, and the rest is cleaning up and organizing."

And when she asks Haï Kaï chef Amélie Darvas, "What makes your food so compelling?" the response she gets is "I'm not afraid of fat."

What most people who come to the bistronomy restaurants don't know is that the majority of the chefs have serious classical French training. Many of them have worked with France's finest chefs: Guy Savoy, Joël Robuchon, Alain Passard. They didn't just walk in off the street with tattoos and tousled hair, turn on a burner, and open the front door. They have knowledge and passion, and an eagerness to create a new world. They are working to weave classic French techniques into a more relaxed and personally inspired style. They are taking advantage of an ecological movement that spotlights locally grown, often organic produce, sustainable fish supplies, and organic wines. Vegetables no longer take a back seat but play a central role, especially root vegetables. We fall in love again with the chefs' alchemy with Jerusalem artichokes, parsnips, beets, radishes, and kale. We discover the wonders of mackerel and hake, and become even greater friends with lentils, white beans, and peas. Herbs, such as lovage and borage, become our new culinary neighbors.

What I love, as well, is that the parade of young chefs—no longer just an all-male French club—includes plenty of women, as well as cooks from Japan, England, America, and Australia. And they don't play an us-versus-them game with the chefs and bistros that came before them, but pay homage to their roots.

The food in this book is thoroughly appealing and totally accessible to the home cook, so much so that you want to grab it and take it into the kitchen and begin cooking right away. That cold fennel soup with chervil (page 34). Tomatoes smoked in a wok over wood chips (page 101). Cod cooked in a casserole with tomatoes, olives, and chorizo (page 134). And then all those lovely recipes with meringue, one of my favorite light and easy desserts.

Fredrika Stjärne's photos are brilliant and so perfectly reflect the true bistronomy movement: bikes parked out front, casually dressed diners perched on bar stools, chefs taking a cigarette break on the curb outside. The interiors and the colorful food carefully capture a movement that's fully grown and working oh so well!

— PATRICIA WELLS

introduction

Opposite (clockwise from top): Angling for a view of chef Daï Shinozuka at Les Enfants Rouges; father of bistronomy Yves Camdeborde on the rooftop of Hôtel Relais Saint-Germain; quayside, overlooking Notre Dame Cathedral.

I spent a year squeezed into Paris's tiny new bistro kitchens, notebook and pen in one hoodie pocket, iPhone in the other. I wanted to meet the city's "bistronomy" chefs—the young, adventurous, and international cooks who are rewriting the rule book of upscale dining. What are their motivations? How do they do it? What's it like to work sixteen-hour maniac days with just cigarette breaks and maybe a nap on the banquette?

But, actually, my research on bistronomie (bistro + gastronomie) started in 1980 when I moved to Paris to go to cooking school. I was twenty-one and didn't ship back my copper tarte Tatin pan, charlotte mold, and asparagus plates until I was thirty-six. During those years, I translated for the buzzy nouvelle cuisine chefs who came to teach at L'École de Cuisine La Varenne. I ate alongside the hugely influential author, cooking teacher, and journalist Patricia Wells as she researched *The Food Lover's Guide to France*. Eventually, I wrote two French cookbooks of my own: *Backyard Bistros, Farmhouse Fare* and *Normandy Gastronomique* (there's even a French edition!).

I came to know an absurd amount about culinary France: I was an expert on raising salt-marsh lambs around Mont-Saint-Michel and I could also tell you where to find the best grilled marrow bones in Paris at two in the morning (Chez Denise). As a result, when I went home to New York and joined *Food & Wine* as a senior food editor, I became the magazine's resident expert on France and the person everyone went to for advice on where to eat in Paris. Now, as a contributing writer at *Food & Wine* and the magazine's France correspondent, I keep tabs on which No. 2 chefs have left which formidable restaurants to open

places of their own. As often as I can, I catch up with extended eating binges.

So I've seen bistronomy's precursors, its emergence, and multiple iterations. And it all began in 1992 with Yves Camdeborde.

FIRST GENERATION

Yves Camdeborde looked like a superhero in a tux shirt against the Left Bank backdrop of dark summer clouds, clay chimney pots, and a distant Eiffel Tower. Risking our necks, Fredrika Stjärne, the book's photographer, her Paris assistant, Romain Diani, and I inched across the slippery steel roof of the chef's boutique Hôtel Relais Saint-Germain, posing Camdeborde for the ultimate portrait. He stood straddling the roof ribs, five stories from extinction. What were we thinking?

But Camdeborde didn't flinch. He's used to taking risks. In 1992, when only twenty-eight, he left the Hôtel de Crillon to strike out on his own. For generations, when a chef with a résumé this exalted wanted to open a restaurant, he'd outfit an elegant dining room in refined western Paris. It was the reliable path to Michelin stars and glory. But Camdeborde didn't feel comfortable in the luxe, buttoned-down environments where he had trained. His idea of a restaurant was a zero-pretense spot where you hang out because you're there to enjoy life. So instead of shopping at Christofle and Porthault and taking on massive debt, he pivoted to low-rent eastern Paris and launched his first bistro, La Régalade.

La Régalade reflected exactly who Camdeborde was: a charcutier's son from Pau, in southwest France, who had worked in some of the best kitchens in Paris. He offered an affordable prix fixe that included

Opposite (clockwise from top): Beak-to-tail cooking; Paris's Mansart roofs, clay chimney pots, and a graceful cupola; no tablecloths at Septime, but folded cloth napkins to covet.

the rustic family terrine (you helped yourself to as much as you wanted) and cooked his heart out, fusing haute cuisine technique with regional culinary traditions and adding smart twists. To keep prices down, he limited the menu, changed it frequently to take advantage of peak produce, and worked with cheaper cuts of meat.

Camdeborde's strategy was counterintuitive, given that diners associated sophisticated French food with crystal and ceremony. One high-profile chef told him, "This will never work."

In fact, people came in droves to Camdeborde's democratic take on fine dining. Against prevailing restaurant conventions, he created a template for eating out that could be high art and fun. Camdeborde's elite posse from the Hôtel de Crillon, including Thierry Breton and Christian Etchebest, took note. They sensed an opportunity and, in 1995 and 1998 respectively, debuted their own bistros. Camdeborde's protégés followed suit, such as Stéphane Jégo, who kicked off L'Ami Jean in 2003. The same year, Camdeborde's mentor from the Hôtel de Crillon, Christian Constant, became a convert, unveiling his first bistro, Café Constant. He now operates a string of restaurants on the rue Saint-Dominique in Paris.

In 2005, Camdeborde took advantage of his own growing reputation and fame to vault into new endeavors, including the Hôtel Relais Saint-Germain and its bistro, Le Comptoir du Relais.

Le Comptoir is still one of the toughest reservations in Paris, and that's the drawback to the success of these small "neo-bistros" (new-style bistros). Getting a table can be slightly painful. The hottest spots with limited space are booked weeks or even months in advance.

SECOND WAVE

Camdeborde and his cohort had liberated good French food from expensive dining rooms. But, for the most part, it was still classic French cooking. Also, Camdeborde had come from a blue-collar family, and cooking had not been his top career choice. (His dream was to play rugby.)

Enter the bearded, lanky, complex-free Inaki Aizpitarte. The Basque-French chef burst onto the Paris stage at La Famille in Montmartre, then, in 2006, as his own boss at Le Chateaubriand on a desolate stretch of the eleventh arrondissement. The space was unremarkable. The furnishings were extraordinarily plain. Nobody wore a uniform, and it was hard to tell the staff from paying customers.

But Aizpitarte turned his new bistro into an idea factory. He combined ingredients that shouldn't be capable of coexisting on the same plate, like slabs of foie gras on raw root vegetable shavings.

The thrillingly unbound Le Chateaubriand expressed a cultural shift. The craft of cooking was now perceived as artsy—even sexy. It was pulling in acolytes from the middle class and from other professions—there are a lot of ex-designers now in restaurant kitchens, many who have never been to culinary school.

"Two months after Le Chateaubriand opened, I went with my friend Sven Chartier [of Saturne]," said Bertrand Grébaut, designer-turned-chef-owner of the Michelin-starred Septime. "We were not even twenty-five, working like lunatics at [three-star] Arpège. Here we were in a cool place with a thirty-six-euro menu. I remember an incredible dessert with mozzarella, petit-suisse [a soft cheese], buttermilk, and basil coulis like it was yesterday. At that moment, something really clicked in our heads."

IT'S A BIG TENT

The second generation of neo-bistro chefs, like Inaki Aizpitarte, Bertrand Grébaut, and Sven Chartier, are reformers, interested in testing received notions not only about food but also about what dining can and should be. Many are abandoning the multicourse lunches and

Above: Thierry Breton's crusty loaves are delivered by bicycle. Below: Summer bounty from market gardener Joël Thiébault. Opposite: Staff meal at Bertrand Grébaut's Michelin-starred restaurant, Septime.

dinners of their parents' generation, offering small plates, keeping their doors open all day, serving food seven days a week, seating guests at the bar.

There's a new inclusiveness, too. For the first time in my life, without even trying, I can name more than twenty-five incredible women chefs who are cooking in Paris right now. What's more, many of the most sought-after restaurants are helmed by foreign cooks.

The vibe in these small kitchens is more group home than military barracks. As Braden Perkins, the American chef-owner of Verjus, put it, "I feel like I'm working with friends. We go on vacation together."

Yet these cooks work long, grueling days in cramped spaces. They get angry. There are rivalries. "We went through forty-seven cooks in one year," Perkins told me. "It sounds OCD, but these people have to be the right ones for you with the same aesthetic. They need to complement you professionally and psychologically. It's not just a job with a paycheck."

SHOP SMART

What is this aesthetic? These chefs are obsessed with product. Each ingredient may well be the best example of its kind you've ever tasted. "In a restaurant, it's twenty percent about the cooking and fifty percent about the buying," said Daniel Rose, an Illinois native and the chef-owner of Spring. "The rest is cleaning and organizing."

New ways of sourcing have helped make super-high-quality ingredients central to the neo-bistro menu. In bistronomy's first act, chefs shopped every Tuesday at Rungis, the vast market out near Orly airport. Now chefs can order through Terroirs d'Avenir, the slow-food purveyor, or contact small producers directly. (Texting has changed buying forever.) "I've never known Rungis," said Bertrand Grébaut of Septime. "It's another school."

The devotion to pristine ingredients has a moral valence. These chefs value caviar and truffles no more than the most ordinary ingredients like onions, parsnips, and radishes. They are sensitive to the conditions under which food is grown and harvested. Whenever possible, they support humane methods of slaughter. They observe the seasons, prefer ingredients that are locally grown, and are strict about traceability.

In terms of the menu, less-expensive, line-caught seafood dominates. There's a preponderance of hake, with its firm, sweet white flesh, and eco-friendly, nutritious mackerel. Another favorite is farmed trout from the Pays Basque, truite de Banka, considered the sustainable alternative to salmon. Crudo is also trendy: "I really like raw seafood," said James Henry of Bones. "With produce so impeccable, I have no hesitation. The prawns are still jumping in the box they arrived in. The scallops are still alive."

The range of what people eat in Paris is enormous—lamb sweetbreads, kidneys, pork bellies, pigeon, guinea hen, capon. Still, something as common as beef is de-emphasized. "I don't use beef," said Spring chef Daniel Rose. "Or sometimes as an accompaniment."

These chefs aren't vegetarian, but they do vegetables right—especially roots, bulbs, and leaves. Even dessert has a hint of the garden. At Bones, chef James Henry prepares a sunchoke (Jerusalem artichoke) ice cream with hazelnut praline and apple.

Yet some of French cuisine's most spectacular achievements have practically vanished. Saucemaking, for instance, which requires expertise and a dedicated work station, is an impossibility with tiny staffs and micro kitchens. Brown butter, simple vinaigrettes, and salsa verde now stand in for the complex mother sauces and their variations, as do swooshes of Vitamix-smooth vegetable purees. "There are hardly any more sauces," Franck Baranger of Le Pantruche and Caillebotte told me.

The cheese course, if it exists at all, is stripped down. Instead of a dozen varieties, the new bistros may serve a single cheese—but a well-aged, rigorously sourced one—

and it may be in a pile of shavings instead of served whole or as a wedge.

Ambitious restaurants usually employ a pastry chef in charge of desserts, her own team, and, often, her own kitchen. But most neo-bistros don't have a pastry chef, let alone a separate dessert space. As a result, intricate confections with multiple components are replaced by homey choices, like crumbles, fruit salads, fromage blanc, and chocolate ganache. In the same spirit, the bistronomy chef's favorite pastry is meringue, the easiest pâtisserie in the baker's repertoire. These dishes can be prepared by any cook in the kitchen or even a dishwasher.

Beverages receive the same laserlike attention as vegetables or fish. Bistronomy chefs are natural (noninterventionist, low-sulphur) wine crusaders. They're just as picky about buying coffee beans from local roasters. The bartender at Septime always offers a vibrant infusion, a nonalcoholic elixir prepared by steeping kitchen scraps in lab beakers. But, in general, cocktails are seen as belonging to bar culture and not fit to accompany serious food.

These chefs may fetishize baby vegetables and picked-right-now freshness, but an ingredient's usefulness exists on a temporal spectrum, explained veteran bistronomy chef Stéphane Jégo of L'Ami Jean, with value at both ends. "You don't use spring onions to make a pot au feu," he said. "You pick an older carrot to make braised beef with carrots, not a spring carrot with its delicate greens."

COOKING ON THE FLY

All this stress on locally produced, organically grown, seasonally available food has completely changed the way menus are composed. "Before, chefs wrote a menu for the season, no matter the price," said Bertrand Grébaut of Septime. "We work from the product to the menu."

Producers text chefs on a daily basis and tell them what's available. "They practically do the thinking for you," said Franck Baranger of Le Pantruche and Caillebotte. "As a result, cooking is much more instinctive than it was in the past."

"There's no time for planning," said Shaun Kelly. "There are general theories. For instance, I get five rabbits a week. First you use the offal, then the prime cuts, then you braise what's left. Once you're used to it, it's really easy."

At Bones, things change fast. "Every Monday I write a new menu for the week," said chef James Henry. "That will evolve over the next five days."

Often the chefs simply try to satisfy themselves with the ingredients that arrive. They ask, "What would we like for dinner?" But Stéphane Jégo of L'Ami Jean takes a different approach. "I've got a taste wheel in my head," he said. "We talk all day long about what we are going to do."

Sometimes, however, a dish tastes like a bunch of ingredients thrown together that have no particular affinity for one another. In fact, chefs need to work with them until they could be codified as a recipe. "It takes five or six days to get it right," admitted Franck Baranger. At Le Pantruche, a dish stays on the menu until an ingredient is no longer perfect, in season, or at the optimum of taste. At least one dish in each category (app, main, dessert) changes every day.

Again, it takes a seasoned chef to lend perspective to the notion of a market menu. For instance, serving fish that's been out of the water barely twenty-four hours in sashimi-like bites is magnificent but it's only one way of putting together a menu. "You have to let time do its work," said Stéphane Jégo of L'Ami Jean.

Sometimes old is gold. Jégo dry-ages steak and suckling pig to make them more tender and develop umami. Le 6 Paul Bert and Comptoir Canailles both have refrigerators just for aging birds and meat. At Le Bal Café chefs Anna Trattles and Alice Quillet marinate most of the meat and poultry that comes in before cooking it. "That way you've always got something to serve," said Quillet. "And it keeps longer if you can't serve it right away."

Above: Legendary chef
Pierre Gagnaire (right) stops
by L'Ami Jean for an early
morning chat with bistrotier
Stéphane Jégo. Below: At Au
Passage, a boatload of herbs
for the night's menu. Opposite:
Flawless technique and
artful plating from Bertrand
Grébaut of Septime.

CRAFTING THE PERFECT PLATE

In order to break the rules, you have to know what they are and understand them. Neo-bistro cooks are fascinated with technique and kitchen science; that is, not just how to do something, but why it works. Many have cooked in Copenhagen, Modena, Brisbane, and Brooklyn, and they come back with ideas and a set of skills spawned in diversity. They have learned all the tricks of modern cooking—old (smoking, fermenting, aging, recycling) and new (cooking sous vide, making foams in a siphon [a canister charged with pressurized gas], freezing individual servings of ice cream or sorbet in a PacoJet)—and they use this knowledge to create new dishes.

New World cooks are especially adept at unlocking technique from their national contexts. "Being an American, you grow up eating French on Monday, Italian on Tuesday," said Braden Perkins of Verjus. "You learn everything because you have to be prepared for anything. So you learn technique: duck confit is really creating gravlax out of meat. It's exactly the same method applied to a different protein; that is, extracting moisture. Once you understand the underlying technique you can manipulate it."

For a lot of cooks who have opened their own bistros, high-tech gear like immersion circulators and induction stoves are too expensive. Still, anyone can create a stovetop smoker using a wok and some hay. Anyone can cure meat with a little salt and sugar. Also, there's an incipient anti-modernist mindset. Cooking trends are always in flux, and today sous vide, many believe, is not "real" cooking.

Presentation, with each ingredient placed just so, is as important to neo-bistro chefs as irreproachable product and precision technique. Today, plating tends to the asymmetrical, with flawless mandoline-sliced vegetables or a dusting of piment d'Espelette. But there's usually a casual perfection to the plate— roughly chopped herbs, smears of puree.

Sometimes the compositions are artfully bewildering. On purpose. It's a way to engage diners and get them to reflect—and have feelings—about what they're eating. A favorite strategy is to disguise or hide ingredients. In Shaun Kelly's cherry and beet Pavlova (pictured page 179), nothing is what it seems, and it's impossible not to marvel when you eat what you think is a summer berry and find out it's a vegetable.

THE CHALLENGES OF STAYING SMALL

Is there an end-stage reckoning? France's move toward a more casual, open society along with a shaky economy fueled the new age of bistronomy. The same forces cut against the preeminence of luxury high-end restaurants. Today, dining rooms with hotel school–trained waitstaff rolling cheese carts between crystal-bedecked tables are increasingly the domain of a few deep-pocketed hotel groups.

Since so many of the neo-bistro chefs gained experience at these haute bastions, who will train the next generation, I wonder. "What's going to be lost is service and décor," said Bertrand Grébaut, the chef of Septime, who worked at the Michelin-three-star restaurant Arpège. He thinks it's neo-bistro chefs like himself who will mentor the new crop of young cooks.

I may worry about France's great culinary heritage, but one of the world's venerable chef-entrepreneurs, Alain Ducasse, is unconcerned. "Do we need more grand restaurants?" said Ducasse, who is also a Paris bistrotier. "I don't think so."

While restaurant cooking may now appeal as a profession to the middle class, I'm not sure for how long. It's a grind. There will be dropouts. "I don't know if I can work sixteen hours a day for the rest of my life," admitted James Henry of Bones.

I ask myself if the rising tide of neo-bistros will capsize the whole idea of

bistronomy. A full reservations book has allowed the chef-owners of such restaurants as Septime, Frenchie, and Le Chateaubriand to create mini empires, including wine bars, sandwicheries, épiceries, bakeries, and seafood bars. Le Chateaubriand chef Inaki Aizpitarte has even opened a restaurant in London's silk-stocking Mayfair district, and there's a Racines outpost in New York City. Are we losing the offbeat, personal qualities that made bistronomy so alluring in the first place?

The triumph of bistronomy has turned some hole-in-the-walls into full-fledged restaurants. The huge popularity of Spring, for instance, compelled chef-owner Daniel Rose to expand what had been a sixteen-seat eatery into a restaurant serving sixty. "We've grown up," said Rose. "I was forced by my success to be more professional. Now we call taxis for people."

Besides the challenge of tight spaces, bistronomy presents a raft of limitations. Even before Frenchie turned five, owner Greg Marchand bristled at what he couldn't do. So when he revamped the original bistro in 2014, he upgraded the décor, brought back the à la carte menu, and raised the prices. "We're bored," he said. "Give me more freedom!"

Yet, as a business model, bistronomy continues to attract young cooks starting out and has begun to win over high-level chefs with gastro restaurants. Some are eliminating the formality of their existing restaurants. Others, like Jean-François Piège, the versatile owner of a chic eponymous restaurant, a brasserie, and a pâtisserie, are growing their empires with neo-bistros. A recent Piège venture, Clover, showcases bistronomy's most admirable qualities: refined and inventive food, relaxed attitude, and scaled-down prices.

My research helped me realize that neo-bistros are multiplying around France—and the globe. In Lyon, a city used to its pork-loving and genially cluttered bouchons (bistros), Mathieu Rostaing-Tayard's menu at Café Sillon is vegetable-centric and prepared with outstanding skill and creativity; his

dining room is tastefully spartan with long unadorned tables. In Nice, the Moroccan-born chef Elmahdi Mobarik of Le Canon cooks Provençal comfort food with mandoline-sharp technique in a space furnished with Formica tables and flea market chairs. Inspired by Paris bistronomy's mission to whack the starch out of fine dining, chefs in Bordeaux, Lille, New York, London, Frankfurt, Copenhagen, and Sydney—to name a few—are riffing on the concept, adapting it to fit their personalities, local cuisines, and customers.

Bistronomy's spread and evolution are perhaps the most promising signs of its vitality. Even as it matures, it remains a tremendously appealing innovation. "Who's the winner in all this?" said Guy Savoy, a Michelin-three-star chef with bistros of his own. "It's the diner."

COOKING BISTRONOMY

Writing about the French food scene has given me a front-row seat to the lives and work of some of the most creative and intriguing chefs of the twentieth and twenty-first centuries. But I am not a chef and I don't try to cook like one. I'm an interpreter—listening, tasting, taking notes, asking questions in the professional kitchen, and then translating for the home cook.

The one hundred-plus recipes here are—and are not—what you find at the restaurants I've profiled. Let me explain. First, I selected only the chefs' dishes that I could prepare in my opposite-of-high-tech kitchen and skipped anything that involved the complicated wrangling of many ingredients or was too much work. I dropped recipes that required special equipment and Internet-sourcing (though I include artisans I like). I also give alternatives for ingredients you might not find at the farmers' market—but don't discount what you can order through your supermarket butcher and produce department. Or I adapted dishes.

Opposite (clockwise from top):
Writing the dinner menu on
the glass storefront at L'Office;
remains of lunch at Tatiana
Levha's neo-bistro, Le Servan;
chef Yves Camdeborde's
abbreviated kitchen notebook:
combine as usual and cook
until done.

For example, Bertrand Grébaut of Septime cooks his pork belly sous vide (pictured on page 160). It's perfect. I braised it the traditional way, and it was sublimely tender.

Two exceptions to the no-special-gear rule: I have a digital scale (twenty bucks). It's one of the most useful gadgets in the kitchen. My recipes do give cup measurements, but the metric weights listed next to them are more accurate. And I love my cheap mandoline because it makes my slicing technique as precise as Sota Atsumi's of Clown Bar. Take a look at how he cuts baby beets into petals on page 63.

The dishes at neo-bistros generally aren't classics. They're ephemeral, changing even within a single meal service, so there's no capturing any recipe definitively. Even Stéphane Jégo's Parmesan Soup with Peas (pictured on page 40), which customers won't let him take off the menu, evolves with the seasons.

Also, a recipe can't fully express the way a dish comes together in a chef's head. Chefs start with the market, then apply technique. So working from recipe back to ingredient is inherently the wrong way around. Still, I am thrilled to have put these ideas down on paper and not let them slip away.

Sometimes the pitfalls of re-creating recipes are more practical. I was shoehorned into kitchens before and during lunch or dinner. But restaurant cooks don't prepare dishes straight through. They may prep part of a recipe in the morning but cook it for dinner, so often I didn't see a recipe from start to finish. Or it was prepared at the same time as six other dishes.

Even getting hold of a written recipe is not always the answer. I'm often given a list of ingredients and weights and told to combine as usual and cook until done. Yves Camdeborde of Le Comptoir and Edward Delling-Williams of Au Passage let me loose in their bulging notebooks. But those are manuals to sous chefs. Many ingredient amounts call for "as much as needed." Or they're restaurant quantities and unsuitable for the home kitchen.

Occasionally, ingredients are missing by mistake or because it's assumed I'll know to add them. Some not-so-basic cooking skills are taken for granted—cutting oranges into supremes, slicing vegetables into julienne—and I fill that in, too. Essentially, I do a lot of reverse engineering, based on what I taste, common sense, and my cooking know-how.

Fortunately, the neo-bistro cook's passion for extraordinary product translates into simple recipes. Chefs do as little as possible in order to highlight an ingredient's flavor, but in a unique and creative way. This is what I have tried to showcase. I would never have thought to whip smoked fish and radish tops into butter as a spread for radishes (pictured on page 49) as Tatiana Levha does at Le Servan. Or to grate feta cheese as a feathery topping for haricots verts and strawberries (pictured on page 61) as Sota Atsumi does at Clown Bar.

Another plus for home cooks: The average bistronomy chef has no more skill as a baker than you do. His kitchen is probably no bigger than yours, he doesn't have fancy baking tools, and he can't afford a pastry chef. He frequently prepares desserts in the same way as savory dishes; that is, without exact amounts—a tip-off that these desserts are uncomplicated. Yves Camdeborde's Fresh Pineapple with Basil Syrup (pictured on page 194) is a good example. Making a simple syrup and blitzing it with basil leaves is hard to mess up, but it transforms the fruit.

I took an iPhone shot of every dish as the chef prepared it, then I reproduced it as if I were expecting her to check my work before letting the food leave my kitchen. Later I returned with photographer Fredrika Stjärne to capture the chefs in action. Fredrika also photographed thirty of the dishes in her studio. In addition, I include notes for each recipe, and longer features explain ingredients and techniques in detail.

These recipes are proof that French cooking is alive and well and living in Paris.

bistronomy timeline

1907

Auguste Escoffier's *Le Guide Culinaire* summarizes and organizes the accumulated knowledge of French cuisine. It's still the foundation of brilliant restaurant kitchens. "I found that knowing traditional French cooking was very reassuring," said Tatiana Levha of neo-bistro Le Servan. "If worse came to worst, and I really didn't know what to do, I could always go back to making something like a beurre blanc and that would work because it's always worked."

1926

The Michelin Guide awards its first stars for restaurant cooking. "It's still the ultimate reference," said new-vanguard bistrotier Franck Baranger of Le Pantruche and Caillebotte. "They continue to inspect seriously without being influenced by trends."

1955

At La Pyramide in Vienne, near Lyon, Fernand Point instills the nascent principles of nouvelle cuisine in the cooks who later become its star practitioners: Georges Blanc, Paul Bocuse, Alain Chapel, Louis Outhier, Jean and Pierre Troisgros, Roger Vergé. Point's forward-thinking ideas, published posthumously as *Ma Gastronomie*, lay the groundwork for bistronomy.

1965

Palace-trained Michel Guérard sets up as his own boss at the unprepossessing Le Pot-au-Feu in suburban Paris, serving dazzling food to all. The bistro wins one Michelin star in 1967, then two, in 1971, but it's a stepping stone to upscale greatness, not an end in itself. In 1974, Guérard moves to classy spa town Eugénie-les-Bains, in southwest France, and invents cuisine minceur.

2003

After a brief retirement in the '90s, star chef Joël Robuchon returns to the kitchen at L'Atelier de Joël Robuchon, serving ultra-luxurious small plates from an open kitchen at a sushi bar–inspired counter. Robuchon, who has a house in Spain, helps establish Iberico ham and other Spanish ingredients in French kitchens.

2001

Alain Passard, one of the most talked-about chefs in the world, launches a vegetable-focused menu at his Michelin-three-star restaurant, Arpège. Fired up by their training, Arpège protégés and bistronomy stars Bertrand Grébaut, Tatiana Levha, Sven Chartier, and Alice Di Cagna consider leaves, bulbs, and roots a worthy place to experiment.

2000

○ Natural wine evangelist Cyril Bordarier reinvents the Paris wine bar in a scrappy storefront. Le Verre Volé becomes the prototype for the new caves à manger—eat-in wine shops—and helps kick off a noninterventionist wine phenomenon.

○ *Le Fooding* (food + feeling), a cheeky restaurant guide, champions small, upstart establishments.

○ Cult chef Pierre Gagnaire teams up with French chemist Hervé This on modernist creations like the dreamy, now-familiar 63°C (145°F) egg.

○ Global restaurant impresario Alain Ducasse helps popularize Mediterranean cooking in Paris, when he stocks white truffles and good olive oil at Alain Ducasse at the Plaza Athénée.

2004

French food writer Sébastien Demorand coins the word bistronomie (bistro + gastronomie) to describe the culture that is changing French food. Its restaurants are called neo-bistros.

2006

○ Cool kid Inaki Aizpitarte opens Le Chateaubriand and touches off a second wave of neo-bistros. The raffish neighborhoods around the Canal Saint-Martin become the epicenter of D.I.Y. style and edgy food in provocative combinations.

○ Raves from French bloggers make it possible for chefs to scrape a bit of paint off the walls and start filling the reservations book without validation from Michelin. Paris becomes a breeding ground for expat talent: Japanese, American, British, Australian, Italian, Brazilian, Spanish, North African.

2008

○ René Redzepi, a student of Michel Bras, debuts Noma in Copenhagen, and sparks a nature-worshipping New Nordic trend around the world.

○ Slow-food purveyor Terroirs d'Avenir sells line-caught fish, rare-breed meat, and heirloom vegetables directly to chefs, bypassing Rungis, the wholesale market near Orly airport.

1968

French students and workers throw cobblestones at the police and demand that France's sclerotic postwar system change. Meanwhile, in restaurants, power shifts from the front of the house to the back. Plating is perfected in the kitchen and replaces tableside service. Cooks, once blue-collar workers, become celebrities.

1973

French journalists Henri Gault and Christian Millau issue the "ten commandments of nouvelle cuisine," a trend map of cooking by pioneering chefs. The tenets identify what makes this movement radical—new ingredients and techniques, concise menus, ultrafresh ingredients, brief cooking times, flourless sauces, flavor boosts from fresh herbs and acidity—and have a deep, lasting effect in restaurant kitchens.

1976

Publisher Robert Laffont debuts its chef cookbook collection *Les Recettes originales de*. Michel Guérard's *La Grande Cuisine minceur* is the first of more than a dozen titles.

1978

After a summer run in the countryside, Michel Bras dreams up the idea for gargouillou, an aesthetically flawless composition of 50 to 60 seasonal greens, herbs, and vegetables. The signature salad eventually reaches far beyond his Michelin-three-star restaurant in remote central France, inspiring global variations whose ingredients reflect the land around them.

1994

St. John in London breaks down whole animals, serves every conceivable part, and makes it groovy. American cooks take notice, and, eventually, so do the French, who are used to having the butcher do this sort of thing. "It feels Jurassic," said Yves Camdeborde, an off-cuts maestro himself. "But we can learn from this."

1992

Yves Camdeborde turns a first-rate CV into La Régalade, a neo-bistro epiphany in the far reaches of the Left Bank. The new format—small space, small menu, out-of-this-world food, modest prices—becomes the blueprint for a whole generation of restaurants. As a judge on French *MasterChef*, Camdeborde helps legitimize the profession of cooking for children of the middle class.

1988

Christian Constant takes over the kitchens at the Hôtel de Crillon, earning two Michelin stars, and mentors the future authors of bistronomy: Yves Camdeborde, Christian Etchebest, Thierry Breton, Éric Fréchon. When people talk about a thread of Basque culture running through bistronomy (piment d'Espelette), it starts with Constant, who was born in Montauban, in southwest France.

1987

Michelin-two-star chef Michel Rostang repurposes a turn-of-the-century épicerie into Le Bistrot d'à Côté, the bistro next door to his eponymous posh restaurant. Rostang's peers, including Guy Savoy, extend their own refined skills and exquisite ingredients to postage stamp–size annexes—forerunners of the neo-bistro. But stellar food in a stripped-down space is not yet sufficiently glorious by itself.

2009

Taking advantage of the neo-bistro model, Adeline Grattard opens a tiny storefront (she cooks fewer than 25 covers a night) in Les Halles and earns a Michelin star for her Paris-meets-Hong Kong tasting menu with tea pairings. Yam'Tcha paves the way for other women chefs to become entrepreneurs.

2010

Inaki Aizpitarte of Le Chateaubriand transforms a nearby café into Le Dauphin, a wine bar with lots of white marble, designed by architect Rem Koolhaas. The offshoot helps create a neo-bistro brand of Monopoly, with chefs expanding into wine shops, seafood bars, sandwicheries, takeout counters, épiceries, pizzerias, coffee bars, and food trucks.

2012

Sandor Ellix Katz writes *The Art of Fermentation*, and every cook on the planet buys it. French chefs who have up to now been content to leave ancient craft traditions like curing, aging meat, and brining to the experts, replace cornichons with house-made "pickles."

2014

Greg Marchand gentrifies his five-year-old neo-bistro, Frenchie. Marchand upgrades the décor, brings back the à la carte menu, and raises the prices, so he can cook more freely (using more expensive ingredients). As Marchand tells it, "We've arrived at the beginning of a new cycle."

GET THE LOOK

retro vs. neo-bistro style

CATEGORY	OLD-TIME BISTRO	NEO-BISTRO
RESTAURANT SIGN	Painted on the storefront or window; printed on the awning.	Often no sign, just a paper menu taped to the front door.
BANQUETTE	Red leatherette.	Bones has a concrete banquette; Le Grand Pan has leatherette.
TABLECLOTHS	Red-checkered or white, starched; sheets of white paper; oilcloth; bare tables.	Bare tables.
NAPKINS	Wide, white, cloth, starched.	Wide, white, cloth, starched.
COMMUNAL TABLE	No sharing tables.	A common feature of bistronomy.
CUTLERY	Serviceable, matching.	Flea-market finds or matching stainless steel.
TABLE KNIVES	Steak knives need to cut through chewy, budget cuts.	Serious, supersharp, heavy knives, preferably from Atelier Perceval.
PLATES	Sturdy, white porcelain from a restaurant supply house like E. Dehillerin.	Hand-thrown, one-of-a kind pottery from Jars, Marion Graux, and J.C. Herman.
BREAD BASKETS	Aluminum, woven reed.	Floppy fabric.
WINEGLASSES	Tumblers or thick, serviceable wineglasses.	Serious glasses to show off curated wine lists.
BAR	Lead- or zinc-topped with a heavy wood frame, for drinking and snacking before dinner.	For drinking, snacking, and eating a full-fledged meal.
FLOOR	Tiled.	Tiled, polished cement.
WALLS	Dozens of coats of lacquer paint; lined with oversize mirrors and framed posters.	Excavated stone, brick. Framed posters.
LIGHTING	Pendant lamps.	Edison-style bulbs, industrial lamps.
CHEF'S OUTFIT	Double-breasted white chef's jacket, checked trousers.	Blue dishwasher's apron (the cheapest you can buy), T shirt, jeans, sneakers, tattoos.
CHEF'S HEADGEAR	Pleated toque.	Bare-headed.
SERVERS' UNIFORMS	Black vest and long white aprons.	Jeans and sneakers.
MENU	Hand-written, sometimes on a mirror or chalkboard, or mimeographed in purple ink.	Fixed or traveling chalkboard or mirror; or printed in tiny type.
RESTROOM SOAP	Liquid or bar soap.	Aesop hand soap.
KITCHEN	Minuscule, hidden.	Minuscule, open.

BISTRO DECODER
the old vs. the new

CATEGORY	OLD-TIME BISTRO	NEO-BISTRO
MENU	Nostalgia-inducing, reassuringly predictable à la carte choices with seasonal specials plus, often at lunch, a prix-fixe.	Ephemeral—changing sometimes within a single service—often choiceless and challenging multicourse menu and/or short à la carte menu.
RECIPE TITLES	Familiar appellations with brief descriptions, often telegraphed by place names or celebrities, like peach Melba (with raspberry puree).	Pithy lists of (sometimes disparate) ingredients, like swordfish/apricots/carrots. Come with lengthy tableside explanations.
TAPAS	You mean hors d'oeuvres! They begin a meal. In ultra-traditional bistros, a half-dozen are served family-style. Foie gras terrine.	Small plates for sharing can be the meal.
SOURCING INGREDIENTS	From Rungis, the increasingly industrialized wholesale market near Orly airport that spans about a square mile (1.6 km).	From Terroirs d'Avenir, the slow-food purveyor of line-caught fish, rare-breed meat, and heirloom vegetables; or direct from the producer, forager, coffee roaster, grower.
STOCKS	Stocks, often developed over months.	Intense broths, made daily.
SAUCES	Escoffier classics: beurre blanc, béchamel, hollandaise, béarnaise, red-wine based.	Simple: broths, jus, brown butter, salsa verde, vinaigrettes, sauce vierge (tomato vinaigrette).
VEGETABLES	Potato puree, potato gratin, french fries, spinach puree, glazed carrots, wild mushrooms. Also, salads, from carottes râpées and céléri rémoulade to leeks vinaigrette and frisée with bacon.	Baby vegetables, root vegetables, bulbs, tubers, heirloom. Raw or semi raw and shaved on a mandoline; in soups, salads, purees. Wild mushrooms.
CONDIMENTS	Dijon mustard, cornichons.	Pickles, preserved lemon.
SMOKE	In the form of purchased smoked bacon, smoked salmon.	Produced in house with a Big Green Egg barbecue, makeshift stovetop smoker, often by burning hay, or blowtorch. Also, in the form of chorizo; leek and eggplant ashes.
BONES	Meat, poultry, and fish are often served on the bone.	Usually boneless, except veal chops and marrow bones.
CHEESE	A large platter of six to eight regional French cheeses, usually left on the table.	Often a single cheese.
WINE	Beaujolais! Basic and the superior cru Beaujolais, sometimes decanted from barrels into thick-bottomed carafes. The small selection can also include wines from the Rhône, Loire, Alsace, and Languedoc-Roussillon, sold by the bottle—often you pay for only what you drink.	Small selection of closely considered natural (low-sulphur) and international wines sold by the glass, bottle (magnum preferred), and, sometimes, carafe. Course-by-course wine pairings.
COFFEE	Coffee, Arabica or Robusta beans, often from whichever manufacturer supplied the coffeemaker.	Locally roasted, for example, at Belleville Brûlerie. Filter coffee made in a Chemex glass is popular.

HAÏ KAÏ

mon HAÏ KAÏ du jour
17 euros   entrée plat OU plat dessert
22 euros entrée, plat et dessert

Chers amis nous travaillons avec des produits frais et avec de l'arrivage
quotidien quand il n'y a plus il n'y a plus et c'est bon signe

entrée

moule du Bouchot, haricot vert

ou

ris de veau
fricassée, linguine

PLATS

Lieu jaune de l'ile vierge

ou

boeuf de Salers

Dessert

pêche , sabayon , citron vert

les plats hors menu

Longe de cochon noir de bigorre 40€

Demi carrelet Finistère rôti 35€

dorade grise entière 40€

service compris , prix ttc

social network

A partial map of Paris bistronomy's interconnected chef mentors and their protégés

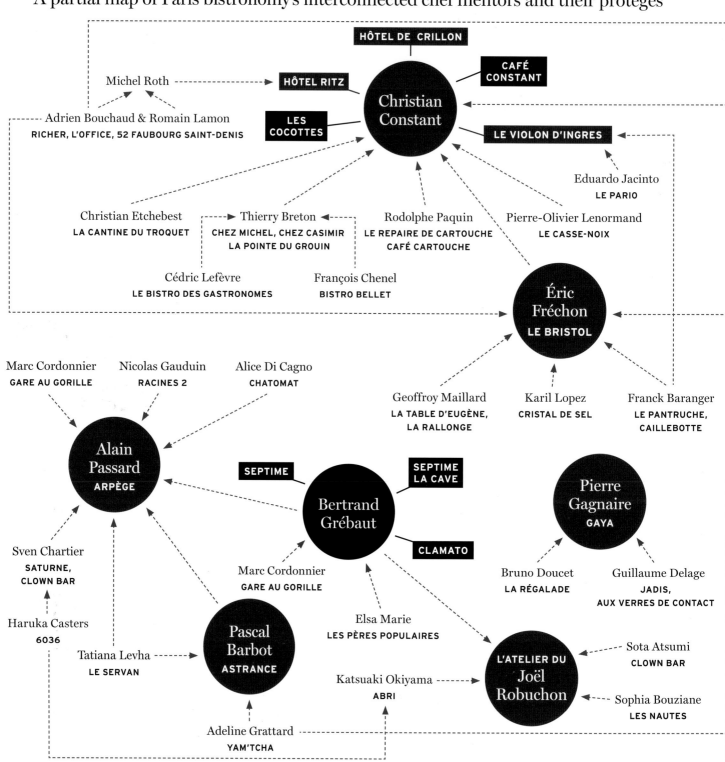

HÔTEL DE CRILLON

Michel Roth

HÔTEL RITZ

CAFÉ CONSTANT

Adrien Bouchaud & Romain Lamon
RICHER, L'OFFICE, 52 FAUBOURG SAINT-DENIS

LES COCOTTES

Christian Constant

LE VIOLON D'INGRES

Eduardo Jacinto
LE PARIO

Christian Etchebest
LA CANTINE DU TROQUET

Thierry Breton
**CHEZ MICHEL, CHEZ CASIMIR
LA POINTE DU GROUIN**

Rodolphe Paquin
**LE REPAIRE DE CARTOUCHE
CAFÉ CARTOUCHE**

Pierre-Olivier Lenormand
LE CASSE-NOIX

Cédric Lefèvre
LE BISTRO DES GASTRONOMES

François Chenel
BISTRO BELLET

**Éric Fréchon
LE BRISTOL**

Marc Cordonnier
GARE AU GORILLE

Nicolas Gauduin
RACINES 2

Alice Di Cagno
CHATOMAT

Geoffroy Maillard
**LA TABLE D'EUGÈNE,
LA RALLONGE**

Karil Lopez
CRISTAL DE SEL

Franck Baranger
**LE PANTRUCHE,
CAILLEBOTTE**

**Alain Passard
ARPÈGE**

SEPTIME

SEPTIME LA CAVE

Bertrand Grébaut

CLAMATO

**Pierre Gagnaire
GAYA**

Sven Chartier
**SATURNE,
CLOWN BAR**

Marc Cordonnier
GARE AU GORILLE

Bruno Doucet
LA RÉGALADE

Guillaume Delage
**JADIS,
AUX VERRES DE CONTACT**

Haruka Casters
6036

Tatiana Levha
LE SERVAN

**Pascal Barbot
ASTRANCE**

Elsa Marie
LES PÈRES POPULAIRES

Katsuaki Okiyama
ABRI

L'ATELIER DU Joël Robuchon

Sota Atsumi
CLOWN BAR

Sophia Bouziane
LES NAUTES

Adeline Grattard
YAM'TCHA

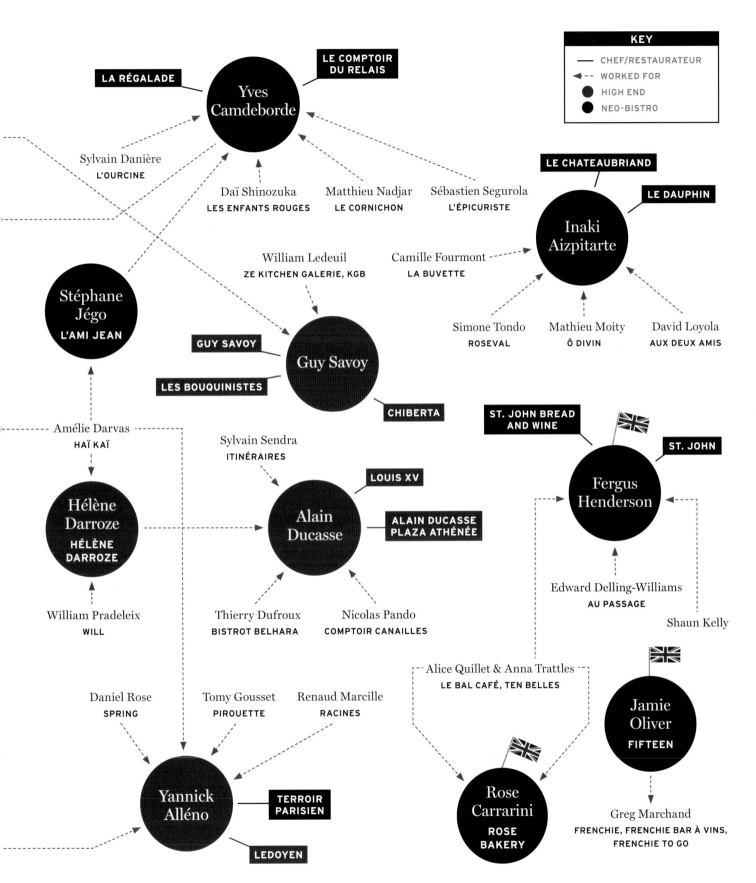

KEY
— CHEF/RESTAURATEUR
◄-- WORKED FOR
◗ HIGH END
● NEO-BISTRO

LA RÉGALADE — Yves Camdeborde — LE COMPTOIR DU RELAIS

Sylvain Danière
L'OURCINE

Daï Shinozuka
LES ENFANTS ROUGES

Matthieu Nadjar
LE CORNICHON

Sébastien Segurola
L'ÉPICURISTE

LE CHATEAUBRIAND — Inaki Aizpitarte — LE DAUPHIN

William Ledeuil
ZE KITCHEN GALERIE, KGB

Camille Fourmont
LA BUVETTE

Stéphane Jégo
L'AMI JEAN

GUY SAVOY — Guy Savoy
LES BOUQUINISTES
CHIBERTA

Simone Tondo
ROSEVAL

Mathieu Moity
Ô DIVIN

David Loyola
AUX DEUX AMIS

Amélie Darvas
HAÏ KAÏ

Sylvain Sendra
ITINÉRAIRES

St. JOHN BREAD AND WINE — Fergus Henderson — ST. JOHN

LOUIS XV — Alain Ducasse
ALAIN DUCASSE PLAZA ATHÉNÉE

Hélène Darroze
HÉLÈNE DARROZE

William Pradeleix
WILL

Thierry Dufroux
BISTROT BELHARA

Nicolas Pando
COMPTOIR CANAILLES

Edward Delling-Williams
AU PASSAGE

Shaun Kelly

Alice Quillet & Anna Trattles
LE BAL CAFÉ, TEN BELLES

Daniel Rose
SPRING

Tomy Gousset
PIROUETTE

Renaud Marcille
RACINES

Jamie Oliver
FIFTEEN

Yannick Alléno — TERROIR PARISIEN
LEDOYEN

Rose Carrarini
ROSE BAKERY

Greg Marchand
FRENCHIE, FRENCHIE BAR À VINS, FRENCHIE TO GO

soups

gazpacho *with* chorizo & pineapple

**Four First-Course or
Eight Hors d'Oeuvre Servings**

—

4 ripe medium tomatoes
(about 1½ pounds/750 g), cut
into chunks

1 medium cucumber, peeled
and chopped

1 red bell pepper, cut into
chunks

½ small fennel bulb, chopped

2 large shallots, halved and
sliced

1 garlic clove, chopped

¼ cup (60 ml) extra-virgin
olive oil, plus more for drizzling

3 tablespoons sherry vinegar,
plus more

Sea salt and freshly
ground pepper

A few drops of hot sauce

2 tablespoons (20 g) small
pearl tapioca (not instant)

½ cup (125 ml) tomato juice

2 tablespoons chopped mint

½ ounce (15 g) Spanish
chorizo, cut into ⅛-inch
(3-mm) dice

¼ cup (45 g) diced fresh
pineapple (⅛-inch/3-mm dice)

Crème fraîche, sour cream,
or Greek yogurt, for garnish

Pickled samphire, for garnish
(optional; see Note)

Piment d'Espelette

—

Note
Samphire is a green, fleshy
seaweed. It's often sold pickled
in specialty food shops.

Make Ahead
The recipe can be prepared
through Step 2 and
refrigerated overnight.

Les Enfants Rouges chef Daï Shinozuka often sends out an amuse-bouche of soup to customers while they wait for their first courses. It's a small but extraordinarily warm gesture, given bistronomy's no-frills ethic. In summer, the soup might be this zingy gazpacho, which Shinozuka marinates before pureeing to release all the tasty vegetable juices. He always adds a "Wait—what's that?" component, like a microscopic dice of sweet pineapple and pimentón-laced sausage, hidden at the bottom of the bowl.

—

1.
In a large gratin dish, combine the tomatoes, cucumber, bell pepper, fennel, shallots, garlic, oil, and vinegar. Sprinkle with 2 teaspoons of salt, season with pepper and hot sauce, and toss to coat. Cover with plastic wrap and let stand at room temperature, stirring occasionally, for at least 1 hour.

2.
Meanwhile, in a small saucepan of boiling salted water, cook the tapioca, stirring occasionally, until translucent and just tender, about 15 minutes. Drain and rinse in cold water.

3.
Working in batches, puree the tomato mixture with the tomato juice and mint in a food processor or blender until very smooth. Strain through a medium sieve into a bowl, pressing on the vegetables. Discard the solids in the sieve. Taste the soup and season again with oil, vinegar, salt, pepper, and hot sauce, if needed.

4.
Spoon the chorizo, pineapple, and tapioca into soup bowls. Ladle the soup into the bowls, top with a quenelle or spoonful of crème fraîche, and garnish with the samphire, if using. Drizzle with oil, sprinkle with piment d'Espelette, and serve.

—

Variation
Chef Daï Shinozuka likes to make a savory whipped cream for topping the soup. He whips heavy cream until it starts to thicken, then drizzles in a little extra-virgin olive oil and continues whipping until the cream holds a firm peak.

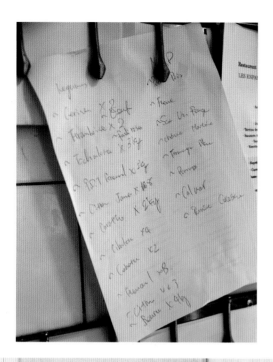

Daï Shinozuka
LES ENFANTS ROUGES

—

CATCHING UP over a drink at Yves Camdeborde's L'Avant Comptoir, cookbook author Dorie Greenspan suggested I check out Les Enfants Rouges. It's a fire-engine-red, mom-and-pop storefront, she said, with café curtains in the windows and bentwood chairs where Monsieur cooks and Madame takes orders. Except that Monsieur and Madame are Japanese. Cooking alongside bistronomy master Camdeborde and then L'Ami Jean's Stéphane Jégo, chef Daï Shinozuka became an expert at conjuring recipes that discreetly push the boundaries. When he opened Les Enfants Rouges, the Tokyo native also embraced his mentors' brand of effervescent hospitality and openness. It's such a pleasure when his wife, Tomo, delivers elegant cups of gazpacho (pictured on page 29) as a giveaway. Having become a stakeholder in the Paris dining scene, what does Daï cook when he's off duty? "I eat the Japanese food my wife prepares," he said.

winter squash soup
with cocoa cream

Four Servings

—

1 tablespoon unsweetened cocoa powder, plus more for dusting

¾ cup (185 ml) heavy cream

4 tablespoons (60 g) unsalted butter

1 small onion, halved and thinly sliced

Sea salt

One 1-pound (500-g) kabocha or butternut squash, peeled, seeded, and cut into 1-inch (2.5-cm) pieces (see Notes)

4 cups (1 L) water or vegetable or chicken stock

4 ounces (125 g) Yukon Gold potato, peeled and diced

2 slices of firm, day-old white bread, crusts removed, cut into ¼-inch (6-mm) cubes

Snipped chives, for sprinkling

Piment d'Espelette

—

Notes
To make prep easier, buy 1 pound (500 g) of peeled, seeded, and cubed winter squash.

The cocoa powder whipped into the cream makes it stiffer than usual.

Make Ahead
The soup can be prepared through Step 2 and refrigerated for up to 2 days. The croutons can be stored in an airtight container for up to 2 days.

"It could be my mother's," says L'Ami Jean's Stéphane Jégo of this simple velouté. "Except the cocoa cream takes it in a completely different direction." Jégo pipes the whipped cream into bowls and sends out the smooth soup separately in a pitcher. The (unsweetened) cream melts as the steaming soup is poured into your bowl, like marshmallows in a cup of hot chocolate.

—

1.
In a medium bowl, whisk the cocoa with 1 tablespoon of the cream to form a thick paste. Whisk in ½ cup (125 ml) of the remaining cream just until smooth. Cover the bowl and refrigerate until very cold, at least 1 hour. Whip the cocoa cream until it holds a firm peak. Cover and refrigerate.

2.
Meanwhile, in a large saucepan, melt 2 tablespoons (30 g) of the butter. Add the onion and a pinch of salt and cook over medium heat, stirring occasionally, until softened, about 5 minutes. Add the squash, cover, and cook over medium-low heat until it begins to soften, about 10 minutes. Add the water and potato and bring to a boil. Simmer, partially covered, over medium heat, stirring occasionally, until the potato is tender, about 20 minutes. Working in batches, puree the soup in a blender until very smooth.

3.
In a medium skillet, melt the remaining 2 tablespoons (30 g) of butter. Add the bread cubes and cook over medium-low heat, stirring occasionally, until crisp and golden, about 5 minutes. Season the croutons with salt, remove from the heat, and let cool.

4.
Return the soup to the saucepan, stir in the remaining 3 tablespoons of cream, and gently reheat. Season with salt. Pour the soup into a tureen or pitcher. Using a pastry bag with a large star tip or a spoon, pipe or dollop the whipped cocoa cream into soup bowls. Dust with cocoa powder and sprinkle with the croutons, chives, and piment d'Espelette. Serve with the soup.

cold fennel soup *with* chervil

Four Servings

—

4 tablespoons (60 ml) extra-virgin olive oil

1 onion, chopped

Sea salt

One 1-pound (500-g) fennel bulb, chopped, plus chopped fennel fronds

1 cup (30 g) packed chervil or parsley leaves

2 garlic cloves, chopped

¼ cup (60 ml) dry white wine

1 bay leaf

3 cups (750 ml) water

1 tablespoon fresh lemon juice

Freshly ground pepper

Crème fraîche, sour cream, or Greek yogurt, for serving

—

Make Ahead
The soup can be prepared through Step 2 and refrigerated for up to 2 days.

The velvety texture of chefs Anna Trattles's and Alice Quillet's fennel soup at Le Bal Café makes you think there must be some trick to it. In fact, it's simply a matter of getting the right ratio of water to fennel and then letting the blender run. Another reason it's so good: the bright chervil lends a greener color to the fennel's faint celadon and deepens the flavor.

—

1.
In a large saucepan, heat 2 tablespoons of the oil. Add the onion and a pinch of salt and cook over medium heat, stirring occasionally, until softened, about 5 minutes. Add the chopped fennel, fennel fronds, chervil, garlic, wine, and bay leaf. Cover and cook over medium-low heat until the fennel begins to soften, about 10 minutes. Add the water and bring to a boil. Simmer, partially covered, over medium heat, stirring occasionally, until the fennel is tender, about 20 minutes. Pick out and discard the bay leaf.

2.
Working in batches, puree the soup in a blender until very smooth. Transfer the soup to a medium bowl and refrigerate until chilled, about 1 hour.

3.
Stir the lemon juice and remaining 2 tablespoons of oil into the soup and season with salt and pepper. Ladle the soup into bowls, top with a quenelle or spoonful of crème fraîche, and serve.

green lentil soup *with* tapioca

Four Servings

—

4 tablespoons (60 ml) extra-virgin olive oil

1 carrot, halved lengthwise and thinly sliced

1 small onion, halved and thinly sliced

Sea salt

1 cup (200 g) green Puy lentils, rinsed and picked over

2 cups (500 ml) heavy cream, light cream, or half-and-half

4 cups (1 L) water or vegetable stock

2 tablespoons (20 g) small pearl tapioca (not instant)

2 slices of firm, day-old white bread, crusts removed, cut into ¼-inch (6-mm) cubes

2 ounces (60 g) foie gras or chicken liver terrine, cut into ¼-inch (6-mm) cubes

Snipped chives, for sprinkling

—

Make Ahead
The soup can be prepared through Step 1 and refrigerated for up to 2 days. The croutons can be stored in an airtight container for up to 2 days.

At Le Comptoir, Yves Camdeborde reimagines sweetly old-fashioned tapioca (one of the chef's pet ingredients) as a savory garnish for soup. You get the teasingly chewy pearls (think: bubble tea), plus croutons for crunch. The high-low juxtaposition of ingredients in progressive bistro cooking is very much apparent here with the luxe foie gras that Camdeborde adds to the bowl along with the homey tapioca before pouring in the hot soup.

—

1.
In a large saucepan, heat 2 tablespoons of the oil. Add the carrot and onion and a pinch of salt and cook over medium heat, stirring occasionally, until softened, about 5 minutes. Add the lentils, cream, and water and bring just to a simmer. Cook, partially covered, over medium-low heat, stirring occasionally, until the lentils are tender but still intact, 30 to 40 minutes. Using a slotted spoon, remove ¼ cup (60 ml) of the lentils and reserve. Working in batches, puree the soup in a blender until very smooth.

2.
Meanwhile, in a small saucepan of boiling salted water, cook the tapioca, stirring occasionally, until translucent and just tender, about 15 minutes. Drain and rinse in cold water.

3.
In a medium skillet, heat the remaining 2 tablespoons of oil until shimmering. Add the bread cubes and cook over medium-low heat, stirring occasionally, until crisp and golden, about 5 minutes. Season the croutons with salt, remove from the heat, and let cool.

4.
Return the soup to the saucepan and gently reheat. Season with salt. Pour the soup into a tureen or pitcher. Spoon the lentils and tapioca into soup bowls. Sprinkle with the croutons, foie gras, and chives. Serve with the soup.

—

Variation
I've also made this soup without the cream and embellishments, and it was still richly smooth. Replace the water with chicken stock and the cream with water. Skip the tapioca, croutons, foie gras, and chives. Add a chunk of butter to each bowl just before serving.

le
comptoir

Relais de Saint

Nos Vi...

NS ET LIQUOREUX
DE...

Eric Caill...

Thierry Pu...

René Moss

Antoine A...

Pierre & C...

Christian a...

Charles Hours

Michelle

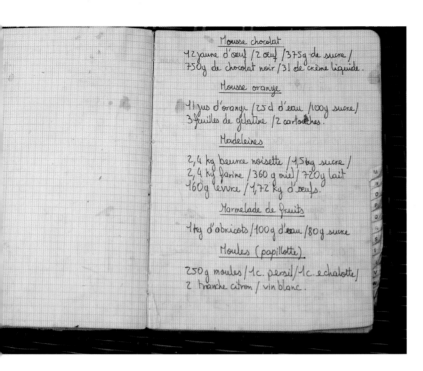

Yves Camdeborde

—

WHEN YVES CAMDEBORDE first opened Le Comptoir du Relais, I shadowed the Béarnais chef, trying to understand why in the world anyone would wait three and four months for his weeknight five-course prix fixe. (And endure the cold. If seated outside, you get a blanket and a bowl of steaming broth to warm your hands.) Camdeborde had already shaken up the staid Paris restaurant scene in 1992 with La Régalade (now operated by Bruno Doucet), serving luxurious dishes like scallops in the shell with citrus butter (page 114) at unprecedentedly low prices. His food and fun aesthetic became a surprise success, and chef friends, protégés, and even his mentor drew on his experience to open their own neo-bistros. After Camdeborde bought the small seventeenth-century Hôtel Relais Saint-Germain and created Le Comptoir, he launched L'Avant Comptoir, a stand-up small-plates holding room for people waiting to get in next door. Why the enduring appeal? It's hard to beat Camdeborde's traditional, regionally accented French cuisine and gift for charming the clientele.

sunchoke soup *with* black truffles

Four Servings

—

1 pound (500 g) sunchokes (Jerusalem artichokes), scrubbed (see Notes)

1 tablespoon extra-virgin olive oil, plus more for drizzling

Sea salt

4 tablespoons (60 g) unsalted butter

1 small onion, halved and thinly sliced

4 cups (1 L) water or chicken or vegetable stock

2 tablespoons (12 g) minced black truffles or truffle peelings, plus 4 black truffle slices (optional; see Notes)

Black truffle sea salt (see Notes)

—

Notes
Rose doesn't peel the gnarled sunchokes, so the soup is flecked with appealing brown specks.

Black truffles are available from dartagnan.com.

Black truffle sea salt is available at specialty food shops and from tfsnyc.com.

Make Ahead
The soup can be prepared through Step 2 and refrigerated for up to 2 days.

In this silky soup, Daniel Rose of Spring marries dirt-cheap sunchokes (Jerusalem artichokes) with extravagant truffles. When France's Tuber melanosporum is at its peak in January, even chefs on a budget can't resist them. Rose stirs in these flavor bombs just before serving—plus he adds slices to the bowl for garnish. But just a sprinkle of black truffle salt on top will give the soup a foraged aroma.

—

1.
Heat the oven to 425°F (220°C). On a small rimmed baking sheet, rub the sunchokes with the oil and season with sea salt. Bake, turning them occasionally, until they are tender when pierced with a knife, about 45 minutes. Let cool slightly, then thinly slice.

2.
In a large saucepan, melt 2 tablespoons (30 g) of the butter. Add the onion and a pinch of sea salt and cook over medium heat, stirring occasionally, until softened, about 5 minutes. Add the sunchokes, cover, and cook over medium-low heat for 10 minutes. Add the water and bring to a boil. Simmer, partially covered, over medium-low heat for 20 minutes. Working in batches, puree the soup in a blender until very smooth.

3.
Return the soup to the saucepan, stir in the remaining 2 tablespoons (30 g) of butter and the minced truffles, if using, and gently reheat. Season with truffle salt. Ladle the soup into soup bowls. Drizzle with oil, top with the truffle slices, if using, and serve.

parsnip soup *with* marcona almonds

Four Servings

—

2 tablespoons (30 g) unsalted butter

1 onion, halved and thinly sliced

Sea salt

1 pound (500 g) parsnips, peeled and diced

4 ounces (125 g) Yukon Gold potatoes, peeled and diced

4 cups (1 L) water or vegetable or chicken stock

½ cup (125 ml) heavy cream

1 tablespoon Marcona almonds, coarsely chopped

½ ounce (15 g) Spanish chorizo, finely chopped

Snipped chives, for garnish

—

Notes
Discard the woody cores if using large parsnips.

If the soup is too thick, thin it with milk when reheating.

Make Ahead
The soup can be prepared through Step 1 and refrigerated for up to 2 days.

La Cantine du Troquet chef Christian Etchebest's bone-white soup, topped with nuggets of smoky chorizo and salty nuts, might have you guessing if you didn't know that parsnips were the main ingredient. Look more deeply, Etchebest seems to say. There's so much flavor in the ordinary.

—

1.
In a large saucepan, melt the butter. Add the onion and a pinch of salt and cook over medium heat, stirring occasionally, until softened, about 5 minutes. Add the parsnips, cover, and cook over medium-low heat until they begin to soften, about 10 minutes. Add the potato and water and bring to a boil. Simmer, partially covered, over medium heat, until the potato is very tender, about 20 minutes. Working in batches, puree the soup in a blender until very smooth.

2.
Return the soup to the saucepan, stir in the cream, and gently reheat. Season with salt. Ladle the soup into bowls, garnish with the almonds, chorizo, and chives, and serve.

parmesan soup *with* peas

Four Servings

—

2 bacon slices, cut crosswise
¼ inch (6 mm) thick

2 slices of firm, day-old white
bread, crusts removed,
cut into ¼-inch (6-mm) cubes

Sea salt

¼ cup (60 g) shelled fresh peas
or thawed frozen baby peas

2 tablespoons (30 g) unsalted
butter

3 shallots, finely chopped

7 ounces (200 g) Parmesan
cheese, preferably aged:
5 ounces (150 g) grated,
2 ounces (50 g) shaved

2 cups (500 ml) heavy cream

1 cup (250 ml) chicken stock

Freshly ground pepper

Snipped chives and chopped
leeks, spring onions, or
scallions, for sprinkling

—

Note
Stéphane Jégo likes adding
chopped raw leeks to almost
all his dishes for color and
snap. He first soaks them in
ice water for 10 minutes to
soften the flavor yet keep the
vegetable crisp.

Make Ahead
The soup and bacon can be
refrigerated, separately,
for up to 2 days. The croutons
can be stored in an airtight
container for up to 2 days.

Stéphane Jégo's soup is like a liquid
version of Parmigiano-Reggiano—the
cheese is melted in cream and chicken
stock. It's incredibly popular at L'Ami
Jean; Jégo pretty much can't take it off
the menu—ever. He can punctuate it,
though, with whatever's just come to
market, like the first-of-season peas
he spooned into my bowl along with the
invariable crisp croutons and bacon.

—

1.
In a medium skillet, cook the bacon over
medium-high heat, stirring occasionally,
until crisp and lightly browned, about
5 minutes. Using a spider or slotted spoon,
transfer the bacon to paper towels.

2.
In the same skillet, cook the bread
cubes over medium-low heat, stirring
occasionally, until crisp and golden,
about 5 minutes. Season the croutons
with salt, remove from the heat, and let
cool in the skillet.

3.
In a small saucepan of boiling salted water,
cook the peas until tender, 1 to 3 minutes.
Drain and rinse in cold water. Drain again
and pat dry with paper towels.

4.
In a medium saucepan, melt the butter.
Add the shallots and a pinch of salt
and cook over medium heat, stirring
occasionally, until softened, 3 to 5 minutes.
Add the grated cheese and cook, stirring
often, until melted, 2 to 3 minutes.
Gradually stir in the cream and stock
and bring to a simmer, scraping up
any cheese stuck to the bottom. Cook,
partially covered, over medium-low
heat, stirring occasionally, for 10 minutes.
Season with pepper.

5.
Working in batches, puree the soup in
a blender until very smooth. Pour it into
a tureen or pitcher. Spoon the shaved
cheese, bacon, peas, and croutons into
soup bowls. Sprinkle with the chives and
leeks and serve with the soup.

1236

CELLPHONE

"I was constantly on the phone with suppliers," chef Stéphane Jégo said. "I couldn't peel an onion without being interrupted. Texting changed my life."

RECIPES

remain on the menu year after year—creamy Parmesan soup (opposite) and the famously over-the-top rice pudding, enriched with crème anglaise and salted caramel cream (pictured on page 199).

WEEKS

Jégo lets hare marinate for nearly a month when preparing lièvre à la royale. Then he cooks it for 12 hours and leaves it in its cooking liquid to develop even more flavor before it is served in a sauce based on hare blood.

MONTHS

Jégo develops his stocks over weeks and weeks, adding a freshly made batch to the deeply flavored original every day.

>10

40 —TO— 50

80

YEARS AGO

when he purchased the Basque pub, Jégo, a Breton, kept the original bric-a-brac, and added his own fun style, like cartoons painted on the walls.

LUNCH CUSTOMERS

come for Jégo's bistro favorites prepared with serious technique, such as winter squash soup (pictured on page 33) and steak worthy of a Flintstone (pictured on page 155).

DINNER GUESTS

plus up to ten walk-ins. At night, Jégo divides the menu between traditional à la carte choices and an inventive tasting menu, with suave dishes such as mackerel with blistered herbs (pictured on page 70).

BAKER *on the* RISE

Thierry Breton is a titan of bistronomy, one of its fiercest proponents, the owner of an expanding hub of establishments near the Gare du Nord. >

Like his posse of first-generation neo-bistro chefs, Yves Camdeborde and Christian Etchebest, Breton had worked under top toques at the Ritz, La Tour d'Argent, Hôtel de Crillon, and Pavillon Ledoyen before opening his own modern bistros Chez Michel and Chez Casimir.

As most cooks do, he had outsourced his bread. But during a lull in 2007, after truffle and game season, Breton began experimenting with artisanal baking. It was a lark, he told me, not a fanboy's dedication to an ancient craft. "We started without a recipe, in our restaurant oven, just for the experience," Breton said.

Yet his tinkering turned into a full-blown obsession. Breton bought a pétrain (a trough for kneading the fermented dough), built a bread oven

at Chez Michel, and even set up a chef's table alongside it. Eventually, other restaurateurs started asking for Breton's darkly crusted loaves, and the chef now operates a full-fledged bakery in the basement next door with a Breton bar, La Pointe du Grouin, on the ground floor. (The bakery is eco-conscious, too. Breads still warm from the oven are packed into an insulated bag fitted to a Danish Bullitt cargo bicycle and delivered all over Paris by a helmeted deliveryman.)

When I stopped by La Pointe du Grouin, Breton was prepping for lunch, a menu of bread-oven–focused snacks, including soups studded with hefty sourdough croutons (pictured on page 45) and sandwiches crafted to pair the right filling with the right bread. Soft smoked salmon and fresh goat cheese were tucked into tender seeded buns that wouldn't overwhelm or squish the filling. Sturdy items like sliced saucisson sec (salami) and andouille were layered into thick-crusted ficelles.

On an étagère next to the bar, large brown rounds of chewy rye bread were stacked after the morning's firing. Deep-dish pies, buttery Breton kouign-amann pastries, and a plum crumble (page 190) sat on the counter. They're slightly charred, having been baked in the diminishing heat of the oven once the bread came out.

Breton now bakes 500 loaves daily for his own three bistros and 70-plus restaurant clients, including Les Enfants Rouges, Au Passage, Clown Bar, and Bistro Bellet. "It wasn't my objective to start an empire," Breton told me. "But if we're going to bake bread, let's be serious about it."

leek & potato velouté *with* bacon cream

Four Servings

—

2 bacon slices, finely chopped

¾ cup (185 ml) heavy cream

Freshly ground pepper

2 tablespoons (30 g) unsalted butter

2 leeks, white and light green parts only, halved lengthwise and thinly sliced

Sea salt

8 ounces (250 g) Yukon Gold potatoes, peeled and diced

4 cups (1 L) water or vegetable or chicken stock

Piment d'Espelette (see Note)

—

Note
Piment d'Espelette, a subtly spicy ground chile pepper, is available at specialty food shops, spice shops, and surlatable.com.

Make Ahead
The soup can be prepared through Step 2 and refrigerated for up to 2 days.

You rarely see leek and potato soup at new bistros; it's too old-school. But Daï Shinozuka of Les Enfants Rouges infuses cream with bacon and lots of black pepper, then whips it to make a voluptuous garnish for the pureed soup.

—

1.
In a small nonstick skillet, cook the bacon over medium-high heat, stirring occasionally, until lightly browned, 3 to 5 minutes. Remove the skillet from the heat and spoon off the fat. Add ½ cup (125 ml) of the cream to the bacon, cover, and let steep for 15 minutes. Season generously with pepper. Transfer the cream and bacon to a medium bowl, cover, and refrigerate until very cold, at least 1 hour. Whip the cream until it holds a firm peak. Cover and refrigerate.

2.
Meanwhile, in a large saucepan, melt the butter. Add the leeks and a pinch of salt, cover, and cook over low heat, stirring occasionally, until softened, about 10 minutes. Add the potatoes and water and bring to a boil. Simmer, partially covered, over medium heat, until the potatoes are very tender, about 20 minutes. Working in batches, puree the soup in a blender until very smooth.

3.
Return the soup to the saucepan, stir in the remaining ¼ cup (60 ml) of cream, and gently reheat. Season with salt. Pour the soup into a tureen or pitcher. Using a pastry bag with a large star tip or a spoon, pipe or dollop the whipped bacon cream into soup bowls and dust with piment d'Espelette. Serve with the soup.

blue crab velouté *with* celery root

Four Servings

—

6 tablespoons (100 ml)
extra-virgin olive oil

2 pounds (1 kg) small blue
crabs, halved crosswise

1 large onion, halved and
thinly sliced

1 large celery rib, finely
chopped

8 large parsley sprigs,
tied in a bundle

Sea salt

1 cup (250 ml) dry white wine

4 cups (1 L) water

4 ounces (125 g) celery root

1 tablespoon fresh lemon juice

4 ounces (125 g) sourdough
bread, torn or cut into rough
1-inch (2.5-cm) cubes

½ cup (125 ml) heavy cream

Micro parsley sprigs or
chopped parsley, for garnish

Piment d'Espelette

—

Make Ahead
The soup can be prepared
through Step 2 and refrigerated
for up to 2 days.

The croutons can be stored
in an airtight container for up
to 2 days.

At La Pointe du Grouin, chef Thierry Breton (the guy behind the bar in a red wool knitted cap, summer or winter) makes a hearty seafood soup with small blue crabs. These are the same as the pricey soft shell crabs you eat whole in spring and summer but with their hard, cold-weather shells, they're a fraction of the price. They don't have much meat on them—you toss them after they're cooked—but they add intense seafood flavor to soups and sauces.

—

1.
In a large sauté pan or skillet, heat 2 tablespoons of the oil. Add half of the crabs to the pan and cook over medium-high heat, turning them once, until they turn red on both sides, about 2 minutes. Transfer the crabs to a bowl. Repeat with 2 tablespoons of the oil and the remaining crabs.

2.
To the same pan, add the onion, celery, parsley bundle, and a pinch of salt. Cover and cook over low heat, stirring occasionally, until softened, 8 to 10 minutes. Return the crabs to the pan with the wine. Bring to a boil and simmer over medium-high heat until nearly evaporated, about 5 minutes. Add the water, bring to a boil, and simmer over medium heat, partially covered, for 30 minutes.

3.
Meanwhile, thickly peel the celery root. Using a mandoline, thinly slice it ⅛ inch (3 mm) thick, then cut into julienne strips. In a medium bowl, toss the celery root with the lemon juice.

4.
In a medium skillet, heat the remaining 2 tablespoons of oil until shimmering. Add the bread cubes and cook over medium-low heat, stirring occasionally, until crisp and golden, about 5 minutes. Season with salt, remove from the heat, and let cool.

5.
Remove the crabs and parsley bundle from the soup and discard. Working in batches, puree the soup in a blender until very smooth. Return the soup to the saucepan, stir in the cream, and gently reheat. Season with salt. Pour the soup into a tureen or pitcher. Spoon the celery root, croutons, and parsley sprigs into bowls. Sprinkle with piment d'Espelette. Serve with the soup.

—

Variation
If you can get your hands on scallops in the shell, save the coral and everything else you're tempted to throw out. Wash them well and use instead of blue crabs to make a fantastic variation of this soup.

small bites and starters

radishes *with* smoked herring butter

Four Servings

—

2 tablespoons (4 g) packed parsley leaves

1½ to 2 ounces (45 to 60 g) smoked fish, such as herring, bluefish, or mackerel, skinned and chopped

1 pound (500 g) multicolored radishes with greens, greens trimmed to ½ inch (1 cm), 2 tablespoons of chopped greens reserved

8 tablespoons (125 g) unsalted butter, softened

1 tablespoon fresh lemon juice

Fine sea salt and freshly ground pepper

Sliced baguette, for serving

Fleur de sel

—

Note
For super-crisp radishes, soak them in ice water an hour before serving.

Make Ahead
The smoked fish butter can be wrapped in plastic and refrigerated for up to 2 weeks or frozen for up to 1 month. Bring to room temperature before serving.

Le Servan chef Tatiana Levha's new take on the iconic radish-sea salt-butter combination is as hard to stop eating as the original. Levha whips smoky fish into the butter, along with herbs and some of the spicy radish tops. That's not much of a recipe, you say. Admittedly, half of the pleasure comes from how it's eaten—the physical act of dipping a crisp radish in fleur de sel, smearing a slice of bread with butter, and tasting successive crunchy, salty, creamy bites.

—

1.
In a mini food processor, pulse the parsley, smoked fish, and reserved 2 tablespoons of chopped radish greens until finely chopped. Add the butter, lemon juice, and a pinch each of salt and pepper and pulse to blend.

2.
Spread the smoked fish butter in a small crock. Serve with the radishes and baguette slices and pass fleur de sel at the table.

Tatiana Levha
LE SERVAN
—

TATIANA LEVHA's bistro, Le Servan, perfectly expresses the Paris restaurant trends of the moment. Levha is young, foreign (Filipina-French), and a veteran of the city's top restaurants (Michelin-three-stars Astrance and Arpège), plus Ferrandi, the capital's haute cuisine feeder school. The space is small, the menu is brief, and there's no restaurant sign (a paper menu is taped to the door instead). Levha ate around Asia for six months before transforming a gritty nineteenth-century café into a pretty, light-filled bistro with window walls. Excavation uncovered stone columns and garlands of ceiling molding, which now encircle delightful trompe-l'oeil clouds. Tatiana does not call attention to herself, preferring to quietly focus on her sublime Paris-via-Manila cooking. It's hard to think of a more compelling argument for multiculturalism than her mahogany-seared guinea hen with a superb ginger-cashew mix stuffed under the skin (page 146). What about the modernist tools she mastered at Astrance and Arpège? "I can't afford a sous vide machine," she said. "And I don't miss it."

smoked eel *&* beet crostini

—

2 medium beets, scrubbed

¼ cup (60 ml) apple juice

¼ cup (60 ml) apple cider vinegar

3 tablespoons (70 g) honey

2 tablespoons crème fraîche or sour cream

4 ounces (125 g) smoked fish, such as eel, mackerel, or bluefish, skinned and cut to fit the beet half slices

Micro herb sprigs, for garnish

—

Note
If the apple vinaigrette hardens, heat it in the microwave until pourable, about 10 seconds.

Make Ahead
The recipe can be prepared through Step 1 and refrigerated overnight.

For this appetite-teaser, Spring chef Daniel Rose layers smoked fish and crème fraîche on slices of beet instead of toast. Drops of nose-tingling apple syrup—a reduction of apple juice, apple cider vinegar, and honey—perfume each bite.

—

1.
In a medium saucepan, cover the beets with 2 inches (5 cm) of water. Bring to a simmer and cook until the beets are tender, 50 to 60 minutes. Drain and let cool slightly. Peel the beets and slice crosswise ¼ inch (6 mm) thick. Cut each slice in half.

2.
Meanwhile, in a small saucepan, bring the apple juice, vinegar, and honey to a simmer and cook over medium-high heat, swirling the pan occasionally, until syrupy, about 4 minutes.

3.
Arrange the beet slices on a platter. Dab each with ¼ teaspoon of crème fraîche and set a piece of fish on top. Spoon a drop of the apple vinaigrette on top, garnish with an herb sprig, and serve.

watermelon & charentais with burrata & basil

Four Servings

—

½ cup (60 g) oil-cured black olives, pitted and chopped

2 teaspoons sherry vinegar

1 tablespoon extra-virgin olive oil, plus more for drizzling

Sea salt and freshly ground pepper

12 ounces (350 g) watermelon, rind removed, flesh cut into 1x1x2½-inch (2x2x6-cm) rectangles

12 ounces (350 g) Charentais or cantaloupe melon, rind removed, flesh cut into 1x1x2½-inch (2x2x6-cm) rectangles

12 ounces (350 g) burrata or mozzarella cheese, torn into 4 pieces

Small mixed basil leaves, such as Genovese, purple, and Thai, for garnish

Fleur de sel

—

Make Ahead
The dehydrated olives can be refrigerated in an airtight container for up to 1 week.

Les Déserteurs chef Daniel Baratier reinterprets the sweet, creamy, and salty tastes in dishes like melon with prosciutto and tomatoes with mozzarella. This is undeniably a chef-y presentation; Baratier cuts the pink and orange melons into precise rectangles and lines them up, alternating the colors, but you can slice the melons and arrange them any way you like. The saltiness comes from pulverized olives, dehydrated in the microwave. They take only minutes to prepare and are phenomenal.

—

1.
Spread the olives on a microwave-safe plate. Microwave at high power, uncovered, in 1-minute intervals until the olives are dehydrated but still plump, 3 to 6 minutes total. Transfer to a food processor and pulse until finely chopped.

2.
In a large bowl, whisk the vinegar with the oil and season with salt and pepper. Add the watermelon and Charentais melon and gently toss to coat. Alternate the two melon rectangles in a tight row on each plate. Top with the burrata and basil and season with fleur de sel. Drizzle with more oil, sprinkle with the dehydrated olives, and serve.

beet dip *with* za'atar & pomegranate molasses

Makes 1½ Cups (375 ml)

—

1 pound (500 g) medium red beets, scrubbed

1 garlic clove, chopped

3 tablespoons extra-virgin olive oil, plus more for drizzling

3 tablespoons Greek yogurt

1 tablespoon pomegranate molasses

1 tablespoon za'atar, plus more for sprinkling (see Notes)

Fine sea salt and freshly ground black pepper

¼ teaspoon cayenne pepper

2 tablespoons (15 g) toasted skinned hazelnuts, chopped (for toasting, see page 105, Step 1)

Sliced toasted sourdough bread, for serving

—

Notes
Cold food requires more seasoning than warm food, so be sure to taste the dip again just before serving and add as much sea salt, black pepper, and cayenne as needed to make the flavors pop.

Za'atar is available at specialty food stores and Mediterranean markets and from penzeys.com.

Make Ahead
The recipe can be prepared through Step 1 and refrigerated overnight.

Marion Graux, who created the distinctive pottery for neo-bistro Clown Bar (see page 63), calls this recipe "ma betterave" ("my beet"). She transforms the earthy root vegetable into a scarlet puree and seasons it with sweet-and-sour pomegranate molasses and a Mediterranean spice blend dominated by tart sumac, sesame seeds, and herbs.

—

1.
In a large saucepan, cover the beets with 2 inches (5 cm) of water. Bring to a simmer and cook until the beets are very tender, about 1 hour. Drain and let cool slightly. Peel the beets and cut each one into 8 pieces.

2.
In a food processor, pulse the beets with the garlic until blended. Add the oil, yogurt, pomegranate molasses, and za'atar and puree until mostly smooth. Season with salt, black pepper, and cayenne. Scrape into a wide, shallow serving bowl. Cover and refrigerate until cold, about 1 hour. Taste and season again with salt, black pepper, and cayenne, if needed. Drizzle more oil around the bowl. Sprinkle with za'atar, scatter the hazelnuts on top, and serve with the bread.

—

Variation
Brush 4 pita breads on both sides with extra-virgin olive oil and dust with za'atar. Grill over medium-high heat until lightly browned, 1 to 2 minutes per side. Cut into wedges and serve with the dip.

Marion Graux

MARION GRAUX POTERIE

—

WITH A CLAY-SMEARED apron tied over her Japanese shift, Marion Graux is finishing the bowls she'll give as party favors at her upcoming wedding. The robin's egg blue vessels have three black drips on the inside and are stamped with the date of the nuptials. Their elegant spontaneity is exactly what compelled small-plates spot Clown Bar to commission this stylist-turned-potter to create the bar's tableware. Graux cites cooking as a key inspiration for her work. In her studio, up a dirt road north of Paris not listed on Google Maps, humble kitchen tools—a sieve, a funnel, a ladle, some whisks—hang on the walls like art. A serious home cook herself—her recipe for Beet Dip with Za'atar and Pomegranate Molasses is pictured on page 55— she is constantly thinking about designing and fabricating dishes that chefs will want to use as a canvas for their food. Graux is a feisty defender of the utilitarian. She believes her cups, plates, bowls, and platters are meant to be seen and used. Her argument: "We eat three times a day."

tomatoes *with* ticklemore cheese & lovage

Four Servings

—

1 tablespoon sherry vinegar

2 tablespoons extra-virgin olive oil

Flaky sea salt, such as Maldon

Pinch of sugar

4 ripe medium tomatoes (about 1½ pounds/750 g)

2 tablespoons thinly sliced lovage or celery leaves, plus lovage flowers (optional)

3 ounces (90 g) Ticklemore cheese or another semi-hard goat cheese, thinly sliced

Freshly ground pepper

At Le Bal Café, chefs Alice Quillet and Anna Trattles serve this very English take on the classic Italian Caprese salad. Instead of basil, there's lovage (a favorite in medieval kitchen gardens), and standing in for the mozzarella is crumbly Ticklemore, a farmstead goat's-milk cheese made in Devon. For seasoning, it gets a sprinkling of Maldon salt flakes from the east coast of Essex. It's a delicious twist that keeps the meal interesting without losing the charm of the original.

—

1.
In a large bowl, whisk the vinegar with the oil and season with salt and sugar. Cut the tomatoes into wedges. Add the tomatoes and lovage leaves and flowers, if using, to the vinaigrette and gently toss to coat.

2.
Spoon the tomatoes and juices into shallow bowls. Top with the cheese, season with salt and pepper, and serve.

baby beet salad *with* fresh cheese *&* basil

Four Servings

—

20 small mixed baby beets with greens (about 1 ounce/ 30 g each), scrubbed, stems discarded and ½ cup (15 g) torn greens reserved

¼ cup (60 ml) red wine vinegar

1 tablespoon crème de cassis

¼ cup (60 ml) extra-virgin olive oil

Sea salt and freshly ground pepper

2 tablespoons chopped basil

Fleur de sel

3 ounces (90 g) crumbly fresh cheese, such as French feta, Roquefort, or goat cheese

—

Note
 If your beet greens are less than perfectly fresh, steam them for a minute or two after removing the beets in Step 1.

Key to Tatiana Levha's salad is a splash of crème de cassis (blackcurrant liqueur), which echoes the sweet, dark beets and contrasts with the cheese. Another trick from Le Servan: Levha weaves the tender beet tops through the marinated beets for complexity.

—

1.
In a large saucepan, set a steamer basket over ½ inch (1 cm) of water and bring to a boil. Add the beets, cover, and cook over medium heat until tender, 20 to 30 minutes. Check the water level in the pan halfway through steaming and add more as needed. Transfer the beets to a plate and let cool slightly. Peel the beets.

2.
In a large bowl, whisk the vinegar and cassis with the oil. Season with salt and pepper. Add the beets and reserved beet greens and toss to coat. Spoon the beet salad and juices into shallow bowls. Sprinkle with the basil and season with fleur de sel. Crumble the cheese on top and serve.

—

Variations
For multidimensional texture, try a mix of beets in different shapes and sizes. Halve, quarter, or cube larger beets to contrast with the smaller whole beets. Or add candied and/or toasted, coarsely chopped walnuts, hazelnuts, pistachios, or pecans (see Rainbow Chard Salad with Candied Walnuts, page 88).

haricots verts salad *with* strawberries *&* feta

Four Servings

—

Coarse sea salt

1 pound (500 g) haricots verts

½ tablespoon fresh lemon juice

½ tablespoon honey vinegar, or a mix of 1 teaspoon honey and ½ tablespoon sherry vinegar

2 tablespoons extra-virgin olive oil

Fine sea salt and freshly ground pepper

4 ounces (125 g) small strawberries, sliced crosswise

1 tablespoon fresh green almond halves or sliced almonds (see Notes)

French feta cheese, for grating

—

Notes
Green almonds are fresh, soft almonds sold in their green fuzzy husks (hence the name). You have to split open the husk to get at the nut. A really young nut is jellylike, but French chefs prefer them slightly firmer. They are often split where they naturally form two halves and served as a delicate spring garnish. Green almonds are available sometime between April and June at farmers' markets where there are almond groves nearby and at some specialty food shops.

Chef Atsumi sometimes replaces the strawberries with skin-on peaches, cut into thin wedges.

Make Ahead
The recipe can be prepared through Step 1 and refrigerated for up to 4 hours.

Chef Sota Atsumi at Clown Bar finely grates creamy, mild (not super-salty) French feta into a small blizzard over lightly dressed haricots verts and strawberries, creating a feathery texture that melts in your mouth. It's a totally different experience from eating crumbled feta.

—

1.
Fill a medium bowl with half ice, half cold water. In a medium saucepan of boiling salted water, cook the haricots verts until crisp-tender, about 3 minutes. Drain and transfer to the ice water to cool for 1 minute; drain. Transfer to a thick kitchen towel and pat dry, then cut in half.

2.
In a large bowl, whisk the lemon juice with the vinegar and oil. Season with fine salt and pepper. Add the haricots verts and strawberries and gently toss to coat. Spoon the salad and juices into shallow bowls and top with the almonds. Finely grate the cheese over the top and serve.

Sota Atsumi
CLOWN BAR

—

WITH ITS STUNNING original zinc
bar, Art Nouveau clown tiles, and
glass ceiling painted with circus
scenes, the converted café annex of
the 1852 Cirque d'Hiver (an indoor
circus arena) is the unlikely setting
for a subtly experimental tapas
bar. Clown Bar's kitchen is powered
by the passion, intelligence, and
disarming humility of Sota Atsumi.
Though we spoke in French (a second
language for us both), I grasped that
the Tokyo native had picked up key
lessons from restaurant greats Joël
Robuchon (flawless craftsmanship)
and Michel Troisgros (smart
ingredient sourcing). Still, the
hallmarks of delicacy and simplicity
in dishes like marinated tuna with
raspberries under a blanket of shaved
golden beets (pictured on page 71)
are distinctly his. The sense of
only-in-this-place extends to the
tactile, slightly irregular handmade
dishes by Parisian potter Marion Graux
(page 57) and to the modern wood
tables with a hidden drawer in which
flatware is tucked away.

summer onions *with* salsa verde

Four Servings

—

1 cup (30 g) packed mixed chopped herbs, such as onion greens (reserved from onions below), parsley, dill, tarragon, and mint

¼ cup (60 ml) extra-virgin olive oil, plus more for brushing

4 shallots: 3 halved and thinly sliced (¾ cup/150 g), 1 finely chopped

1 tablespoon fresh lemon juice

1 oil-packed anchovy, finely chopped

½ tablespoon salt-packed capers, rinsed and finely chopped

½ garlic clove, finely chopped

Sea salt and freshly ground pepper

Grapeseed oil, for frying

6 to 10 small spring or early summer onions of every shape and color, green tops reserved for the salsa verde

2 cups (500 ml) buttermilk

Fleur de sel

—

Note
Chef Delling-Williams is not a fan of grill pans. "They add grill marks but no caramelized flavor," he says.

Make Ahead
The onions can be blanched up to 4 hours ahead. The salsa verde can be refrigerated overnight; it will solidify, so let it come to room temperature before serving.

Onions, especially spring and early summer onions with their greens still attached, are headlining menus all over Paris. At Au Passage, chef Edward Delling-Williams treats them as seriously as any protein. They turn sweet, in their onion-y way, when he blanches them in water and then simmers them in buttermilk leftover from their house-made butter. For crunch, they're served with crisp, fried shallots.

—

1.
In a small bowl, combine the herbs with the olive oil, chopped shallot, lemon juice, anchovy, capers, and garlic. Season the salsa verde with salt and pepper.

2.
In a medium skillet, heat ¼ inch (6 mm) of grapeseed oil until very hot but not smoking. Add the sliced shallots and fry over medium-high heat, stirring occasionally, until crisp and browned, about 2 minutes. Using a spider or slotted spoon, transfer the fried shallots to paper towels to drain. Season with salt.

3.
In a large saucepan of boiling water, blanch the onions for 3 minutes; drain. In the same saucepan, bring the buttermilk to a simmer. Add the blanched onions, partially cover, and cook over medium heat until crisp-tender, about 5 minutes; drain.

4.
Heat a grill. Cut the onions in half from top to bottom. Brush them with olive oil and grill over high heat until lightly charred on both sides and tender but still intact, 2 to 4 minutes per side. Transfer the onions to plates, season with fleur de sel and pepper, and drizzle with the salsa verde. Sprinkle the fried shallots alongside and serve.

—

Variation
You can also make this dish with winter onions. Cook them in their skins in Step 3, which helps them stay intact. Peel them just before grilling.

leeks vinaigrette *with* vin jaune sabayon

Four Servings

—

1 tablespoon sherry vinegar

3 tablespoons grapeseed oil

1 teaspoon Dijon mustard

Sea salt and freshly ground pepper

12 baby leeks (white and light green parts only), spring onions, or large scallions

8 tablespoons (125 g) unsalted butter, sliced

2 large egg yolks

1 tablespoon warm water

2 tablespoons vin jaune (see Note) or Gewürztraminer

Fleur de sel

Snipped chives and shaved black truffle (optional), for garnish

—

Note
Vin jaune is a complex white wine from the Jura region in eastern France made with the Savagnin grape in a process similar to making sherry but without the addition of spirits.

Make Ahead
The leeks vinaigrette can be prepared through Step 2 and refrigerated for up to 4 hours.

Auguste Escoffier called this egg-rich sauce a hollandaise. Frenchie chef-owner Greg Marchand froths it in a siphon and calls it a sabayon. Fluffy (whisked by hand) or supremely fluffy (foamed in a siphon), it's magnificent with marinated leeks.

—

1.
In a medium gratin dish, whisk the vinegar with the oil and mustard. Season with salt and pepper.

2.
In a large skillet of boiling salted water, cook the leeks until tender, about 8 minutes. Drain, transfer the leeks to a thick kitchen towel, and pat dry. Transfer the warm leeks to the gratin dish and turn to coat in the vinaigrette.

3.
In a small saucepan, melt the butter over high heat. Skim the froth from the surface and remove the pan from the heat. In a medium saucepan, bring 2 inches (5 cm) of water to a simmer. In a medium heatproof bowl, mix the egg yolks with the warm water. Set the bowl over the saucepan of simmering water and whisk the yolks continuously until thickened slightly and bright yellow, about 1 minute. Remove the bowl from the heat.

4.
Gently reheat the butter in the pan, if needed. Very gradually, whisk the butter into the yolks until a slightly thick sauce forms. Whisk in the vin jaune and season with fleur de sel and pepper.

5.
Arrange 3 leeks side by side on each plate. Spoon the sabayon crosswise on top. Sprinkle with the chives, decorate with the truffles, if using, and serve.

—

Variation
Try fat, peeled asparagus in lieu of the leeks. To keep them bright green, shock the cooked asparagus in a medium bowl of half ice, half water for 1 minute, then drain and pat dry.

66 small bites and starters

grilled sesame shiitake mushrooms

Four Servings

—

1 tablespoon plus 1 teaspoon toasted sesame oil

1 tablespoon plus 1 teaspoon tamari

20 shiitake mushrooms of the same size, stems removed

Fleur de sel and freshly ground pepper

Thinly sliced scallions, for sprinkling

When Semilla opened, chef Éric Trochon seduced customers with a five-ingredient dish that practically cooks itself. It was so successful it never left the menu.

—

1.
In a small bowl, combine the sesame oil and tamari.

2.
Heat a griddle or large cast-iron skillet until very hot. Reduce the heat to medium, add the mushrooms, cap-side down, and cook until moisture appears on the surface, 1 to 2 minutes. Turn the mushrooms, set a large skillet on top to flatten them, and cook until tender, about 1 minute.

3.
Transfer the mushrooms to plates, arranging them slightly overlapping in a circle. Season with fleur de sel and pepper. Drizzle with the sesame oil mixture, sprinkle with the scallions, and serve.

—

Variation
These mushrooms are also great with other toasted nut oils, such as hazelnut or walnut.

smoked herring tartare *with* fava beans *&* lime

Four Servings

—

Coarse sea salt

8 ounces (250 g) fava beans in the pod (see Note), shelled (½ cup/125 g)

2 tablespoons crème fraîche or sour cream

½ tablespoon fresh Meyer lemon juice

Fine sea salt

8 ounces (250 g) smoked fish, such as herring or blue fish, skinned and cut into ¼-inch (6-mm) pieces

2 tablespoons micro or baby basil leaves

2 tablespoons micro or baby amaranth or spinach leaves

2 tablespoons herb oil (see page 116, Step 1)

2 tablespoons fresh lime juice

Freshly ground pepper

Piment d'Espelette

—

Note
You can skip the blanching and peeling of the fava beans in Step 1 if you use 3 ounces (90 g) thawed frozen baby peas (about ½ cup/125 ml).

Make Ahead
The peeled favas and the lemon cream can be refrigerated separately overnight.

This recipe from Amélie Darvas at Haï Kaï is "tartare" like you've never had it before—she starts with smoked fish and pairs it with a swoosh of crème fraîche sparked with Meyer lemon. The smoke, herbs, cream, and acidity (Meyer lemon juice and lime juice) produce waves of flavor.

—

1.
Fill a small bowl with half ice, half cold water. In a small saucepan of boiling salted water, blanch the fava beans for 1 minute. Drain the favas and add to the ice water to cool for 1 minute. Drain again, then peel them.

2.
In a small bowl, whisk the crème fraîche with the lemon juice. Season with fine salt.

3.
In a medium bowl, combine the favas with the smoked fish, basil, amaranth, herb oil, and lime juice and gently toss to coat. Season with fine salt, pepper, and piment d'Espelette. Spoon the tartare in a line down the center of each plate. Spoon the lemon cream next to the tartare and serve.

mackerel *with* blistered herbs

Four Servings

—

1 large mini cucumber, sliced ¹⁄₁₆ inch (1.5 mm) thick on a mandoline

½ small carrot, peeled and cut into ⅛-inch (3-mm) dice

1 teaspoon sugar

1 teaspoon coarse sea salt

1 tablespoon white wine vinegar

½ small onion, thinly sliced

Four 4-ounce (125-g) skin-on mackerel, salmon, or bluefish fillets

Extra-virgin olive oil, for brushing

Fine sea salt and freshly ground pepper

8 bay leaves

8 thyme sprigs

8 rosemary sprigs

Piment d'Espelette and nigella seeds (optional), for sprinkling

—

Note
You won't get quite the same drama, but the herbs can be carefully broiled close to the heating element for a similar effect.

Make Ahead
The cucumber salad can be refrigerated for up to 4 hours.

Stéphane Jégo blasts bay leaves and rosemary and thyme sprigs halfway to cinders atop a mackerel fillet and pickled cucumbers. The smoldering herbs turn heads in the dining room at L'Ami Jean, but the real revelation is the suave fish beneath.

—

1.
In a small bowl, toss the cucumber slices and carrot with the sugar and coarse salt and let stand for 5 minutes. Add the vinegar and onion and gently toss to coat. Refrigerate for 10 minutes.

2.
Meanwhile, in a steamer, cook the fish fillets, covered, until medium-rare, 3 to 5 minutes. Transfer the fillets to a platter, skin-side up, brush them with oil, and season with fine salt and pepper.

3.
On a cutting board, pile the bay leaves, thyme, and rosemary and bruise them with a rolling pin. Spoon the cucumber salad on individual wooden boards or heatproof plates. Sprinkle with the piment d'Espelette and nigella seeds, if using. Set a fish fillet skin-side up on the cucumber salad. Top each fillet with 2 bay leaves, 2 thyme sprigs, and 2 rosemary sprigs. Using a kitchen blowtorch, set the herbs aflame and serve when the herbs are smoldering.

tuna *with* raspberries & shaved golden beets

Four Servings

—

8 small golden baby beets (each about 1 ounce/30 g), scrubbed

1 Fuji or Golden Delicious apple, peeled, cored, and cut into eighths

1 tablespoon sake vinegar or sherry vinegar

1 tablespoon apple juice

Sea salt and freshly ground pepper

2 tablespoons fresh lemon juice

2 tablespoons extra-virgin olive oil

1 tablespoon finely sliced scallion, white part only

8 ounces (250 g) well-chilled, ultra-fresh tuna steak, cut into ½-inch (1-cm) cubes

6 ounces (180 g) raspberries

Fleur de sel

Parmesan cheese, for grating

—

Note
Cooked beets can easily be peeled by rubbing off the skin with paper towels.

Make Ahead
The steamed beets can be refrigerated overnight. The apple puree can be refrigerated for up to 4 hours.

Petals of beetroot conceal delicate marinated tuna and fresh raspberries as well as raw apple puree underlying it all. (Apple puree with marinated tuna may not sound promising, but it's magical.) This gracefully composed plate is typical of chef Sota Atsumi's cooking at Clown Bar.

—

1.
In a medium saucepan, set a steamer basket over 1 inch (2.5 cm) of water and bring to a boil. Add the beets, cover, and cook over medium heat until tender, 20 to 30 minutes. Check the water level in the pan halfway through steaming and add more as needed. Transfer the beets to a plate and let cool slightly. Peel the beets and slice them ¹⁄₁₆ inch (1.5 mm) thick on a mandoline.

2.
Meanwhile, in a food processor, puree the apple with the vinegar and apple juice until smooth. Season with salt and pepper.

3.
In a medium bowl, whisk the lemon juice with the oil and scallion and season with salt and pepper. Add the tuna and raspberries and gently toss to coat. Dollop the apple puree into shallow bowls. Spoon the tuna and raspberries on top and season with fleur de sel and pepper. Drape the beet slices over the tuna, slightly overlapping them so they completely cover the tuna. Finely grate the cheese on top and serve.

smoked tomato *&* tuna salad

Four Servings

—

2 pounds (1 kg) medium heirloom tomatoes of every color: 1 pound (500 g) chopped, 1 pound (500 g) peeled, halved, and seeded

Sea salt

1 teaspoon honey

1 tablespoon julienned spring onion, white part only

½ cup (40 g) hardwood chips, such as applewood

8 ounces (250 g) well-chilled, ultra-fresh tuna steak, cut into ½-inch (1-cm) cubes

1 small tomatillo, husk folded back, quartered lengthwise

Extra-virgin olive oil, for drizzling

1 lime

Fleur de sel and coarse freshly ground pepper

—

Notes
Use very ripe, even overripe, tomatoes to make the tomato water; they'll give up even more juice.

Also, add the seedy insides from the peeled, halved, and seeded tomatoes to the sieve with the chopped tomatoes in Step 1. They're full of flavor.

Make Ahead
The tomato water can stand at room temperature for up to 4 hours.

This bright, light, sweet, and citrusy seafood salad mixes sashimi-quality tuna with tomatoes and tart tomatillos. Spring chef-owner Daniel Rose likes to play tricks: the cubes of fish look like pieces of red tomato—until you spear one with a fork. Another surprise: the tuna is more delicate than the tomatoes, which are smoked.

—

1.
Set a fine sieve over a medium bowl. Add the chopped tomatoes and season with ¾ teaspoon of salt. Let stand, stirring occasionally, until about ¾ cup (185 ml) of tomato water has collected in the bowl, 30 to 40 minutes. Discard the chopped tomatoes. Stir the honey and spring onion into the tomato water.

2.
Meanwhile, line the inside of a wok and its lid with foil, leaving about 2 inches (5 cm) of overhang. Add the wood chips to the wok and set a small cake rack on top. Cover and heat the chips over medium-high heat until the edges are slightly burned and smoke starts billowing out, 8 to 10 minutes. Arrange the tomato halves in a gratin dish. Transfer the dish to the rack and quickly cover with the lid. Smoke the tomatoes over medium heat for 5 to 10 minutes. Transfer the tomatoes to a cutting board and cut into wedges.

3.
Divide the tomatoes, tuna, and tomatillo among shallow bowls and pour in the tomato water. Drizzle with the oil and finely grate the lime zest over the top. Season with fleur de sel and pepper and serve.

—

Variation
If raw fish doesn't appeal, try this dish with a tuna steak seared in olive oil or grilled over medium-high heat until browned on the outside and still rare within, 2 to 3 minutes per side.

Daniel Rose
SPRING

—

SPRING IS THE only kitchen I know where, in the middle of dinner service, the cooks burst out singing when Jacques Dutronc's '60s pop hit "J'aime les filles" comes on the soundtrack. The playful spirit flows from the top down. Chicago-born chef-owner Daniel Rose opens Champagne bottles with a saber every time the sparkler is ordered. Rose's American informality and consciously classic French sensibility coupled with super-high-quality ingredients were a megahit with critics at Spring's first incarnation, a tiny sixteen-seat restaurant with a staff of one. In the move to a larger space—almost ten times the size of the original—the former art history student built a roomy open kitchen and hired a team to help him cook his personal, always-changing tasting menu with dishes like Rack of Lamb with Chickpea Puree and Red Onion Relish (page 168). Culinary legends Auguste Escoffier, Alain Chapel, and Louis Outhier are his heroes. "I figure it will take a lifetime just to understand the five fines herbes," Rose said.

tomato salad *with* cockles & marcona almonds

Four Servings

—

Sea salt

2 tablespoons (20 g) small pearl tapioca (not instant)

2 tablespoons fresh lime juice

2 tablespoons extra-virgin olive oil

Freshly ground pepper

2 tablespoons pine nuts

2 tablespoons (30 g) unsalted butter

1 shallot, finely chopped

1 garlic clove, finely chopped

1 thyme sprig

1 bay leaf

1 pound (500 g) cockles or small mussels, scrubbed, mussels debearded

¼ cup (60 ml) dry white wine

1½ pounds (750 g) ripe tomatoes of every size, shape, and color

2 tablespoons Marcona almonds

Small purslane or basil sprigs, for garnish

Balsamic vinegar pearls and extra-virgin olive oil pearls, for garnish (optional; see Note)

Finely grated lime zest, for garnish

Fleur de sel

—

Note
Balsamic vinegar pearls and extra-virgin olive oil pearls are available at specialty food shops.

Make Ahead
The recipe can be prepared through Step 3 up to 4 hours ahead.

At Le Comptoir on the carrefour de l'Odéon, Yves Camdeborde's super-fresh, unfussy cooking draws a line out the door from noon to two, seven days a week for dishes like this one: briny cockles (tiny clams) with tomato wedges, agreeably sour purslane, and toasted almonds and pine nuts.

—

1.
In a small saucepan of boiling salted water, cook the tapioca, stirring occasionally, until translucent and just tender, about 15 minutes. Drain and rinse in cold water.

2.
Meanwhile, in a large bowl, whisk the lime juice with the oil. Season the vinaigrette with salt and pepper.

3.
In a small, dry skillet, toast the pine nuts over medium-high heat until fragrant, about 4 minutes. Transfer to a plate and let cool.

4.
In a medium saucepan, melt the butter. Add the shallot, garlic, thyme, and bay leaf and cook over medium heat, stirring occasionally, until the vegetables soften, about 2 minutes. Add the cockles and wine, cover, and cook over high heat, shaking the pan a few times, until they open, 3 to 5 minutes.

5.
Shuck the cockles and discard the shells. Transfer the meat, dripping with broth, to the vinaigrette. Cut the tomatoes into wedges, add to the vinaigrette along with the tapioca, and gently toss to coat. Spoon the tomato salad and juices into shallow bowls. Garnish with the almonds, toasted pine nuts, purslane, balsamic pearls and olive oil pearls, if using, and lime zest. Season with fleur de sel and pepper and serve.

cured beef fillet *with* celery root salad *&* watercress

Four Servings

—

3 tablespoons (35 g) sugar

Sea salt

One 8-ounce (250-g) trimmed beef tenderloin tip

½ tablespoon whole black peppercorns

1½ teaspoons coriander seeds

½ cup (125 ml) homemade mayonnaise (see page 83, Step 3)

2 tablespoons Dijon mustard

1 tablespoon plus 1 teaspoon fresh lemon juice

1 pound (500 g) celery root, thickly peeled and cut into fine julienne strips (see Note)

Freshly ground pepper

1 teaspoon extra-virgin olive oil

2 ounces (60 g) watercress with tender stems

—

Note
The best way to make a fine julienne is to slice the celery root (or other vegetable) ⅛ inch (3 mm) thick using a mandoline, then stack a few of the slices at a time and cut them into ⅛-inch (3-mm) strips.

Make Ahead
The recipe can be prepared through Step 2 and refrigerated for up to 1 week.

The celery root salad can be refrigerated overnight.

At Le Bal Café, chefs Anna Trattles and Alice Quillet cure their own beef in sugar and sea salt, then encrust it with peppercorns and coriander seeds. It's rather effortless and infinitely better than most deli meat. Slices of the stunning mahogany beef come with creamy, textbook céléri rémoulade.

—

1.
In a small bowl, mix the sugar with 2 tablespoons (25 g) of the salt. In a medium gratin dish, spread half the sugar mixture. Set the beef tenderloin on top and spread the remaining sugar mixture over the top. Cover the dish with plastic wrap and refrigerate for 3 to 6 days.

2.
In a small dry skillet, toast the peppercorns and coriander seeds over medium heat, shaking the skillet occasionally, until fragrant, 2 to 3 minutes. Transfer to a spice mill and let cool, then grind to a powder. Remove the meat from the sugar mixture, rinse in cold water, and pat dry with paper towels. Transfer the meat to a plate and rub it all over with the peppercorn mixture. Cover with plastic wrap and refrigerate.

3.
Meanwhile, in a medium bowl, combine the mayonnaise with the mustard and 1 tablespoon of the lemon juice. Add the celery root and stir to coat. Season with salt and pepper. Cover and refrigerate for at least 1 hour.

4.
Transfer the cured beef to a cutting board and thinly slice it across the grain. In a medium bowl, whisk the oil and remaining 1 teaspoon of lemon juice and season lightly with salt and pepper. Add the watercress and toss to coat. Mound the celery root on plates and lean the cured beef slices on top. Garnish with the watercress and serve.

—

Variation
Quillet and Trattles sometimes swap in sliced cooked red beets tossed in a vinaigrette for the creamy celery root salad.

warm pea salad *with* fresh pear & prosciutto

Four Servings

—

2 tablespoons (30 g) Kiri cheese or cream cheese

2 tablespoons extra-virgin olive oil

2 tablespoons fresh lemon juice

Sea salt and freshly ground pepper

8 ounces (250 g) shelled fresh peas or thawed frozen baby peas (1 cup/250 g)

1 juicy pear, peeled, cored, and cut into ¼-inch (6-mm) dice

1 ounce (30 g) thinly sliced prosciutto, cut into thin strips

2 tablespoons chopped mint, plus tiny leaves for garnish

1 tablespoon snipped chives

—

Make Ahead
The vinaigrette can be refrigerated overnight. Give it a stir before using.

Before the lunch or dinner service at Haï Kaï, the staff sits down to the kind of meal they grew up with—a platter of fried eggs, a green salad, and, for dessert, a yogurt or foil-wrapped cube of Kiri. Yes, the soft industrial cheese. Chef Amélie Darvas uses the processed food as a subversive ingredient in her vinaigrette. Its creaminess marries the flavors of salty ham and sweet, crunchy pear.

—

1.
In a blender, puree the cheese with the oil and lemon juice until smooth. Season the vinaigrette with salt and pepper.

2.
If using fresh peas, fill a small bowl with half ice, half cold water. In a medium saucepan of boiling salted water, blanch the fresh peas until tender, 1 to 3 minutes. Drain and transfer to the ice water to cool for 1 minute; drain. Transfer to a thick kitchen towel and pat dry.

3.
In a medium saucepan, combine the peas, pear, prosciutto, and vinaigrette and season with salt and pepper. Cook over medium heat, tossing, until just warmed through. Remove the pan from the heat and stir in the chopped mint and chives. Spoon the mixture into bowls, garnish with the remaining mint leaves, and serve.

mint
magazine

The Italian Issue
Finding Fulvio | Carlo Mirarchi's Famiglia
Sardinia Back to the future | Puglisi | Petra
Niko Romito | Football, Pizza & Quinto Quarto

eggs, salads, and a sandwich

eggs en cocotte *with* watercress cream

Four Servings

—

2 slices of sourdough bread (each about ½ inch/1 cm thick)

1 tablespoon (15 g) unsalted butter, softened

6 ounces (180 g) watercress with tender stems, 4 small sprigs reserved for garnish

¼ cup (60 ml) crème fraîche or sour cream

Sea salt and freshly ground pepper

4 large eggs

Fleur de sel

—

Note
It's important to cool the watercress under cold running water immediately after blanching because it loses flavor and color. But you don't need to be too diligent about draining the blanched cress before adding it to the blender. Water helps the cress puree smoothly.

Make Ahead
The watercress puree can be refrigerated overnight. Gently reheat before using.

People who know about Yannick Alléno's Michelin-starred palaces Pavillon Ledoyen (and before that Le Meurice) and Le Cheval Blanc, in Courchevel, may be surprised to hear the chef say he was born in a bistro. His parents were bistrotiers in the Paris suburbs, and in 2008 he helped revive locavorism in the capital at his chic bistro Terroir Parisien. "People don't realize there is true Parisian terroir," he says. "I wanted to rediscover those products before they disappeared." For Alléno, bistro cooking is as serious as a three-star's. Even in a dish this simple, the peppery watercress comes from Méréville, the capital of cresson, in the Île de France (the farms and fields that surround Paris). The eggs, too, are local and they're prepared with exactitude— Alléno cooks them in the shell in a steam oven at 145°F (63°C) for precisely 30 minutes. My eggs are ultratraditional— baked in ramekins in a water bath. Either way, the whites are just set and the wobbly yolks spill into the soft, pungent greens.

—

1.
Heat the broiler to high. On a baking sheet, brush the bread slices on both sides with the butter. Broil, turning once, until lightly toasted, 1 to 2 minutes. Remove the bread from the broiler. Halve each bread slice crosswise, then lengthwise into thirds. Turn off the broiler and heat the oven to 375°F (190°C).

2.
In a large saucepan of boiling water, blanch the watercress, stirring gently with a wire skimmer, for 3 minutes. Drain the watercress and rinse in cold water. Transfer the watercress, still dripping wet, to a blender and puree with the crème fraîche until very smooth. Season with salt and pepper.

3.
Spoon the watercress puree into four ½-cup (125-ml) ramekins. Make a hollow in each ramekin and carefully crack in an egg. Set the ramekins in a medium gratin dish and transfer to a baking sheet. Pour boiling water into the gratin dish to reach halfway up the sides of the ramekins. Transfer to the oven and bake the eggs until the whites are set but the yolks are still soft, about 10 minutes.

4.
Carefully remove the ramekins from the water bath and set on plates. Season the eggs with fleur de sel and pepper, garnish with the reserved watercress sprigs, and serve immediately with the toasts.

skillet eggs *with* black trumpet mushrooms

Two Servings

—

4 tablespoons (60 g) unsalted butter

1 slice of firm, day-old white bread, crusts removed, cut into ¼-inch (6-mm) cubes

Sea salt

1 tablespoon extra-virgin olive oil

10 ounces (300 g) mixed black trumpet or chanterelle and button mushrooms, sliced

Freshly ground pepper

1 shallot, finely chopped

2 tablespoons chopped parsley

4 large eggs

2 tablespoons heavy cream

Fleur de sel

You may prefer the relative posh of Chez Michel or Chez Casimir, Thierry Breton's other spots near the Gare du Nord, but the no-reservations, no-service policy at La Pointe du Grouin guarantees a (shared) table at the last minute—and the food's excellent. Like his cohort from the Hôtel de Crillon (Yves Camdeborde, Christian Etchebest), Breton cooks with great generosity; his fried eggs are heaped with wild mushrooms.

—

1.
In a small skillet, melt 1 tablespoon (15 g) of the butter. Add the bread cubes and cook over medium-low heat, stirring occasionally, until crisp and golden, about 5 minutes. Season with salt, remove from the heat, and let cool.

2.
In a medium nonstick skillet, melt 1 tablespoon (15 g) of the butter in the oil. Add the mushrooms, season with salt and pepper, and cook over medium-high heat, stirring occasionally, until golden, 10 to 12 minutes. Add the shallot and parsley and cook, stirring, for 1 minute. Transfer the mushroom mixture to a plate and wipe out the skillet.

3.
Heat the broiler to high. In the same skillet, melt the remaining 2 tablespoons (30 g) of butter. Crack the eggs into the skillet and cook over medium-low heat until the whites are set, 1 to 2 minutes. Pour the cream over the eggs, transfer the skillet to the broiler, and cook until the yolks are slightly set but still soft, about 30 seconds. Carefully transfer the eggs to a platter and sprinkle with fleur de sel. Spoon the mushrooms on top, sprinkle with the croutons, and serve.

crispy five-minute eggs
with butternut purée

Four Servings

—

1 slice of day-old sourdough bread, crusts removed, cut into ½-inch (1-cm) cubes

4 tablespoons (60 g) unsalted butter

1 garlic clove, finely chopped

Sea salt

1 large shallot, finely chopped

One 1-pound (500-g) butternut squash, peeled, seeded, and cut into 1-inch (2.5-cm) dice

2 cups (500 ml) chicken stock

5 large eggs, 1 lightly beaten with 1 teaspoon water

Grapeseed oil, for frying

¼ cup (30 g) all-purpose flour

¾ cup (45 g) panko

Freshly ground pepper

1 teaspoon fresh lemon juice

1 teaspoon extra-virgin olive oil

Fleur de sel

2 ounces (60 g) watercress with tender stems

—

Note
In Step 5, when adding the eggs to the hot oil, hold the spider or slotted spoon just above the oil so it doesn't splash.

Make Ahead
The butternut squash puree and boiled eggs can be refrigerated overnight. The garlic crumbs can be stored in an airtight container for up to 3 days.

Because chef Nadia Igué works alone in her kitchen with the help of one dishwasher-assistant, she makes food that can be prepared ahead at any stage and finished during the meal service as orders arrive. In fact, the butternut puree and soft-boiled eggs here can be refrigerated overnight to make it even easier on the cook, but Igué starts from scratch every day: "When I run out, I run out," she says.

—

1.
Heat the broiler. Spread the bread cubes in a pie pan and toast under the broiler, stirring occasionally, until dried, 2 to 3 minutes. In a small skillet, melt 2 tablespoons (30 g) of the butter. Add the dried bread cubes and cook over medium-high heat, stirring occasionally, until the bread is crisp and golden, 3 to 5 minutes. Add the garlic and cook, stirring, until fragrant, about 30 seconds. Remove from the heat, season with salt, and let cool. Transfer to a food processor and pulse the garlic bread into coarse crumbs.

2.
In a medium saucepan, melt the remaining 2 tablespoons (30 g) of butter. Add the shallot and cook over medium heat until softened, 2 to 3 minutes. Add the squash and season with a pinch of salt. Cover and cook, stirring occasionally, for 3 minutes. Add the stock and bring to a boil, then uncover and simmer over medium heat until the squash is tender and the stock nearly evaporates, about 35 minutes. Scrape the squash into a food processor and puree until very smooth. Gently reheat before serving.

3.
In a small saucepan of simmering water, cook 4 of the eggs in the shell for 5 minutes. Meanwhile, fill a small bowl with half ice, half cold water. Using a spider or slotted spoon, transfer the eggs to the ice water and let cool completely. Carefully peel the eggs.

4.
In a large saucepan, heat 2 inches (5 cm) of grapeseed oil to 375°F (190°C) over medium heat. Meanwhile, pour the flour, beaten egg, and panko into 3 separate baking pans. Season 1 boiled egg with salt and pepper. Dust it with the flour and dip it in the beaten egg, letting the excess drip back into the pan. Coat generously with the panko, pressing gently to help the crumbs adhere. Transfer to a sheet of parchment paper. Repeat with the remaining eggs.

5.
Line a plate with paper towels. Using a spider or slotted spoon, carefully lower the eggs into the hot oil and fry, stirring occasionally, until golden, 3 to 5 minutes. Using a spider or slotted spoon, transfer the eggs to the paper towels.

6.
In a medium bowl, combine the lemon juice and olive oil and season lightly with fleur de sel and pepper. Add the watercress and toss to coat. Spoon some of the squash puree into each shallow bowl. Carefully set an egg alongside and mound the watercress next to it. Sprinkle the eggs with the garlic crumbs and serve.

haricots verts à la niçoise

Four Servings

—

2 large whole eggs

1 pound (500 g) haricots verts

1 large egg yolk

3 tablespoons lemon juice

1 tablespoon red wine vinegar

1 tablespoon Dijon mustard

½ garlic clove, chopped

Sea salt and freshly ground pepper

3 tablespoons grapeseed oil

5 tablespoons (80 ml) extra-virgin olive oil

One 7-ounce (200-g) jar olive-oil packed tuna, tuna flaked, oil reserved (see Notes)

2 tablespoons finely chopped parsley

4 ounces (125 g) cherry tomatoes, halved

¼ cup (60 g) pitted black olives, preferably Niçoise, halved or quartered if large

4 oil-packed anchovies, halved lengthwise

—

Notes

Please note that the egg yolk in the mayonnaise is not cooked.

Chef Delling-Williams saves the oil from his homemade tuna confit to make the mayonnaise; you can use some of the oil from the jarred tuna.

Make Ahead

The mayonnaise can be refrigerated for up to 2 days; it thickens slightly when chilled.

Edward Delling-Williams of Au Passage tweaks the straight-up salade niçoise by putting slender green beans in the center of the plate. Small change, big difference. He also uses his own homemade mayonnaise (included in the recipe below) and his own tuna confit, but I call for good olive oil–packed tuna here.

—

1.
Fill a medium saucepan with water, add the eggs in the shell, and bring to a simmer, then cook until hard-boiled, about 10 minutes. Using a spider or slotted spoon, remove the eggs and let cool slightly. Peel the eggs and halve them lengthwise. Keep the water boiling.

2.
Fill a medium bowl with half ice, half cold water. Add the haricots verts to the boiling water and cook until crisp-tender, about 3 minutes. Drain and transfer to the ice water to cool for 1 minute; drain. Transfer the haricots verts to a thick kitchen towel and pat dry.

3.
In a mini food processor, puree the egg yolk with 1 tablespoon of the lemon juice, the vinegar, mustard, and garlic. Season with a pinch each of salt and pepper. Gradually blend in the grapeseed oil, then 3 tablespoons of the olive oil (from the tuna jar, if desired) until the mayonnaise is thick. In a small bowl, combine the tuna and parsley with just enough of the mayonnaise to lightly coat.

4.
In a large bowl, whisk the remaining 2 tablespoons of lemon juice with the remaining 2 tablespoons of olive oil and season with salt and pepper. Add the haricots verts and gently toss to coat. Transfer the haricots verts to plates and spoon the tuna on top. Decorate with the tomatoes, olives, anchovies, and egg halves and serve.

—

Variation
Swap a dice of rare, pan-seared fresh tuna steak for the jarred tuna.

roast asparagus *with* trofie, radicchio pesto *&* egg

Four Servings

—

Trofie

⅓ cup (50 g) fine semolina flour, plus more for sprinkling

⅓ cup (50 g) all-purpose flour

1 large egg, beaten to mix

Pesto, Asparagus, and Egg

½ cup (15 g) packed chopped radicchio

½ cup (15 g) packed basil

2 tablespoons (15 g) freshly grated Parmesan cheese, plus more for sprinkling

2 tablespoons (15 g) pine nuts, toasted

1 tablespoon plus 1 teaspoon fresh lemon juice

½ garlic clove, grated

Sea salt and freshly ground pepper

¼ cup (60 ml) plus 1 teaspoon extra-virgin olive oil

8 medium asparagus spears, each cut crosswise into 4 or 5 pieces

Baby greens, such as pea shoots, nasturtium leaves, and spinach leaves, for garnish

4 large egg yolks

Brioche breadcrumbs, toasted, for sprinkling (see Notes)

Fleur de sel

—

Notes
Mastering the art of the trofie curl takes some practice. Just keep scraping until you get the hang of it.

To make breadcrumbs, cut the bread into cubes, then pulse it in a food processor.

It's the soft egg yolk that ties together the contrasting textures, temperatures, and flavors in this spring pasta dish. "It's hard to take a bite without breaking the yolk," says chef Braden Perkins of Verjus and Ellsworth, who tried three versions of this dish before getting it right (see Anatomy of a Recipe, opposite). "You have to push through the yolk to get to the pasta and pesto at the bottom of the bowl."

—

1. Trofie
Combine both flours in the bowl of a food processor and pulse a few times. Add the egg and pulse until clumps of moist dough form. Cover a work surface with a silicone mat or parchment paper. Scrape the dough onto the prepared work surface (unfloured) and gently knead a few times to form a dough that just holds together and is slightly sticky. Flatten into a disk, wrap in plastic, and let stand at room temperature for at least 30 minutes or up to 2 hours.

2.
Sprinkle a baking sheet with semolina flour. Cut the dough into 4 equal pieces. Cover with plastic wrap. Working with one piece at a time on a silicone mat or parchment paper, roll the dough into a log about ½ inch (1 cm) thick. Slice crosswise into ¼-inch (6-mm) pieces. Using your hand, roll each piece into a strand with tapering ends slightly wider than your palm. Pull a bench scraper across the dough into a spiral, like curling a ribbon with scissors. Transfer to the prepared baking sheet.

3. Pesto
In a food processor, combine the radicchio with the basil, cheese, pine nuts, 1 tablespoon of the lemon juice, and the garlic, and season with salt and pepper. Process until finely chopped. Add ¼ cup (60 ml) of the oil and puree until smooth.

4.
In a medium saucepan of boiling salted water fitted with a colander, cook the pasta until al dente. Remove and drain the pasta; keep the water boiling. Meanwhile, heat a medium cast-iron skillet until very hot. Add the remaining 1 teaspoon of oil and the asparagus, season with salt, and cook over high heat until slightly charred and crisp-tender, 1 to 3 minutes. Add the remaining 1 teaspoon of lemon juice and remove the pan from the heat.

5.
Spoon the pesto into shallow bowls, then top with the asparagus, pasta, and baby greens. Remove the pan of boiling water from the heat. Using a slotted spoon, carefully add the egg yolks one at a time to the hot water and cook until just set on the outside and soft within, about 1 minute. Transfer one yolk to each bowl and sprinkle with the breadcrumbs. Season with fleur de sel, sprinkle more cheese over the top, and serve.

—

Variation
You can substitute artisanal dried pasta. If you can't find trofie, try hearty pasta shapes like cavatelli or fusilli. You'll need only about 4 ounces (125 g).

ANATOMY *of a recipe*

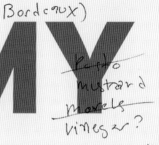

Handwritten margin notes:
Seafood / vegetables /
Butter
Pam
eggs (yolk)

pesto
mustard
morels
vinegar? |

usry
already
too tst$

2 kilo
Yes
all /herbs
cream
Feb
onions /shallots
ramps
keep it vegetarian!

heavy prers (creamy sauce)
risotto eggy dishes
no! again?

Pasta (pappadelle) fried eggs
been dubaile for pasta!

Sharp cheeses! pecorino / Gouda

e is
ean /refreshing herbal /vegetable

Quick finish
by things that stick to it!
Sauces, egg Yolk,
Soft rice dishes

Unctuous

toasted hazelnuts?

shaved
raw asparagus
frisee

warm
ess Yolk / salt
roast asparagus
lemon / butter
brown butter
S&P

Body text

When I ask about menu planning, most chefs just laugh. >

"There's no time for that," Shaun Kelly told me. It's constraint that inspires the menu at Le Servan, chef-owner Tatiana Levha said. So I was thrilled when Braden Perkins volunteered to walk me through how a dish comes together at Verjus, his two-story restaurant and wine bar opposite the seventeenth-century Palais Royal.

Perkins serves a seven-course tasting menu at dinner, and changes to any one recipe ripple through the entire meal. That's impetus enough to keep a dish on the menu as long as it works. But when new ingredients appear at the market—a weekly, or even daily, event—the American chef starts talking to his team.

In late April, it was dewy asperges vertes du Poitou that triggered a brainstorming session. Perkins thinks the green asparagus from the Atlantic Coast is so fantastic he doesn't want to do much to it.

His first question—What's the best asparagus you've ever had?—elicits an outpouring of taste memories, from risotto by someone's mom to a dish from Chez Panisse in Berkeley. Perkins homes in on the answers. "Why did you like it?" he asks.

He wants to tease out what made these recipes unforgettable and combine the elements in a new way. "What goes with asparagus?" he asks. Perkins draws up a list: butter, Parmesan, eggs, herbs, cream, crab, seafood, hollandaise sauce, onions/shallots/ramps, pesto, mustard, morel mushrooms, pasta. Crab is immediately eliminated to keep the dish vegetarian and avoid repetition with the course that follows, clams from Mont-Saint-Michel. Morels are out too; they're already served with the clams and they're expensive.

No risotto, says Hannah Kowalenko, Braden's number two in the kitchen. She's the logistics person, and risotto would require heavy prep early in the meal. Also, she points out, we want people to walk away feeling comfortable. Keep the first courses light and move on to heavier tastes.

By the end of the meeting, a dish begins to take shape. The group decides on a warm salad with shaved raw asparagus, roasted asparagus, pasta, frisée lettuce, fermented black beans, lemon, brown butter, and egg yolk.

But the recipe needs work. The fermented beans obliterate the asparagus. "It's like eating a few different ingredients, one at a time," someone comments. "The shaved asparagus is too crunchy." "The egg floats without combining the flavors." Visually, there's too much white space, and they can't add dots or a swoosh of sauce. (The presentation possibilities are reduced with a tasting menu because chefs don't want to repeat the same plating flourishes.) Is asparagus too hard to serve without being a side dish, they wonder?

On the second try, the cooks decide to keep the pasta and egg and replace the fermented beans with pesto, an herbal element that coats everything. But which pasta? Linguine? Does super-Italian pappardelle look odd in the menu now? This iteration, with skillet-charred asparagus, squiggles of trofie pasta, slightly bitter radicchio pesto, and barely poached egg yolk, gets appreciative murmurs. Still, something's missing, they agree. Crunch.

The crispy component reveals itself in some Emperor Norton brioche buns, left over from the fried chicken sandwich served in the wine bar downstairs. Perkins grinds the bread into crumbs, toasts them, and sprinkles them over the top. A little recycling magic and voilà, a new dish: Roast Asparagus with Trofie, Radicchio Pesto, and Egg (opposite).

3

DINNER COOKS

prepare the nightly five-course menu plus room service orders.

3 -OR- 4

MONTHS

The wait for Camdeborde's gloriously delicious weeknight multicourse prix fixe. But the chef saves tables for guests of the hotel, and hopefuls who show up between 6 and 7 p.m. occasionally get a same-day dinner reservation.

STATS — *le comptoir*

10

ESPRESSOS

The number of cups chef-owner Yves Camdeborde drinks in a day. No cream. No sugar. "It's the warmth I like," said the bistrotier. His beans come from Paris coffee roaster L'Arbre à Café, 10 rue du Nil, 2nd arrond.; larbreacafe.com.

60

HORS D'OEUVRES

plus 10 daily specials and 70 wines are offered at L'Avant Comptoir, Camdeborde's stand-up wine bar adjoining his bistro and hotel. A discreet plaque defines the word "hors d'oeuvre" for anyone who insists on calling the spot a tapas bar. "We have a perfectly good French word for small plates," said the chef.

240

PLATES

are ferried up the stairs (and down) on napkin-lined trays during the dinner service by Le Comptoir's hard-working runner-dishwasher, Richard. That's two plates every minute.

300

LUNCH CUSTOMERS

eat reinvented bistro standards like Smoked Salmon Croque Monsieur (opposite) and Fresh Pineapple with Basil Syrup (pictured on page 194) at Le Comptoir on sunny days.

2,000

BOOKS

Camdeborde's collection of current and vintage cookbooks in his office, hotel library, and home.

smoked salmon croque monsieur

Four Servings

—

1 tablespoon thinly sliced red onion

1 tablespoon sherry vinegar

Sea salt

1 tablespoon extra-virgin olive oil

1 tablespoon chicken pan juices (see Note) or extra-virgin olive oil

Freshly ground pepper

8 slices of firm white bread

6 ounces (180 g) Gruyère cheese, very thinly sliced on a mandoline

8 ounces (250 g) sliced lightly smoked salmon

2 tablespoons (30 g) caviar, such as smoked herring, paddlefish, or lumpfish

4 heads of Little Gem lettuce (sucrine), halved lengthwise

—

Note
I always save leftover juices from roast chicken. They add great depth of flavor to vinaigrettes and sauces.

Make Ahead
The vinaigrette can be prepared through Step 1, covered with plastic wrap, and refrigerated for up to 2 hours.

After seeing Eric Ripert at Le Bernardin in New York replace the ham in croque monsieur with smoked salmon and caviar, Yves Camdeborde came up with this everyman version for Le Comptoir with modest smoked herring roe. He also grills the sandwich in a panini press instead of frying it, to make it lighter.

—

1.
In a small bowl, toss the onion with the vinegar and a pinch of salt and let stand for 5 minutes. Whisk in the oil and pan juices and season the vinaigrette with pepper.

2.
Arrange 4 bread slices on a work surface. Layer the cheese, smoked salmon, and caviar on top. Close the sandwiches with the remaining 4 bread slices.

3.
Heat a sandwich press. Cook the sandwiches until the bread is lightly browned and crisp on the outside and the cheese is melted within, about 3 minutes. Cut each sandwich in half on the diagonal and arrange, slightly overlapping, on plates. Arrange the lettuce halves, slightly overlapping, next to the sandwich halves on each plate. Drizzle the lettuce with the vinaigrette and serve.

rainbow chard salad
with candied walnuts

Four Servings

—

Sea salt

Two 4- to 6-inch (10- to 15-cm) dried kombu seaweed strips

1 pound (500 g) tender young rainbow chard, stems cut into 2-inch (5-cm) lengths

½ cup (30 g) walnut halves, toasted (for toasting, see page 105, Step 1)

2 tablespoons (25 g) sugar

2 tablespoons water

1 large egg yolk

1 tablespoon red wine vinegar

1 tablespoon fresh lemon juice

1 tablespoon Dijon mustard

½ garlic clove, chopped

Freshly ground pepper

3 tablespoons grapeseed oil

3 tablespoons extra-virgin olive oil

Radish sprouts or chervil sprigs, for garnish

—

Note
Delling-Williams makes the vinaigrette extra thick, because the boiled chard, even carefully dried, naturally dilutes it. Blending it at high speed in a food processor helps make a strong emulsion. What about whisking? "Doesn't compare," says the chef.

Make Ahead
The chard and vinaigrette can be refrigerated separately for up to 4 hours. The candied walnuts can be kept in an airtight container for up to 5 days. Assemble the salad just before serving.

Rainbow chard, barely cooked in a seaweed broth, is an excellent (and colorful) base for this salad from Au Passage chef Edward Delling-Williams. The sugary, crunchy walnuts are a great foil for the greens' earthiness and delicate saline flavor, but any nut or a mix of pistachios, almonds, and pecans would be terrific here, too.

—

1.
Bring a large pot of salted water to a boil with the kombu. Line a large baking sheet with a thick kitchen towel. Using a spider or slotted spoon, remove the kombu from the water. Add the chard stems to the boiling water and cook until crisp-tender, 3 to 4 minutes. Using a spider or slotted spoon, transfer the stems to the prepared baking sheet. Add the chard leaves to the boiling water and cook, stirring occasionally, until just tender, 1 to 2 minutes. Drain in a large colander, lightly pressing out any water. Spread the chard on the prepared baking sheet, pat dry, and let cool completely.

2.
Line a small plate with a piece of parchment paper. In a skillet, stir the walnuts with the sugar and water. Bring to a simmer and cook over high heat, shaking the pan occasionally, until the nuts have caramelized and all the liquid has evaporated, about 4 minutes. Transfer the walnuts to the parchment-lined plate to cool, spreading them in a single layer. Very coarsely chop the nuts.

3.
In a mini food processor, puree the egg yolk with the vinegar, lemon juice, mustard, and garlic. Season with a pinch each of salt and pepper. Gradually blend in the grapeseed and olive oils until thick. Arrange the chard leaves and stems on plates and dot with the vinaigrette. Garnish with the candied walnuts and radish sprouts and serve. Pass the remaining vinaigrette separately.

—

Variation
To make a more substantial dish, crumble 3 ounces (90 g) of fresh chèvre, French feta cheese, or Roquefort on top before serving.

Edward Delling-Williams

—

THE FIRST TIME I tried Edward Delling-Williams's cooking at Au Passage, I thought it was someone else's. (The place is a revolving door for expat talent.) But I loved it. The chef packed so many thoughtful ideas onto the chalkboard menu, I ordered practically every dish— all small plates meant for sharing. Delling-Williams, who is English, doesn't cook French but uses all the same ingredients, so it's intriguing to see what he comes up with. His food is an international adventure with Mediterranean and Asian influences, like rainbow chard simmered in a kombu (seaweed) broth (pictured on page 89). Au Passage and its even more casual satellite, Martin, are saturated with an Old World artisanal ethos. For example, the cultured butter—and resulting buttermilk—are made in-house. For this alum of nose-to-tail innovator St. John in London, the grungy dive-bar décor at Au Passage and Martin is just fine. "I love it when beautiful food is served on shitty plates," he told me. "I hate putting on a dress shirt."

pan-seared gnocchi salad
with burrata & tomatoes

Four Servings

—

Gnocchi

Coarse sea salt

2 russet (baking) potatoes (each about 8 ounces/250 g), scrubbed

¾ cup (100 g) all-purpose flour, plus more for dusting

1 large egg yolk

1 teaspoon fine sea salt

⅛ teaspoon freshly ground pepper

Parsley Oil

1 cup (30 g) packed parsley leaves

¼ cup (60 ml) grapeseed oil

Sea salt

2 tablespoons (30 g) unsalted butter

Salad

1 large beefsteak tomato, cut crosswise into 8 slices ¼ inch (6 mm) thick

12 ounces (350 g) burrata or mozzarella cheese, torn into 4 pieces

1 tablespoon (15 g) toasted pine nuts

Fleur de sel and freshly ground pepper

Pea shoots, micro herbs, or small herb leaves, for garnish

Pirouette chef Tomy Gousset's signature potato gnocchi would be unrecognizable in Rome. In April, he pairs the tender dumplings with fresh morels and seasonal English peas. In July, they're browned in butter and arranged around slices of beefsteak tomato topped with a burrata pillow. The intense parsley oil Gousset pours on the plate has a thousand uses. Drizzle it on fish, vegetables, eggs, or grilled meats.

—

1. Gnocchi
Heat the oven to 450°F (230°C). Spread ¼ inch (6 mm) of coarse salt in a pie pan. Set the potatoes on top of the salt and bake until they are tender, about 45 minutes. Let cool slightly. Halve the potatoes and scoop the flesh into a ricer. Pass them through the ricer into a large bowl. Add the flour, egg yolk, fine salt, and pepper and stir until a stiff dough forms. Gently knead a few times until the dough is smooth but slightly sticky.

2.
Lightly dust a baking sheet with flour. Cut the dough into 4 equal pieces. Working with one piece at a time on a silicone mat or parchment paper, roll the dough into a log ¾ inch (2 cm) thick. Slice crosswise into ¾-inch (2-cm) pieces and transfer to the prepared baking sheet.

3.
Bring a large skillet of salted water to a boil. Boil the gnocchi until they rise to the surface, then cook for 2 minutes longer; drain.

4. Parsley Oil
In a food processor, puree the parsley with the oil and salt until very smooth. Scrape into a small saucepan and cook over medium-low heat for 2 to 3 minutes. Strain the hot oil through a mesh coffee filter into a small bowl. (Discard the parsley.) Let cool.

5.
In a medium nonstick skillet, melt 1 tablespoon (15 g) of the butter. Add half of the gnocchi and cook over medium heat, stirring occasionally, until browned on 2 sides, about 5 minutes. Transfer to a platter and repeat with the remaining 1 tablespoon (15 g) of butter and gnocchi.

6. Salad
Center 2 tomato slices slightly overlapping on each plate and top with a piece of burrata. Drizzle with the parsley oil and sprinkle with the pine nuts. Line up the gnocchi around the tomatoes. Season with fleur de sel and pepper, garnish with the pea shoots, and serve.

—

Variations
Tomy Gousset likes to add a meat jus to the plate along with the parsley oil for deeper flavor. I've had excellent results baking the potatoes in a microwave oven for 10 minutes instead of a conventional oven.

Make Ahead

This recipe makes more gnocchi than you'll need for four first-course servings, but it's tricky to reduce the quantities. So you have a few choices: the uncooked gnocchi can be frozen on the baking sheet, then transferred to a resealable plastic bag and frozen for up to 1 month. Boil them without defrosting. Or the recipe can be prepared through Step 5 and refrigerated overnight; toss the boiled gnocchi with olive oil. Bring the gnocchi to room temperature before continuing. At my house the gnocchi never make it to the freezer. I sauté the entire batch in butter and eat the leftovers the next day in an omelet or baked in a gratin dish topped with pesto or a bit of heavy cream and grated Gruyère cheese.

green lentils *with* beets & labneh

Four Servings

—

1 pound (500 g) small beets, such as Chioggia, red, and/or golden, scrubbed

½ cup (100 g) green Puy lentils, rinsed and picked over

1 onion, halved

1 thyme sprig

2 cups (500 ml) water

Sea salt

1 tablespoon red wine vinegar

1 tablespoon fresh lemon juice

1 tablespoon Dijon mustard

1 garlic clove, finely chopped

Freshly ground pepper

6 tablespoons (100 ml) extra-virgin olive oil

¼ cup (8 g) chopped mint leaves, plus more for sprinkling

2 tablespoons chopped dill, plus more for sprinkling

½ cup (125 ml) labneh (Lebanese strained yogurt) or Greek yogurt

Fleur de sel

—

Make Ahead
The salad can be prepared through Step 3 up to 4 hours ahead. Assemble it just before serving.

Au Passage chef Edward Delling-Williams's vegetable dishes are just as bold and satisfying as his meaty ones. Many have a Mediterranean accent, like this earthy, sweet salad with dollops of Lebanese yogurt and tons of fresh herbs.

—

1.
Heat the oven to 400°F (200°C). Wrap the beets in a single layer in a sheet of foil, transfer to a baking sheet, and roast until tender, 50 to 60 minutes. Let cool slightly, then peel and crush lightly with the bottom of a small bowl.

2.
Meanwhile, in a medium saucepan, combine the lentils, onion, thyme, water, and a pinch of salt. Bring to a boil and simmer over medium heat until the lentils are tender but still intact, about 25 minutes. Drain the lentils and discard the onion halves and thyme. Return the lentils to the pan.

3.
In a small bowl, whisk the vinegar with the lemon juice, mustard, and garlic. Season with a pinch each of salt and pepper. Gradually whisk in the oil. Stir three-fourths of the vinaigrette into the warm lentils. Stir in the mint and dill just before serving.

4.
Spread the lentils on a platter or plates and arrange the beets on top. Drizzle with the remaining vinaigrette and dollop the labneh around the platter. Season with pepper, sprinkle with fleur de sel and herbs, and serve.

eggplant carpaccio *with* summer vegetables

Four Servings

—

One 12-ounce (350-g) eggplant

½ teaspoon finely chopped garlic, plus 1 garlic clove, thinly sliced

2 tablespoons fresh lemon juice

2 tablespoons extra-virgin olive oil, plus more for drizzling

Piment d'Espelette

Sea salt and freshly ground pepper

1 ounce (30 g) haricots verts or green beans

4 ounces (125 g) mixed favas beans and green peas in the pod, shelled (¼ cup/60 g), or 2 ounces (60 g) frozen baby peas

Grapeseed oil, for frying

1 slice of firm white bread, crusts removed, cut into ½-inch (1-cm) cubes

1 large hard-boiled egg, yolk and white finely grated separately

4 cherry tomatoes, halved

½ small yellow tomato, cut into 4 thin wedges

Pea shoots, radicchio leaves, herb leaves, red currants, sliced pitted black olives, chopped anchovies, shaved Parmesan cheese, and edible flowers, for garnish

Fleur de sel

—

Make Ahead
The marinated eggplant can be refrigerated for up to 3 days. The recipe can be prepared through Step 4 up to 4 hours ahead.

This salad from L'Office has marinated eggplant as its heart but it's topped with a gorgeous, wildly varied array of flavors and textures. Pick a few of the listed garnishes and make it look pretty.

—

1.
Heat the oven to 450°F (230°C). Using a fork, poke holes all over the eggplant. Put the eggplant on a foil-lined baking sheet and roast, turning occasionally, until the skin is charred and the eggplant is very soft and collapsed, 30 to 40 minutes. Transfer to a cutting board and let cool slightly. Peel the eggplant and cut it into ½-inch (1-cm) dice.

2.
In a medium bowl, whisk the chopped garlic with the lemon juice, olive oil, and a pinch of piment d'Espelette. Season with salt and pepper. Add the eggplant and toss to coat.

3.
Fill a small bowl with half ice, half cold water. In a small saucepan of boiling salted water, cook the haricots verts until crisp-tender, about 3 minutes. Using a spider or slotted spoon, transfer them to the ice water to cool for 1 minute. Using a spider or slotted spoon, transfer the haricots verts to a thick kitchen towel and pat dry. Blanch the fava beans and peas in the boiling water until tender, 1 to 3 minutes. Drain and transfer to the ice water to cool for 1 minute; drain. Transfer to the kitchen towel and pat dry. Peel the fava beans.

4.
In a small skillet, heat ¼ inch (6 mm) of grapeseed oil until shimmering. Add the garlic slices and fry over medium heat until crisp and golden, 2 to 4 minutes. Using a spider or slotted spoon, transfer the garlic to paper towels to drain. Add the bread cubes to the skillet and fry until crisp and golden, 2 to 4 minutes; drain on paper towels.

5.
Spread the eggplant in shallow bowls and drizzle olive oil around the edge. Top with some of the egg yolk and white, haricots verts, favas, peas, garlic, bread cubes, cherry tomato halves, and yellow tomato wedges. Decorate with the garnishes, sprinkle with fleur de sel, and serve.

ricotta *with* kale salsa verde & sprouting broccoli

Four Servings

—

2 quarts (2 L) whole milk

4 tablespoons (60 ml) fresh lemon juice

Sea salt

2 ounces (60 g) sprouting broccoli, broccoli rabe, or broccolini florets, cut into 2-inch (5-cm) lengths

1 cup (30 g) packed baby kale or tender radish, turnip, or carrot tops

¼ cup (60 ml) extra-virgin olive oil

1 small shallot, quartered

½ tablespoon salt-packed capers, rinsed

½ garlic clove, coarsely chopped

⅛ teaspoon ground fennel seeds

Pinch of crushed red pepper

Freshly ground black pepper

Fleur de sel

8 anchovy fillets in extra-virgin olive oil from Cantabria (see Notes)

—

Notes
The homemade ricotta can be replaced with 8 ounces (250 g) of fresh, whole milk ricotta.

Hand-packed Cantabrian anchovies are available from tienda.com.

Make Ahead
The fresh ricotta can be refrigerated for up to 2 days. The salsa verde can be refrigerated overnight; it will solidify, so let it come to room temperature before serving.

At Bones, James Henry drapes plump, buttery anchovies from Cantabria, Spain, over his house-made ricotta. (I've included an easy recipe for ricotta below.) If you've got ordinary oil-packed anchovies, instead pulse just one into the salsa verde (what the French call sauce verte); you'll get a whiff of anchovy without being overwhelmed by its pungency.

With its sweet florets, sprouting broccoli is not as bitter as broccoli rabe and tastier than both broccoli and broccolini. It's also leafier than broccoli but not as leafy as broccoli rabe.

—

1.
Line a colander with dampened cheesecloth, leaving about 1 inch (2.5 cm) of overhang, and set it in the sink. In a large saucepan, warm the milk over medium-high heat until bubbles appear around the edge. Add 3 tablespoons of the lemon juice and cook over low heat, stirring gently, until curds form and rise to the surface, about 3 minutes. Remove the pan from the heat, cover, and let stand for 5 minutes; the curds will firm up slightly.

2.
Gently pour the curds into the prepared colander and let drain for 10 minutes. Transfer the ricotta to a bowl and season with salt.

3.
In a medium saucepan of boiling salted water, cook the sprouting broccoli until crisp-tender, 2 to 3 minutes. Drain it and rinse in cold water. Drain again, transfer to a thick kitchen towel, and pat dry.

4.
In a food processor, puree the kale with the oil, shallot, capers, garlic, and remaining 1 tablespoon of lemon juice until finely chopped. Season with the fennel seeds, crushed red pepper, salt, and black pepper.

5.
Spoon the ricotta into shallow bowls and lay the anchovies on top. Sprinkle with fleur de sel and pepper. Drizzle the kale salsa verde around each plate and top with the broccoli.

—

Variation
James Henry prefers Tuscan kale in the salsa verde. He removes the tough stems and blanches the leaves in boiling water until just tender, 1 to 2 minutes. The kale is then chilled in ice water, drained, and patted dry before continuing. He also adds some of the blanching water to the salsa verde.

green beans & mussels *with* curry oil

Four Servings

—

½ cup (125 ml) grapeseed oil

2 tablespoons Madras curry powder

Sea salt and freshly ground pepper

1 pound (500 g) green beans

2 tablespoons (30 g) unsalted butter

1 shallot, finely chopped

1 garlic clove, finely chopped

1 thyme sprig

1 bay leaf

1 pound (500 g) small mussels, scrubbed and debearded

¼ cup (60 ml) dry white wine

Fleur de sel

Piment d'Espelette

1 lime

Mixed herbs, such as nasturtium leaves, dill flowers, and purslane, for garnish

—

Make Ahead
The recipe can be prepared through Step 2 up to 4 hours ahead. The strained curry oil can be refrigerated for up to 1 month.

Haï Kaï's Amélie Darvas gives her blanched bean salad deep flavor with warm-spice-infused oil, sweet briny mussels, and a hit of fragrant lime zest finely grated over the top. Try some of the leftover oil with other salads or cooked vegetables and eggs of any kind.

—

1.
In a small skillet, gradually stir the oil into the curry powder. Warm over very low heat, stirring occasionally, for 30 minutes. Line a fine sieve with a double layer of cheesecloth and set it over a small jar. Add the curry oil and strain, pressing on the spices with the back of a spoon to extract as much oil as possible. Season the curry oil with salt and pepper. Discard the cheesecloth. Pour 2 tablespoons of the curry oil into a large bowl. Seal the jar of remaining curry oil and refrigerate for another use.

2.
Fill a medium bowl with half ice, half cold water. In a medium saucepan of boiling salted water, cook the green beans until crisp-tender, 3 to 4 minutes. Drain and transfer to the ice water to cool for 1 minute; drain. Transfer the green beans to a thick kitchen towel and pat dry.

3.
In a medium saucepan, melt the butter. Add the shallot, garlic, thyme, and bay leaf and cook over medium heat, stirring occasionally, until the vegetables soften, about 2 minutes. Add the mussels and wine, cover, and cook over high heat, shaking the pan a few times, until they open, 3 to 5 minutes.

4.
Shuck the mussels and discard the shells. Transfer the meat, dripping with broth, to the bowl with the curry oil. Add the green beans to the bowl, season with fleur de sel, pepper, and piment d'Espelette, and gently toss to coat. Mound the green beans and mussels on plates and finely grate lime zest over the top. Garnish with the mixed herbs and serve.

smoked tomatoes *with* crab *&* soppressata

Four Servings

—

Tomato Sauce

2 tablespoons extra-virgin olive oil

½ small onion, finely chopped

2 garlic cloves, finely chopped

Pinch of crushed red pepper

Pinch of paprika

Sea salt and freshly ground black pepper

⅓ cup (125 ml) dry white wine

1 pound (500 g) ripe red tomatoes, halved and grated on a box grater down to the skin, skin discarded

1 large basil sprig with stems

2 ounces (60 g) fresh (uncured) soppressata or spicy Italian sausage, casing removed, crumbled

Salad

½ cup (40 g) hardwood chips, such as applewood

1½ pounds (750 g) heirloom tomatoes of every shape and color, peeled

Fleur de sel and freshly ground pepper

4 ounces (125 g) lump crabmeat, preferably peekytoe, picked over for bits of shell

Purple basil sprigs and flowers, for garnish

—

Note
Find the freshest crab available in your local seafood shop or supermarket refrigerated fish counter. This dish doesn't work with canned crabmeat.

Make Ahead
The tomato sauce can be refrigerated for up to 2 days.

Bones chef James Henry's tomato salad looks like a full immersion in summer— a no-cooking-required salad of crabmeat, ripe tomatoes, and basil—which, partly, it is. But the tomato slices are lightly smoked and hide a tomato sauce larded with spicy soppressata sausage.

—

1. Tomato Sauce
In a medium saucepan, heat the oil until shimmering. Add the onion and garlic and season with the crushed red pepper, paprika, salt, and black pepper. Cook over medium heat, stirring occasionally, until softened, about 5 minutes. Add the wine and simmer until nearly evaporated, about 3 minutes. Add the grated tomatoes and basil, bring to a simmer, then cook over medium heat, stirring occasionally, until the sauce thickens, 20 to 30 minutes. Discard the basil. Add the sausage and cook, stirring, until it melts into the sauce, about 3 minutes.

2. Salad
Line the inside of a wok and its lid with foil, leaving about 2 inches (5 cm) of overhang. Add the wood chips to the wok and set a small cake rack on top. Cover and heat the chips over medium-high heat until the edges are slightly burned and smoke starts billowing out, 8 to 10 minutes. Arrange the tomatoes in a gratin dish. Transfer the dish to the rack and quickly cover with the lid. Smoke the tomatoes over medium heat for 5 to 10 minutes. Transfer the tomatoes to a cutting board and slice crosswise into rounds.

3.
Spoon the tomato sauce into large shallow bowls. Arrange the tomato slices slightly overlapping on top and season with fleur de sel and pepper. Spoon the crabmeat on top, garnish with the basil, and serve.

—

Variations
You can skip the smoking step altogether. The spicy tomato sauce by itself sets off the sweet crabmeat and ripe tomatoes. The chile-accented tomato sauce is worthy of multiple partners: try it with other vegetables such as summer squash, cauliflower, and (not-too-crunchy) green beans; eggs of any kind; grilled fish or steak; and, yes, pasta, too.

olive oil-poached squid salad
with potatoes, celery & capers

Four Servings

—

1 cup (250 ml) extra-virgin olive oil

2 garlic cloves, crushed

1 tablespoon mixed pickling spice, tied in a cheesecloth bundle

1 onion, chopped

2 large celery ribs, chopped, plus 2 tender ribs, thinly sliced on the diagonal

1 fennel bulb, cut lengthwise into eighths and cored

1 strip of lemon or orange zest

Sea salt

1 pound (500 g) cleaned small squid, bodies halved lengthwise

2 medium Yukon Gold potatoes (12 ounces/350 g total), peeled and sliced ½ inch (1 cm) thick

1 cup (250 ml) dry wine wine, preferably Sauvignon Blanc

¼ cup (8 g) celery leaves

2 tablespoons capers, drained

3 tablespoons fresh lemon juice

1 tablespoon finely chopped preserved lemon (see page 132, Step 1)

Fleur de sel

—

Make Ahead
The recipe can be prepared through Step 1 and refrigerated for up to 4 hours. Reheat it gently before continuing.

If the two paths to squid tenderness are to cook it quick or cook it slow, Alice Quillet's and Anna Trattles's winter salad at Le Bal Café is the long-cooked option—though not too long; this squid is tender in less than an hour. Here, it's sliced lengthwise instead of crosswise into rings, so it curls appealingly as it braises with warm spices, citrus zest, and wedges of fennel. The ingredients cook long enough for their flavors to commingle; for contrast, the chefs toss them with a lively dice of preserved lemon and caper berries before serving.

—

1.
Heat the oven to 325°F (160°C). In a medium enameled cast-iron casserole, warm the oil. Add the garlic and cook over medium-low heat until very lightly browned, about 2 minutes. Add the spice bundle and cook, stirring, for 30 seconds. Add the onion, chopped celery, fennel, and lemon zest and season with salt. Cover and cook, stirring occasionally, until the onions are softened, 8 to 10 minutes. Add the squid, potatoes, and wine to the casserole and bring to a simmer. Transfer to the oven and cook, covered, until the squid is tender, about 45 minutes. Remove and discard the spice bundle. Drain the squid, fennel, and potatoes, reserving the cooking liquid.

2.
In a large bowl, gently toss the squid, fennel, and potatoes with the sliced celery, celery leaves, capers, lemon juice, preserved lemon, and ½ cup (125 ml) of the reserved cooking liquid. Spoon into shallow bowls, season with fleur de sel, and serve.

asparagus *with* smoked trout & toasted hazelnuts

Four Servings

—

3 tablespoons (25 g) skinned hazelnuts

1 large egg yolk (see Notes)

1 teaspoon Dijon mustard

Sea salt

½ cup (125 ml) grapeseed oil

2 tablespoons hazelnut or grapeseed oil

2 tablespoons finely chopped shallots

2 tablespoons fresh lemon juice

20 large green asparagus spears, peeled

Fleur de sel and freshly ground pepper

4 ounces (125 g) smoked fish, such as trout or salmon, skinned and torn into pieces

Micro herb sprigs with their flowers, if available, or snipped chives, for garnish

—

Notes
Please note that the egg yolk in the mayonnaise is not cooked.

You can swap in ½ cup (125 ml) store-bought mayonnaise for the homemade.

Make Ahead
The recipe can be prepared through Step 3 and refrigerated overnight.

Richer chefs Adrien Bouchaud and Romain Lamon take the springtime pairing of asparagus and egg—which can be anything from a runny yolk to a hollandaise sauce or, as in this recipe, egg in the form of homemade mayonnaise—as a starting point, then add smoke and crunch. They also shower the plate with micro herbs—as well as pretty herb flowers—for a shot of concentrated flavor.

—

1.
Heat the oven to 375°F (190°C). Spread the hazelnuts in a pie plate and toast in the oven, stirring occasionally, until lightly browned, about 7 minutes. Coarsely chop the hazelnuts.

2.
In a blender, puree the egg yolk with the mustard and a pinch of sea salt. With the machine on, slowly add the grapeseed oil, then the hazelnut oil. Scrape the mayonnaise into a bowl and whisk in the shallots and lemon juice; refrigerate.

3.
In a large skillet of boiling salted water, cook the asparagus until crisp-tender, about 6 minutes. Drain, rinse in cold water, and drain again. Transfer to a thick kitchen towel and pat dry.

4.
Arrange 5 asparagus spears side by side on each plate. Lightly brush with the mayonnaise and season with fleur de sel and pepper. Arrange the smoked fish on top and sprinkle with the hazelnuts. Garnish with the herbs and serve.

—

Variation
Steamed artichoke bottoms would also be excellent topped with the smoked fish, homemade mayonnaise, and toasted hazelnuts.

Adrien Bouchaud & Romain Lamon

RICHER
L'OFFICE
52 FAUBOURG SAINT-DENIS

—

ADRIEN BOUCHAUD could have continued his tour of Paris palace hotels; he'd already cycled through Le Bristol and Hôtel de Crillon, plus Michelin-one-star restaurant Chiberta. But he (left in photo opposite) and fellow line cook Romain Lamon decided to ditch their safe perch at the Ritz for the freewheeling possibilities at Richer, thirty-something restaurateur Charles Compagnon's no-reservations corner café. Bouchaud let me hang out in the kitchen (it's the size of a walk-in closet) where he and Lamon began developing their affordable tweezer-style cooking, employing tricks like smoking fish to serve with mayonnaise-slicked asparagus (pictured on page 104). "We don't really have the space," Bouchaud said. "But we have fun anyway." Bouchaud and Lamon's culinary expertise now extends throughout Compagnon's burgeoning bistro universe in the gritty outer ninth and tenth arrondissements, including Richer, L'Office, and 52 Faubourg Saint-Denis.

baby razor clams *with* cucumbers *&* dill flowers

Four Servings

—

1 cup (30 g) packed fennel fronds, dill leaves, or a mix

¼ cup (60 ml) grapeseed oil

Sea salt

4 ounces (125 g) European cucumber, halved lengthwise, seeds scraped, and sliced crosswise into half-moons ¼ inch (6 mm) thick

1 teaspoon sugar

2 tablespoons fresh lemon juice, mirin, or a mix

2 pounds (1 kg) small razor clams or steamers, scrubbed

½ cup (125 ml) dry sake

2 teaspoons finely chopped parsley

1 teaspoon salt-packed capers, rinsed

Freshly ground pepper

Dill or fennel flowers and/or dill sprigs or fennel fronds, for garnish

Crusty bread, for serving

—

Make Ahead
The fennel oil can be refrigerated for up to 5 days.

The clams' natural juices, scented with sake and pickle juice (from homemade pickles), make a wonderful broth. Au Passage chef Edward Delling-Williams enriches the shellfish flavor with a drizzle of fennel oil.

—

1.
In a food processor, puree the fennel fronds with the oil and salt until very smooth. Scrape into a small saucepan, bring to a simmer, and cook over medium-low heat for 2 to 3 minutes. Strain the hot oil through a mesh coffee filter or a fine sieve into a small bowl. Let cool.

2.
In a medium bowl, toss the cucumber slices with the sugar and 1 teaspoon of salt and let stand for 5 minutes. Add the lemon juice and toss to coat. Refrigerate for 30 minutes.

3.
In a medium saucepan, combine the clams with the sake, cover, and cook over high heat, shaking the pan a few times, until the clams open, 3 to 5 minutes. Remove from the heat and let cool slightly in the pan. Shuck the clams and discard the shells. Cut the razor clams into 2 or 3 pieces on the diagonal; leave steamers whole. Strain the cooking liquid into a bowl, leaving the grit behind. Add the clams to the bowl with the liquid.

4.
Add the parsley, capers, and clams, dripping with the cooking liquid, to the cucumbers. Season with pepper and gently toss to coat. Spoon the clam mixture into shallow bowls and drizzle with the fennel oil. Garnish with the flowers and serve with bread.

—

Variations
This lemony, herb-flecked shellfish salad makes a great topping for tartines, the open-face sandwiches you often see at Parisian cafés. Pick a good loaf of bread, like sourdough, slice it ¼ inch (6 mm) thick, and toast it before spooning the salad on top. To turn tartines into two-bite hors d'oeuvres, slice them crosswise into strips.

heirloom tomato salad
with skate & basil

Four Servings

—

Skate

Four 4-ounce (125-g) skinless skate fillets

Sea salt and freshly ground pepper

1 cup (250 ml) clam broth

1 cup (250 ml) water

½ cup (125 ml) dry white wine

Extra-virgin olive oil, for brushing

12 or more large basil leaves

Tomato Salad

¼ cup (60 g) oil-cured black olives, pitted and chopped

1 tablespoon sherry vinegar

2 tablespoons extra-virgin olive oil

Sea salt and freshly ground pepper

1½ pounds (750 g) ripe tomatoes of every size, shape, and color

1 small spring onion, white part only, halved lengthwise and thinly sliced

Micro arugula or baby arugula, for garnish

—

Make Ahead
The dehydrated olives can be refrigerated in an airtight container for up to 1 week. The fish terrine can be refrigerated overnight. Bring it to room temperature before slicing.

When ultrafresh skate can be found in the market, why not try this satisfying and light salad from Caillebotte? Sous chef Thibault Eurin poaches the underutilized fish in a tangy broth to give the skate lots of flavor when it's served cold. The poached fillets are layered with fresh basil in a terrine and chilled until firm to accompany marinated tomatoes.

—

1. Skate
Spread the fish fillets in a large skillet and season with salt and pepper. Pour the broth, water, and wine over the fish and bring to a bare simmer. Poach over medium-low heat until the fillets are opaque throughout, about 3 minutes. Using a slotted spatula, transfer the fillets to paper towels to drain. Discard the broth. Let the fish cool slightly.

2.
Brush a medium loaf pan with oil. Lay one layer of fish fillets in one half of the pan, trimming them to fit, and season with salt and pepper. Cover with basil leaves. Continue layering the fish fillets and basil, finishing with the fish. Press a piece of plastic wrap on the fish, set a 14-ounce (425-g) can on top to weight it down, and refrigerate until firm, at least 2 hours.

3. Tomato Salad
Spread the olives on a microwave-safe plate. Microwave on high power, uncovered, in 1-minute intervals until the olives are dehydrated but still plump, 3 to 6 minutes total. Transfer to a food processor and pulse until finely chopped.

4.
In a large bowl, whisk the sherry vinegar with the oil and season with salt and pepper. Cut the tomatoes into wedges. Add the tomatoes and spring onion to the vinaigrette in the bowl and gently toss to coat. Run a knife around the chilled fish terrine and turn it out onto a cutting board. Cut the fish crosswise into 4 slices. Arrange 1 slice on each plate. Spoon the tomatoes, onions, and juices on top and sprinkle with the dehydrated olives. Garnish with the arugula and serve.

Barbue salsie,
Bouillon de coquillages et chou pointu

Poulpe de St-Jean de Luz,
Betteraves, arroche et cassis

Ris d'agneau,
Poisson fumé, girolles et pommes de terre

***

Faux-Filet de veau,
Shitake, graine de courge, vin jaune et carotte

Gigot d'agneau de Bourgogne,
Brocoli, pêche et faisselle

½ pigeonneau,
Cresson, radis et beurre d'anchois

***

Fromage du jour

Cannoli au citron de Sicile, sorbet au fromage frais
Soupe froide de pastèque, granité à la tagette et gi
Fraises, oseille, meringue et sorbet rhubarbe

Le restaurant est ouvert tous les soirs du mardi au
Et tous les midis du mercredi au samedi (12h/14h)

seafood

mussels *with* chopped romesco

Four Servings

—

½ large red bell pepper, halved lengthwise

3 tablespoons (30 g) whole almonds

4 pounds (2 kg) small mussels, scrubbed and debearded (see Notes)

1 small plum tomato, peeled, seeded, and chopped

1 garlic clove, finely chopped

2 tablespoons fresh lemon juice

2 teaspoons thyme leaves

Extra-virgin olive oil, for drizzling

Fine sea salt and piment d'Espelette

Crusty sourdough bread, for serving

—

Notes
Farmed mussels require very little prep work before cooking. Discard any mussels with broken shells, then give the others a quick rinse and and pull out the beards. In all, this takes only a few minutes for several pounds of mussels.

If you can find only large mussels, steam them in Step 3 for an extra minute or two after they open, until they're cooked through.

Do not be tempted to use roasted red bell peppers from a jar; they are too vinegary.

Make Ahead
The roasted bell peppers can be refrigerated overnight; bring them to room temperature before serving. The toasted almonds can be kept in an airtight container for up to 1 week.

Bones chef James Henry plays with your expectations of Spanish romesco in this dish. Instead of finely grinding the ingredients—almonds, garlic, grilled red pepper, and tomato—into the classic thick sauce, he chops them into a genius topping for sweet steamed mussels.

—

1.
Heat the broiler to high. Line a small baking sheet with foil. Arrange the bell pepper pieces on the foil skin-side up and broil until the skin is mostly black, 10 to 15 minutes. Remove the peppers from the oven and wrap them in the foil to steam the skin loose, 10 to 15 minutes. Remove the roasted peppers from the foil and reserve any roasting juices. Peel off the skin and cut the flesh into ¼-inch (6-mm) dice. Leave the broiler on.

2.
Spread the almonds on the same baking sheet. Transfer to the oven and broil, stirring the almonds occasionally, until toasted, 2 to 3 minutes. Transfer the almonds to a cutting board and let cool. Coarsely chop.

3.
In a large pot, cook the mussels, covered, over high heat, stirring once or twice, until they open, 3 to 5 minutes. Remove the pot from the heat and spoon the mussels and juices into bowls. Sprinkle the bell pepper, almonds, tomato, garlic, lemon juice, and thyme over the top. Drizzle with oil and season with salt and piment d'Espelette. Serve immediately with plenty of crusty bread.

sea scallops *with* citrus butter

Four Servings

—

4 tablespoons (60 g) unsalted butter, softened

Finely grated zest of 2 Meyer lemons

Fine sea salt

¾ cup (185 g) coarse sea salt

12 large sea scallops (about 1 pound/500 g), side muscle removed

Fleur de sel

Piment d'Espelette

12 toasted almond slices

—

Note
You need 12 scallop shells to make this recipe. Buy them separately or, if you can find them, buy sea scallops in the shell.

Make Ahead
The citrus butter can be shaped into a log, wrapped in plastic, and refrigerated for up to 3 days or frozen for up to 1 month. The scallops can be assembled in the shell, covered, and refrigerated for up to 4 hours.

During the winter months, Yves Camdeborde often works these fast and easy broiled scallops into his legendary five-course dinner at Le Comptoir. For a citrus kick, he dots the tops with yuzu butter from Breton dairy Bordier. This adaptation uses a homemade citrus butter suffused with aromatic Meyer lemon.

—

1.
In a small bowl, beat the butter with the lemon zest and ½ teaspoon of fine salt.

2.
Heat the broiler to high. Using 1 tablespoon of coarse salt for each, make 3 neat mounds of salt on each of 4 large plates, spacing the mounds well apart. Arrange 6 clean scallop shells on each of 2 baking sheets. Set 1 scallop in each shell and dot with the citrus butter. Transfer the baking sheets to the oven and broil, rotating the sheets halfway through, until the scallops are barely opaque in the center, 3 to 5 minutes.

3.
Transfer the scallop shells to the plates, nestling each into a mound of salt. Season the scallops with fleur de sel and piment d'Espelette, set an almond slice on each scallop, and serve immediately.

scallops *with* bacon, cauliflower puree & onions

Four Servings

—

1 pound (500 g) cauliflower, cored and cut into 1-inch (2.5-cm) florets

4½ tablespoons (65 g) unsalted butter

Sea salt and freshly ground pepper

12 spring onions, white part only, or peeled pearl onions

12 large sea scallops (about 1 pound/500 g), side muscle removed

6 bacon slices, halved crosswise

1 tablespoon extra-virgin olive oil

2 thyme sprigs, preferably lemon thyme

2 tablespoons fresh lemon juice

Fleur de sel

—

Make Ahead
The cauliflower puree and glazed onions can be refrigerated separately for up to 4 hours. The scallops can be assembled and refrigerated for up to 4 hours; cook just before serving.

La Rallonge's teeny kitchen has barely enough room for one cook and one dishwasher, but chef Marine Thomas sends out mini versions of French classics like she commands a brigade. Her solo efforts, like bacon-wrapped scallops with a satiny puree and small glazed onions, make a persuasive argument for bringing back old-fashioned pleasures.

—

1.

In a large saucepan of boiling water, cook the cauliflower until very tender, 8 to 10 minutes. Drain, reserving ¼ cup (60 ml) of the water, and return the cauliflower to the pan. Using an immersion blender, puree with 2 tablespoons (30 g) of the butter until smooth, adding the reserved cooking water by tablespoons to loosen, if needed. Season with salt and pepper. Gently reheat before serving.

2.

In a small skillet, combine the onions and 1½ tablespoons (20 g) of the butter. Season with salt and add just enough water to coat the bottom of the pan. Cover, bring to a simmer, and cook over medium heat until the onions are tender, 5 to 7 minutes. Uncover and cook until lightly browned, about 3 minutes.

3.

Season the scallops with salt and pepper. Wrap each scallop around the circumference in a bacon slice and secure with a toothpick. In a large nonstick skillet, heat the oil until shimmering. Add the scallops and cook over medium-high heat until golden on the bottom, about 2 minutes. Reduce the heat to medium. Turn the scallops, add the thyme and remaining 1 tablespoon (15 g) of butter, and cook, tilting the skillet and spooning the butter over the scallops until they are just opaque throughout, about 2 minutes. Season with the lemon juice. Remove the toothpicks.

4.

Mound the cauliflower puree on plates and lean the scallops on top. Add the onions to the plate and season with fleur de sel. Drizzle with the brown butter and serve.

charred squid *with* boudin noir, peas & herb oil

Four Servings

—

½ cup (15 g) packed parsley leaves

½ cup (15 g) packed mint leaves

¼ cup (60 ml) grapeseed oil

Fine sea salt and freshly ground pepper

8 ounces (250 g) French boudin noir or morcilla sausage (blood sausage), casing removed, at room temperature

1 pound (500 g) small cleaned squid with tentacles

1 pound (500 g) green peas in the pod, shelled (1 cup/250 g)

1 tablespoon fresh lemon juice

1 tablespoon extra-virgin olive oil, plus more for brushing

Fleur de sel

—

Make Ahead
The herb oil can be refrigerated for up to 3 days.

I am in love with Shaun Kelly's use of color on the plate and unbelievably fresh ingredients. Here, the chef spoons black sausage into white pockets of squid, then flash-grills them and serves tiny garden peas and a house-made herb oil alongside—the herbs simply blitzed with oil and strained. His use of boudin noir is clever: the sausage is creamy, flavorful, and sold precooked (no last-minute sautéing necessary)—a perfect readymade filling.

—

1.
In a food processor, puree the parsley with the mint and grapeseed oil until very smooth. Pour into a mesh coffee filter or a fine sieve set over a small bowl and strain the oil, pressing on the herbs with the back of a spoon. (Discard the herbs.) Season with salt and pepper.

2.
In a medium bowl, beat the boudin noir with a wooden spoon until smooth. Using a small spoon, very loosely stuff the squid bodies with the boudin. Using toothpicks, attach the tentacles to the bodies, sealing in the boudin.

3.
In a steamer, cook the peas, covered, until barely tender, 1 to 3 minutes. Transfer to a small bowl and toss with the lemon juice and olive oil. Season with salt and pepper.

4.
Meanwhile, heat a grill or a grill pan. Brush the squid with olive oil and season with salt and pepper. Grill over high heat until they are lightly charred, about 30 seconds per side. Remove the toothpicks and transfer the squid to plates; sprinkle with fleur de sel. Spoon the peas alongside, drizzle the herb oil around the plate, and serve.

—

Variation
Instead of blood sausage, try stuffing the squid with fresh Mexican chorizo. Remove the sausage casing, crumble the meat, and sauté it in olive oil until browned and cooked through.

tuna *with* shell beans & mussels in celery broth

Four Servings

—

2 shallots: 1 halved,
1 finely chopped

2 garlic cloves: 1 crushed,
1 finely chopped

1 carrot, quartered crosswise

1 tomato, chopped

1 bacon slice, finely chopped

2 thyme sprigs

2 bay leaves

4 cups (1 L) chicken stock

1 cup (180 g) fresh shell beans,
such as cranberry or cannellini
(about 1 pound/500 g in the pod),
or ¾ cup (150 g) dried beans

Sea salt

2 tablespoons (30 g) unsalted
butter

1 pound (500 g) small mussels,
scrubbed and debearded

1 cup (250 ml) dry white wine

1 tablespoon extra-virgin olive
oil, plus more for drizzling

Four 4- to 5-ounce (125- to
150-g) skinless tuna steaks

1 tender celery rib, finely diced

¼ cup (8 g) chopped parsley

Fleur de sel and freshly
ground pepper

Dill sprigs, for garnish

—

Make Ahead
**The beans can be refrigerated
overnight in their cooking
liquid. Gently rewarm over
medium heat before using.**

Even though his cooking is wholly French, Les Déserteurs chef Daniel Baratier's set menu evokes a Japanese kaiseki experience in its expression of the season. In summer, creamy shell beans right out of the pod come with rare-seared tuna in a shellfish broth made from steaming mussels. It's a whiff of a day at the beach.

—

1.
Tie the shallot halves, crushed garlic, carrot, tomato, bacon, 1 thyme sprig, and 1 bay leaf in a cheesecloth bundle. In a large saucepan, combine the herb bundle with the stock, fresh or dried beans, and a pinch of salt and bring to a boil. Reduce the heat to medium-low and simmer, partially covered, until the beans are tender, 20 to 30 minutes for the fresh beans and 1 to 1½ hours for the dried beans, depending on the age. Remove the pan from the heat and leave the beans in the cooking liquid.

2.
In a medium saucepan, melt the butter. Add the chopped shallot, chopped garlic, and remaining thyme sprig and bay leaf and cook over medium heat, stirring occasionally, until the vegetables soften, about 2 minutes. Add the mussels and wine, cover, and cook over high heat, shaking the pan a few times, until they open, 3 to 5 minutes. Let cool slightly in the pan, then shuck the mussels and discard the shells. Strain the cooking liquid into a small saucepan, leaving the grit behind, and add the mussels to the pan.

3.
In a large nonstick skillet, heat the oil until hot. Add the tuna steaks and cook over medium heat until lightly browned on the outside and still rare within, 2 to 3 minutes per side. Gently reheat the mussels in the cooking liquid. Drain the beans (save the liquid to make soup) and discard the herb bundle. Spoon the beans into shallow bowls and add the celery and parsley. Ladle the mussels and their cooking liquid into the bowls and drizzle oil around the edge. Set the tuna on top and season with fleur de sel and pepper. Garnish with the dill and serve.

bonito *with* green lentil *&* summer squash salad

Four Servings

—

½ cup (100 g) green Puy lentils, rinsed and picked over

2 shallots, halved

2 garlic cloves, crushed

1 thyme sprig

1 bay leaf

2 cups (500 ml) water

Coarse sea salt

2 tablespoons red wine vinegar

2 teaspoons Dijon mustard

Flaky sea salt, such as Maldon, and freshly ground pepper

6 tablespoons (100 ml) lemon olive oil (see Note)

Four 4- to 5-ounce (125- to 150-g) bonito loins or skinless tuna steaks

8 ounces (250 g) yellow summer squash, sliced ¼ inch (6 mm) thick on the diagonal

8 ounces (250 g) zucchini, sliced ¼ inch (6 mm) thick on the diagonal

3 ounces (90 g) baby spinach

1 tablespoon finely chopped preserved lemon (see page 132, Step 1)

—

Note
Many lemon oils are artificial tasting, but Pasolivo citrus oils (there are tangerine and lime varieties, too) have a super-fresh flavor. They're available from pasolivo.com.

Make Ahead
The lentil salad can be prepared through Step 2 up to 4 hours ahead.

At Le Bal Café, chefs Anna Trattles and Alice Quillet created this citrusy dish (they add lemon olive oil and preserved lemon peel) with bonito, a tuna-like fish, but tuna steaks or bluefish fillets can also be used.

—

1.
In a medium saucepan, combine the lentils, shallots, garlic, thyme, bay leaf, water, and a pinch of coarse salt. Bring to a boil and simmer over medium heat until the lentils are tender but still intact, about 25 minutes. Drain the lentils and discard the vegetables, thyme, and bay leaf. Return the lentils to the pan.

2.
In a small bowl, whisk the vinegar with the mustard. Season with a pinch each of flaky salt and pepper. Gradually whisk in ¼ cup (60 ml) of the oil. Stir the vinaigrette into the warm lentils in the pan.

3.
Heat a grill or a grill pan. Brush the bonito loins with 1 tablespoon of the oil. Season with flaky salt and pepper. Grill over medium-high heat, turning once, until lightly charred on the outside and rare within, 2 to 3 minutes per side. Transfer to a cutting board. Leave the grill on or clean the grill pan.

4.
In a medium bowl, toss the squash and zucchini with 2 teaspoons of the oil and season with flaky salt and pepper. Grill the squash and zucchini over medium-high heat until grill marks form, about 2 minutes. Turn the squash and zucchini and grill until tender, about 2 minutes.

5.
In a large bowl, season the remaining 1 teaspoon of oil lightly with flaky salt and pepper. Add the spinach and toss to coat. Add the lentils, squash, zucchini, and preserved lemon and gently toss to combine. Mound the lentil salad on plates and lean the bonito loins on top. Season with flaky salt and serve.

swordfish *with* carrots & apricot puree

Four Servings

—

8 dried apricots

1 tablespoon unseasoned
rice vinegar

⅛ teaspoon turmeric

Sea salt

2 tablespoons plus 2 teaspoons
extra-virgin olive oil

Splash of fresh orange juice

8 ounces (250 g) tender
young carrots, tops trimmed
to ½ inch (1 cm)

2 tablespoons buttermilk

1 teaspoon hazelnut oil

Freshly ground pepper

4 spring onions, white part
only, halved lengthwise

Fleur de sel

One 1-pound (500-g) skinless
swordfish loin

½ cup (125 ml) carrot juice,
warmed

Edible orange marigold flowers
or nasturtiums, for garnish

—

Make Ahead
The recipe can be prepared
through Step 2 and
refrigerated overnight.

Louis-Philippe Riel of Le 6 Paul Bert
fools you into thinking his apricot puree
is made with some kind of orange
vegetable. It's not. It's a piquant condiment
of dried fruit steeped in rice vinegar
with turmeric and olive oil. Just a dab
on your knife gives the semi-raw
swordfish a sweet-and-sharp boost.

—

1.
In a small bowl, combine the apricots
with the vinegar and turmeric and season
with salt. Let soak, stirring occasionally,
for 2 hours. In a mini food processor, puree
the apricot mixture with 1 tablespoon of
the olive oil and a splash of orange juice
until very smooth.

2.
Set 2 of the smaller carrots aside. Cut
off the tops of the remaining carrots
and discard; cut the carrots into 1-inch
(2.5-cm) pieces. In a medium saucepan,
combine the carrot pieces with water to
cover by 1 inch (2.5 cm). Bring to a boil
and cook over medium heat until tender,
about 10 minutes; drain. In a food
processor, puree the cooked carrots with
the buttermilk, hazelnut oil, and a pinch
of salt until very smooth. Season with salt
and pepper.

3.
In a medium skillet, heat 1 teaspoon of
the olive oil until shimmering. Add the
2 reserved carrots, cover, and cook over
low heat, turning them occasionally, until
tender, about 10 minutes. Transfer the
carrots to a cutting board and season with
salt. Halve the carrots lengthwise.

4.
Heat a medium cast-iron skillet until
very hot. Add 1 teaspoon of the olive oil
and the onions, season with salt, and
cook over high heat until slightly charred
and crisp-tender, about 4 minutes per
side. Season with fleur de sel and pepper.

5.
In a large nonstick skillet, heat the
remaining 1 tablespoon of olive oil until
hot. Add the fish and cook over medium
heat until lightly browned on the outside
and rare within, 1 to 2 minutes per side.
Transfer to a cutting board and cut
crosswise into 8 slices.

6.
Spoon 1½ tablespoons of the carrot juice
onto each plate. Lay one carrot half
vertically across one third of the plate.
Alternate the swordfish slices and onion
halves in a row alongside the carrot. Set
a spoonful of the apricot puree on one slice
of fish. Set a spoonful of carrot puree on
the other side of the carrot. Sprinkle with
fleur de sel and pepper, garnish with the
flowers, and serve.

Louis-Philippe Riel

LE 6 PAUL BERT

—

"IT WOULD BE a scandal if the fries disappeared from the menu at Bistrot Paul Bert," said owner Bertrand Auboyneau (opposite page, bottom left). But at Le 6 Paul Bert, the indie offshoot of Auboyneau's iconic bistro, self-taught chef Louis-Philippe Riel shows a healthy disregard for old-school cooking. Cream is replaced with buttermilk, and broths stand in for sauces. Many of Riel's dishes are raw to highlight the ultra-freshness of the ingredients. Still, the clean, bold food from this reserved Canadian takes more talent than buying from the best farmers. Riel showed off the basement meat locker where he ages meat and birds. I watched cooks roast vegetables and fish bones for profound flavor. Riel extracted taste from every scrap: ham trimmings, scallop shells, and even hazelnut shells (simmered in milk to enhance a dessert). The upshot: genuinely unusual, spot-on pairings, like barely touched swordfish with a kicky apricot puree (pictured on page 121). Riel's menu is propelled by change. "After three days of the same thing," he said, "I get bored."

marinated salmon *with* fennel salad *&* ricotta

Four Servings

—

Marinade and Salmon

1 star anise pod

1 teaspoon coriander seeds

1 teaspoon dried juniper berries

1 cup (200 g) sugar

1 cup (200 g) sea salt

1 cup (30 g) mixed packed chopped parsley with stems, tarragon with stems, and fennel fronds

Finely grated zest and juice of 1 orange

Finely grated zest and juice of 1 lime

1 lemongrass stalk, tender inner bulb only, finely chopped

One 1-inch (2.5-cm) piece of fresh ginger, peeled and finely chopped

1 teaspoon piment d'Espelette

One 1-pound (500-g) center-cut salmon fillet, skinned

Les Enfants Rouges chef Daï Shinozuka's fragrant, citrusy marinade spiced with star anise and fresh ginger almost cures the salmon, which Shinozuka briefly sears to create a fantastic mix of raw and cooked. The marinade is packed with so much flavor, you can leave out an herb or spice if it's not on hand or easy to find. And while there are several components to this dish, everything but searing the salmon can be done in advance.

—

1. Marinade and Salmon

In a small dry skillet, toast the star anise, coriander, and juniper berries over medium heat, shaking the skillet occasionally, until fragrant, 2 to 3 minutes. Transfer to a spice mill and let cool, then grind to a powder. Transfer the spice mix to a medium gratin dish, add all the remaining marinade ingredients, and stir to mix. Add the salmon and spoon half of the marinade over the top. Cover the dish with plastic wrap and refrigerate for 8 to 10 hours, turning the salmon and redistributing the marinade occasionally.

Salad

¼ small red onion, thinly sliced

2 tablespoons red wine vinegar

Sea salt and freshly
ground pepper

4 ounces (125 g) fava beans in
the pod, shelled (¼ cup/60 g) or
2 ounces (60 g) frozen baby peas

4 ounces (125 g) green peas in
the pod, shelled (¼ cup/60 g) or
2 ounces (60 g) frozen baby peas

1 cup (30 g) packed chopped
baby sorrel or arugula

¼ cup (60 ml) water

3 tablespoons extra-virgin
olive oil

2 tablespoons fresh lemon juice

½ small shallot, finely chopped

½ oil-cured anchovy, sliced
crosswise

½ fennel bulb, cored and
sliced 1/16 inch (1.5 mm) thick
on a mandoline

Flying fish roe (tobiko), for
garnish (optional)

2 tablespoons fresh ricotta
cheese mixed with
2 tablespoons crème fraîche
or sour cream

Piment d'Espelette

—

Make Ahead
The recipe can be prepared
through Step 4 and
refrigerated overnight.

2. Salad

In a small bowl, combine the red onion and
vinegar and season with salt and pepper.

3.

Fill a small bowl with half ice, half cold
water. In a small saucepan of boiling
salted water, blanch the fava beans and
peas until tender, 1 to 3 minutes. Drain
and transfer to the ice water to cool for
1 minute; drain. Transfer to a thick kitchen
towel and pat dry. Peel the fava beans.

4.

In a food processor, puree the sorrel with
the water and a pinch of salt. Pour into a
fine sieve set over a small bowl and strain
the mixture, pressing on the pureed
sorrel with the back of a spoon. Discard
the sorrel in the sieve.

5.

Scrape the marinade off the salmon.
Transfer the salmon to a cutting board and
discard the marinade. Cut the fillet into
4 equal pieces. In a large nonstick skillet,
heat 1 tablespoon of the oil until hot.
Add the fish to the skillet skinned-side
down and cook over medium heat until
rare, about 2 minutes per side.

6.

Spoon the sorrel water into shallow bowls.
In a medium bowl, whisk the lemon juice
with the remaining 2 tablespoons of oil,
the shallot, and anchovy and season with
salt and pepper. Add the favas and peas,
gently toss to coat, and spoon them into
the bowls. Add the fennel slices to the
vinaigrette, gently toss to coat, and add
them to the bowls. Set a piece of salmon
on top and garnish with the pickled red
onion and flying fish roe. Set a quenelle
or spoonful of ricotta cream on top, sprinkle
with piment d'Espelette, and serve.

mackerel *with* confit potatoes & yuzu cream

Four Servings

—

14 tablespoons (225 g) unsalted butter, sliced

2 thyme sprigs

1 bay leaf

12 small red or new potatoes, scrubbed (about 12 ounces/ 350 g total)

Sea salt

2 ounces (60 g) small sprouting broccoli or broccolini florets, cut into 1-inch (2.5-cm) lengths

6 tablespoons (100 ml) crème fraîche or sour cream

1½ tablespoons bottled yuzu juice, fresh Meyer lemon juice, or fresh lemon juice

Fleur de sel

1 tablespoon grapeseed oil

Four 4- to 5-ounce (125- to 150-g) skin-on mackerel, salmon, or bluefish fillets

Freshly ground pepper

Piment d'Espelette

Baby chard leaves, for garnish

—

Note
To keep the potatoes from wrinkling once they're tender, take the saucepan off the heat and cover it with a lid.

Amélie Darvas of Haï Kaï poaches potatoes in butter suffused with thyme and bay leaf. (You've heard of butter-poached lobster, right?) Save any leftover butter for drizzling over fried eggs, steak, or cooked vegetables.

—

1.
In a large saucepan, melt 11 tablespoons (180 g) of the butter. Stir in the thyme and bay leaf. Add the potatoes and season with salt. Cover and cook over medium-low heat, swirling the pan occasionally, until the potatoes are tender, 15 to 20 minutes. Reduce the heat if the butter starts to brown. Drain, reserving the butter, and discard the herbs. Cover the potatoes in the pan.

2.
Meanwhile, heat the oven to 350°F (175°C). In a medium saucepan of boiling salted water, cook the sprouting broccoli until crisp-tender, 2 to 3 minutes. Drain it and rinse in cold water. Drain again, transfer to a thick kitchen towel, and pat dry.

3.
In a small bowl, whisk the crème fraîche with the yuzu juice. Season with fleur de sel.

4.
In a large ovenproof skillet, heat the oil until shimmering. Season the fish with salt and pepper. Add the fish to the skillet skin-side down and cook over medium-high heat without moving it, pressing gently on the fillets with a spatula to ensure the skin is in full contact with the pan, until the skin is crisp and browned, about 5 minutes. Add the remaining 3 tablespoons (45 g) of butter to the skillet, transfer it to the oven (do not turn the fish over), and roast until the fish is still slightly raw on top, 3 to 4 minutes. Remove the skillet from the oven and spoon the brown butter over the fish.

5.
Set a fish fillet skin-side up on one side of each plate, drizzle the brown butter over the fish, and season with fleur de sel and piment d'Espelette. Spoon some of the yuzu cream next to the fish. Garnish with the chard leaves and broccoli. In separate small bowls, arrange the potatoes, season with fleur de sel, and drizzle with the reserved butter. Serve with the fish.

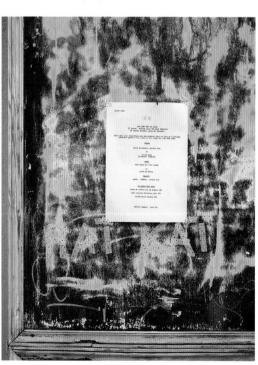

Amélie Darvas

HAÏ KAÏ

—

WE TRIED SHOOTING Amélie Darvas's portrait on the Canal Saint-Martin across from her restaurant, Haï Kaï, but the waterway's romantic peaked iron bridges and enchanting locks didn't suit this biker chef. The Parisian came up working hard at both ends of the restaurant spectrum, from haute (Le Bristol, Le Meurice, Hélène Darroze) to low (L'Ami Jean, Ribouldingue). Then, at only twenty-four, she teamed up with a girlfriend and created something strikingly different: a bright, white, D.I.Y. space with a graffiti facade and "Haï Kaï" spelled out in colorful masking tape. Darvas and her crew treat cooking like an extreme sport—I watched one cook pull the pin feathers out of ducks for hours. Yet she shops like a French housewife, buying only what she needs for the day, changing the market menu at lunch and dinner, and paring it down to essentials (like haïkaï/haiku)—just three or four starters and three main courses. What makes her food so compelling? "I'm not afraid of fat," she said.

monkfish *with* asparagus & parmesan cream

Four Servings

—

2 tablespoons (30 g) unsalted butter

1 shallot, finely chopped

Sea salt

2 ounces (60 g) Parmesan cheese, finely grated

½ cup (125 ml) heavy cream or half-and-half

¼ cup (60 ml) chicken stock

Freshly ground pepper

8 large green asparagus spears, peeled

Fleur de sel

1 tablespoon grapeseed oil

Four 6-ounce (180-g) monkfish loins, trimmed of outer membranes

Baby amaranth or spinach leaves, for garnish

Chopped roasted pistachios, for garnish

—

Make Ahead
The Parmesan sauce can be refrigerated for up to 2 days.

Amélie Darvas learned to make Stéphane Jégo's Parmesan cream (page 40) when she worked at L'Ami Jean. At Haï Kaï, it's transformed into a rich counterpoint to peak-season asparagus.

—

1.
In a small saucepan, melt 1 tablespoon (15 g) of the butter. Add the shallot and a pinch of salt and cook over medium heat, stirring occasionally, until softened, 2 to 3 minutes. Add the cheese and cook, stirring often, until melted, 2 to 3 minutes. Gradually stir in the cream and stock and bring to a simmer, scraping up any cheese stuck to the bottom. Cook, partially covered, over medium-low heat, stirring occasionally, until reduced to ½ cup (125 ml), about 10 minutes. Season with pepper. Using an immersion blender, puree the sauce until very smooth.

2.
In a large skillet of boiling salted water, cook the asparagus until crisp-tender, about 4 minutes. Drain and rinse in cold water. Drain, transfer to a thick kitchen towel, and pat dry. In the same skillet, melt the remaining 1 tablespoon (15 g) of butter. Add the asparagus and cook over medium-high heat until lightly browned all over, about 2 minutes. Season with fleur de sel and pepper. Cut the asparagus crosswise in half on the diagonal.

3.
Heat the oven to 400°F (200°C). In a large ovenproof skillet, heat the oil until shimmering. Season the monkfish with salt and pepper. Add the fish to the skillet and cook over medium-high heat until lightly browned on 3 sides, about 6 minutes total. Transfer the skillet to the oven and roast the fish until a metal skewer inserted in the center feels warm to the touch, about 5 minutes.

4.
Gently reheat the sauce and spoon it onto plates. Arrange the asparagus and amaranth leaves on one side of the plates. Set the monkfish alongside, sprinkle with the pistachios, and serve.

roasted & raw asparagus *with* hake & grilled bread sauce

Four Servings

—

¼ cup (15 g) panko

8 tablespoons (125 g) unsalted butter, diced

Fine sea salt and freshly ground pepper

12 medium asparagus spears, peeled

1 tablespoon extra-virgin olive oil, plus more for drizzling

1 tablespoon fresh lemon juice

Four 4- to 5-ounce (125- to 150-g) skin-on hake or sea bass fillets

4 ounces (125 g) pencil-thin asparagus spears, sliced crosswise ⅛ inch (3 mm) thick

Chervil sprigs or snipped chives, for garnish

—

Make Ahead
The panko can be toasted, the butter browned, and the asparagus blanched up to 4 hours ahead.

You'd be excused for ordering the hake just to get a taste of Septime chef Bertrand Grébaut's meticulously prepared asparagus served alongside. Grébaut thinly slices raw skinny asparagus to eliminate any tough strings yet keep their just-picked flavor. As a foil, medium asparagus are roasted just long enough to develop some char. Lemon juice escapes from the vegetables to keep the rich sauce in check.

—

1.
Heat the oven to 400°F (200°C). Spread the panko in a pie plate and toast in the oven until dark brown, about 5 minutes. Remove the panko from the oven. Leave the oven on.

2.
In a small saucepan, melt the butter over medium-high heat, then cook, swirling the pan occasionally, until the milk solids brown, 3 to 4 minutes. Just before serving, gently reheat the brown butter, stir in the toasted panko, and season the grilled bread sauce with salt and pepper.

3.
In a large skillet of boiling salted water, blanch the medium asparagus for 1 minute. Drain and rinse in cold water, then transfer to a thick kitchen towel and pat dry. Spread on a baking sheet, drizzle with oil and roast in the oven until crisp-tender, about 4 minutes. Remove from the oven and drizzle with the lemon juice. Season with salt and pepper. Leave the oven on.

4.
Meanwhile, in a large ovenproof skillet, heat the 1 tablespoon of oil until shimmering. Season the fish with salt and pepper. Add the fish to the skillet skin-side down and cook over medium heat for 5 to 7 minutes. Transfer the skillet to the oven (do not turn the fish over) and roast the fish until still slightly raw on top, 2 to 4 minutes.

5.
Arrange 3 roasted asparagus spears on each plate and brush with some of the grilled bread sauce. Lean a fish fillet on the asparagus, sprinkle with the sliced asparagus, and drizzle with more of the sauce. Garnish with the chervil and serve.

hake *with* caramelized endives & preserved lemon

Four Servings

—

Quick Preserved Lemon

1 large lemon, cut crosswise into slices ¼ inch (6 mm) thick

½ cup (125 ml) fresh lemon juice (from 2 large lemons)

1 tablespoon sea salt

Hake and Endives

8 tablespoons (125 g) unsalted butter

2 slices of firm white bread, cut into ¼-inch (6-mm) cubes

Sea salt and freshly ground pepper

4 small Belgian endives, red or yellow, halved lengthwise

1 tablespoon grapeseed oil

Four 4- to 5-ounce (125- to 150-g) skin-on hake or sea bass fillets

Fleur de sel

Thinly sliced scallion, white and light green parts only, for garnish

—

Make Ahead
The preserved lemon can be refrigerated for up to 1 week. The cooked endives can stand at room temperature for up to 2 hours; reheat in the oven when baking the fish.

At Le Bal Café, chefs Anna Trattles's and Alice Quillet's thick hake fillets and endive halves (pictured on page 111) are burnished on top of the stove before a quick pass in the oven to cook through. Preserved lemons add beautiful brightness to the plate.

You can use store-bought preserved lemons instead of making the quick preserves here, or, if you can wait three months, prepare them as Trattles and Quillet do: Quarter lemons lengthwise, keeping one end intact. Add 1 teaspoon of sea salt to the center of each lemon. Add a large pinch of sea salt to a jar large enough to hold the lemons you are preserving. Pack the lemons into the jar and seal. Turn the jar upside down two times a day for 3 days. Add fresh lemon juice if needed to cover the lemons. Store in a cool place for 3 months before using. Please note that these traditional preserved lemons are not refrigerated.

—

1. Quick Preserved Lemon
In a small saucepan, bring the lemon slices, lemon juice, and salt to a boil over high heat, swirling the pan to dissolve the salt. Cover, reduce the heat to low, and simmer until the lemon slices are almost tender and the peel is translucent, 8 to 10 minutes. Pour the mixture into a small heatproof bowl, cover, and refrigerate until cool, at least 1 hour. Just before cooking the fish, remove 1 lemon slice. Discard the pulp and mince the peel. Reserve the remaining lemon slices for another use.

2. Hake and Endives
Position racks in the upper and lower thirds of the oven and heat the oven to 350°F (175°C). In a small ovenproof skillet, melt 2 tablespoons (30 g) of the butter in

the oven. Remove the skillet from the oven and stir in the bread cubes, spreading them in a single layer. Transfer the skillet to the upper rack of the oven and bake, stirring once or twice, until the bread cubes are crisp and golden, about 10 minutes. Remove from the oven and season with salt and pepper. Leave the oven on.

3.
In a large ovenproof skillet, melt 3 tablespoons (45 g) of the butter. Arrange the endive halves cut-side down in the skillet and season with salt and pepper. Cook over medium-high heat until nicely browned on the bottom, 3 to 4 minutes. Transfer the skillet to the lower rack in the oven and bake until just tender, about 10 minutes.

4.
Meanwhile, in another large ovenproof skillet, heat the oil until shimmering. Season the fish with salt and pepper. Add the fish to the skillet skin-side down and cook over medium-high heat without moving it, pressing gently on the fillets with a spatula to ensure the skin is in full contact with the pan, until the skin is crisp and golden, about 5 minutes. Add the remaining 3 tablespoons (45 g) of butter to the skillet, transfer it to the upper rack in the oven (do not turn the fish over), and roast until the hake is still slightly raw on top, 3 to 4 minutes. Remove the skillet from the oven and spoon the brown butter over the fish.

5.
Arrange 2 endive halves, slightly overlapping, on each plate and lean a hake fillet on top, skin-side up. Sprinkle the fleur de sel, croutons, scallions, and preserved lemon around the plates and serve.

hake *with* cucumbers, pistachios *&* runner beans

Four Servings

—

Sea salt

8 ounces (250 g) green
runner beans

1 lime

2 tablespoons extra-virgin
olive oil

Freshly ground pepper

1 large mini cucumber, sliced
⅛ inch (3 mm) thick on
a mandoline and cut into
half-moons

2 tablespoons roasted
skinned pistachios

2 tablespoons small dill sprigs

1 tablespoon grapeseed oil

Four 4- to 5-ounce (125- to
150-g) skinless hake, flounder,
or sea bass fillets

Confectioners' sugar,
for dusting

Fleur de sel

—

Note
Tatiana Levha dusts the fish
fillets with confectioners'
sugar before searing them
to get rich caramelization.
The sugar doesn't really leave
a noticeable taste; it just
makes the skinned fish fillets
nice and brown.

Make Ahead
The runner beans can be
prepared up to 4 hours ahead.

Chef Tatiana Levha of Le Servan worked
at top Paris restaurants Arpège and
Astrance, but some of her best dishes are
extraordinarily simple. For the side salad
here, she folds pistachios, dill, and lime
(zest, juice, and segments) into slices of
mini cucumber with skin so tender it
doesn't need peeling. The result: a light,
elegant bistro dish that's so easy to make.

—

1.
Fill a medium bowl with half ice, half
cold water. In a medium saucepan of
boiling salted water, cook the beans until
crisp-tender, 4 to 6 minutes. Drain
and transfer to the ice water to cool for
1 minute; drain. Transfer to a thick
kitchen towel and pat dry.

2.
Finely grate the zest from half the lime
into a medium bowl. Using a small, sharp
knife, cut the skin and all of the bitter
white pith off the lime. Working over
the bowl, cut in between the membranes
to release the segments. Squeeze the
juice from the membranes into the bowl.
Whisk in the olive oil and season with
salt and pepper. Cut the lime segments
crosswise ¼ inch (6 mm) thick and add
to the bowl. Add the cucumber, pistachios,
and dill and toss to coat.

3.
In a large nonstick skillet, heat the
grapeseed oil. Season the fish with salt
and dust with confectioners' sugar. Add
the fish to the skillet skinned-side down
and cook over medium-high heat until
golden, about 3 minutes. Turn the fillets
and cook until the fish is just white
throughout, about 2 minutes. Mound the
beans on plates and lean the fish fillets on
top. Sprinkle with fleur de sel and pepper.
Spoon the cucumber salad on the fish
and serve.

—

Variation
If you can't find flat runner beans, use
any color snap, wax, or French beans and
reduce the cooking time.

cod en cocotte *with* tomatoes, olives & chorizo

Four Servings

—

2 medium Yukon Gold potatoes
(12 ounces/350 g total)

6 plum tomatoes, peeled,
seeded, and chopped

1½ ounces (45 g) Spanish
chorizo, cut into ⅛-inch
(3-mm) dice

12 small black olives, such as
Niçoise, pitted

1 large garlic clove, chopped

Four 4- to 5-ounce (125- to
150-g) skinned cod fillets

4 thyme sprigs

¼ cup (8 g) chopped parsley

4 tablespoons (60 g) unsalted
butter, sliced

3 tablespoons extra-virgin
olive oil

2 tablespoons fresh lemon juice

Sea salt and freshly
ground pepper

—

Make Ahead
**The casserole can be
assembled and refrigerated for
up to 4 hours before baking.**

The current fondness for artfully composed plates has virtually killed the casserole, but La Rallonge chef Marine Thomas serves this cod in adorable mini cast-iron pots. I reconfigured her recipe to make one large family-style dish. All the flavors come together in the brief time it takes to cook the fish.

—

1.
Heat the oven to 350°F (175°C). In a medium saucepan of boiling water, cook the potatoes until tender, about 20 minutes. Drain and let cool slightly, then peel and cut into slices ¼ inch (6 mm) thick.

2.
In a medium enameled cast-iron casserole, spread the potato slices, tomatoes, chorizo, olives, and garlic. Set the fish on top and add the thyme, parsley, butter, oil, and lemon juice. Season with salt and pepper. Cover and bring to a simmer on the stove, then transfer the pot to the oven and cook until the fish is just opaque throughout, 10 to 15 minutes. Serve directly from the casserole.

PAULBERT

poultry
and meat

SEPTIME

crisp chicken *with* potato salad & anchovy vinaigrette

Four Servings

—

12 small red or new potatoes, scrubbed (12 ounces/350 g total)

2 tablespoons red wine vinegar

2 tablespoons minced shallot

3 oil-packed anchovy fillets, chopped

1 teaspoon Dijon mustard

1 garlic clove, minced

⅓ cup (80 ml) plus 1 teaspoon extra-virgin olive oil

Sea salt and freshly ground pepper

2 tablespoons grapeseed oil

4 large skin-on boneless chicken thighs

5 ounces (150 g) large amaranth leaves, thick central veins removed, or baby spinach

Fleur de sel

1 teaspoon fresh lemon juice

Small amaranth or baby spinach and mixed baby lettuce leaves, for garnish

½ cup (125 g) fromage blanc or Greek yogurt, preferably goat's or sheep's milk

—

Make Ahead
The recipe can be prepared through Step 2 up to 4 hours ahead.

Only Septime chef Bertrand Grébaut can make chicken salad taste like a groovy improvisation instead of a safe dish. The boneless thigh meat is moist, crunchy—it develops crackling skin in a cast-iron pan—and rousing when tumbled with anchovy-spiked potatoes. The kicker: a dollop of fromage blanc (or yogurt), plus a mix of raw and sautéed greens on the plate.

—

1.
In a medium saucepan, cover the potatoes with water and bring to a boil. Cook over medium-high heat until tender, 15 to 20 minutes. Drain and cut the potatoes in half.

2.
Meanwhile, in a blender, combine the vinegar with the shallot, anchovies, mustard, and garlic and puree until smooth. With the blender on, drizzle in ⅓ cup (80 ml) of the olive oil until the vinaigrette is emulsified. Season with salt and pepper. Scrape the vinaigrette into a large bowl. Add the warm potatoes and toss to coat.

3.
In a large cast-iron or other heavy skillet, heat the grapeseed oil over high heat until smoking. Season the chicken generously with salt and pepper. Add the chicken to the skillet skin-side down and set another large heavy skillet on top. Reduce the heat to medium and cook the chicken until browned and crisp on the bottom, 6 to 8 minutes.

4.
Remove the top skillet and turn the chicken over, then replace the skillet and cook the chicken for 2 to 3 minutes. Transfer the chicken to a cutting board and let rest for 5 minutes. Slice the chicken into pieces 1 inch (2.5 cm) thick. Add the chicken with any juices to the potatoes and gently toss to coat.

5.
In the same skillet, cook the large amaranth leaves over medium heat, stirring, until just wilted, about 1 minute. Season with fleur de sel and pepper.

6.
In a medium bowl, combine the lemon juice and remaining 1 teaspoon of olive oil and season lightly with fleur de sel and pepper. Add the small fresh amaranth and baby lettuce leaves and toss to coat. Mound the chicken and potato salad on plates. Top with the wilted amaranth and the fresh amaranth and lettuce. Set a quenelle or spoonful of the fromage blanc on each plate, season the fromage blanc generously with pepper, and serve.

chicken breast *with* lemon verbena & peas à la française

Four Servings

—

Sauce Suprême

1 tablespoon (15 g) unsalted butter

1 tablespoon (10 g) all-purpose flour

1 cup (250 ml) chicken stock

Sea salt and freshly ground pepper

2 tablespoons heavy cream

2 tablespoons fresh lemon juice

Chicken and Peas

Two 8-ounce (250-g) skin-on boneless chicken breast halves

2 large lemon verbena or basil sprigs, 8 leaves and remaining stems and leaves reserved separately

Fleur de sel and freshly ground pepper

1 tablespoon grapeseed oil

2 garlic cloves, crushed with skin

3 tablespoons (45 g) unsalted butter

1 tablespoon extra-virgin olive oil

2 ounces (60 g) thinly sliced pancetta or bacon, cut crosswise ¼ inch (6 mm) thick

1 large spring onion, white part only, halved and thinly sliced

8 ounces (250 g) shelled fresh peas or thawed frozen baby peas (1 cup/250 g)

1 head of butter lettuce, cut into ½-inch (1-cm) strips

¼ cup (60 ml) chicken stock

Sea salt

¼ cup (8 g) mixed chopped tender herbs, plus more micro or small herb leaves for garnish

2 tablespoons fresh lemon juice

This springtime dish deftly balances traditional and ambitious elements. Alongside tender spring peas braised with lettuce and bacon—a classic accompaniment to squab in France— Le Pantruche chef Franck Baranger serves succulent, pan-seared chicken with perfumey lemon verbena leaves tucked under the skin.

—

1. Sauce Suprême
In a small saucepan, melt the butter. Stir in the flour. Add the stock, bring to a simmer, and cook over medium-high heat, stirring occasionally, until reduced by half, 5 to 10 minutes. Season with salt and pepper. Just before serving, gently reheat the sauce. Remove the pan from the heat, add the cream and lemon juice, and, using an immersion blender, mix until frothy. Taste for seasoning.

2. Chicken and Peas
Gently run your fingers under the skin of each chicken breast to form a pocket. Slip 4 lemon verbena leaves under the skin of each breast. Smooth the skin over the leaves so they lie flat and season all over with fleur de sel and pepper.

3.
In a medium skillet, heat the grapeseed oil until shimmering. Add the chicken breasts skin-side down and cook over medium-high heat until richly browned, about 5 minutes. Turn the breasts, add the garlic, reserved lemon verbena leaves and stems, and 2 tablespoons (30 g) of the butter and cook over medium heat until the butter is foamy. Carefully tip the skillet and, using a large spoon, baste the chicken repeatedly with the melted butter just until cooked through, about 5 minutes. Transfer the chicken and brown butter mixture to a platter and let rest for 5 minutes. Wipe out the skillet.

4.
In the same skillet, melt the remaining 1 tablespoon (15 g) of butter in the olive oil. Add the pancetta and cook over medium heat, stirring occasionally, until lightly browned, about 5 minutes. Stir in the spring onion. Add the peas, lettuce, and stock and season with salt. Cover and cook over medium-high heat until the lettuce is tender but not completely wilted, 2 to 3 minutes. Remove the skillet from the heat and stir in the chopped herbs. Season with salt, pepper, and lemon juice.

5.
Transfer the chicken breasts to a cutting board and halve them lengthwise. Spoon the pea mixture onto plates, lean a chicken breast half on top, and drizzle with the brown butter. Season with fleur de sel and pepper. Spoon the sauce suprême around the plates, garnish with the herb leaves, and serve.

Herb Primer

The role of fresh herbs in French cooking ranges from a sprinkling of chopped parsley to variations of Michel Bras's massively influential gargouillou, a dish of fifty or sixty garden and foraged greens. Neo-bistro chefs use an array of little leaves far beyond the basic parsley, thyme, chives, tarragon, and chervil of fines herbes to add dimension to soups and salads, boost marinades, and transform desserts and cocktails. These herbs are available at many farmers' markets and most are easy to cultivate. Check local nurseries for seeds and shoots. In the summer, grow them in garden beds or pots. Here's a primer of chef favorites and how to get the most out of them.

1
AMARANTH
Spinach-like amaranth can be plain green, but chefs are in love with the dramatic ruby and multihued varieties. Septime chef Bertrand Grébaut serves it wilted and fresh with his chicken salad (pictured on page 139). At Le 6 Paul Bert, Louis-Philippe Riel likes the seedlings raw with crudo.

2
BORAGE
The leaves and vivid blue flowers of the borage plant both taste uncannily like cucumber. Show off the pretty blossoms in salads or sprinkle them over a finished fish dish.

3
CHERVIL
Le Bal Café chefs Anna Trattles and Alice Quillet simmer this licorice-scented fine herbe in fennel soup (pictured on page 34) to add color and flavor. But most chefs prefer it raw, roughly chopped in a compound butter or in small sprigs as a lacy garnish for eggs and vegetables. Au Passage chef Edward Delling-Williams scatters it over a warm salad of rainbow chard (page 88).

4
CHICKWEED
Sweet, wispy chickweed appears in backyards in early spring. It makes a delightful salad green or delicate garnish for beef stew (page 152) or tea-poached apricots (page 191).

5
FENNEL FRONDS
Many chefs pair the feathery leaves of plump fennel bulbs with seafood. Au Passage chef Edward Delling-Williams boosts the flavor of steamed razor clams with the anisey herb. And at Les Enfants Rouges, Daï Shinozuka uses it in a quick salmon cure (page 124). But fennel fronds as a dessert ingredient? Septime chef Bertrand Grébaut tosses sprigs into fruit salad (pictured on page 185).

6
LEMON VERBENA
The ultrafragrant leaves are usually steeped to make tisanes as well as flavored whipped cream, custards, and sugar syrup. Try also muddling them in a cocktail. Le Pantruche chef Franck Baranger stuffs them under the skin of chicken breasts (page 140).

Herb Primer

7
LOVAGE
Lovage tastes very much like celery, but with an infinitely more complex flavor that hints at celery seed, citrus, and mint. Le Bal Café chefs Anna Trattles and Alice Quillet swap celery-scented lovage leaves for basil in a Caprese-style salad (pictured on page 58), while at Bones, James Henry purees the leaves with sugar syrup to make a pleasantly grassy granité accompaniment for summer berries (pictured on page 187).

8
MUSTARD GREENS
In their petite form, the frilly leaves add texture, spice, and color (especially the pink variety) to winter dishes like Le 6 Paul Bert chef Louis-Philippe Riel's Pork Chops with Salt-Roasted Carrot Puree (page 157). Use the mature leaves in pesto instead of basil or substitute them for parsley in salsa verde.

9
NASTURTIUM
The spicy green leaves and orange flowers are equally delicious. Haï Kaï chef Amélie Darvas adds the round leaves to her green bean salad with curry oil for a hit of fresh, peppery flavor (pictured on page 99). At Le 6 Paul Bert, Louis-Philippe Riel likes the way the orange blossoms look with Swordfish with Carrots and Apricot Puree (pictured on page 121).

10
OXALIS
This tart herb, a.k.a. wood sorrel, can be red, green, or a mix. Bones chef James Henry decorates fruit salad and granité with the clover-shaped leaves (pictured on page 187).

11
PURSLANE
The fleshly leaves of this summer weed add a puckery note to salads and seafood. Le Comptoir chef Yves Camdeborde scatters them on heirloom tomatoes and briny clams (pictured on page 74). They also make a phenomenal vichyssoise; discard the tough stems and simmer the tender tops with a mix of leeks and potatoes.

12
SWISS CHARD
Amélie Darvas of Haï Kaï finishes plates of seared mackerel (pictured on page 127) with the earthy, brightly hued shoots. The next time you're making a salad, toss in a handful of these tender greens.

13
WILD GARLIC
The pretty white blossoms (they taste like a less potent version of the greens) appear in spring, so they're good with pretty much everything else that sprouts then, too: asparagus, artichokes, potatoes. Puree the greens with grapeseed oil to create a concentrated, Technicolor elixir that's ideal for whisking into vinaigrettes and drizzling over fish, eggs, or vegetables.

foie gras–stuffed chicken breast
with carrots & spring turnips

Four Servings

—

Two 8-ounce (250-g) skin-on boneless chicken breast halves

Fleur de sel and freshly ground pepper

¼ cup (8 g) parsley leaves

8 ounces (250 g) foie gras or chicken liver terrine, cut into 2 slices to fit in chicken pocket

8 baby turnips, peeled, tops trimmed to ½ inch (1 cm)

8 baby carrots, peeled, tops trimmed to ½ inch (1 cm)

4 tablespoons (60 g) unsalted butter

1 tablespoon grapeseed oil

2 garlic cloves, crushed with skin

2 large thyme sprigs

—

Make Ahead
The chicken breasts can be prepared through Step 1 and refrigerated overnight.

Bruno Doucet's focus at his triple La Régalade franchise isn't innovation, it's the stellar product and laser-sharp technique of a seasoned chef. To maximize the flavor of chicken breasts, for instance, he simply spoons sizzling butter over them as they cook to create an exceptional crust and an herb-and-garlic-infused sauce.

—

1.

Using a sharp knife, cut horizontally along the thicker side of each chicken breast half, slicing it almost in half. Open the breasts and season with fleur de sel and pepper. Spread the parsley leaves on one half of each breast. Top with a terrine slice and season with fleur de sel and pepper. Close the breasts and seal with toothpicks. Season all over with fleur de sel and pepper. Refrigerate.

2.

In a medium skillet, combine the turnips, carrots, 2 tablespoons (30 g) of the butter, and just enough water to barely coat the bottom of the pan. Cover, bring to a simmer, and cook over medium heat until the vegetables are tender and the liquid evaporates to a shiny glaze, about 10 minutes. Season with fleur de sel and pepper.

3.

In another medium skillet, heat the oil until shimmering. Add the chicken breasts skin-side down and cook over medium-high heat until browned, about 5 minutes. Turn the breasts, add the garlic, thyme, and remaining 2 tablespoons (30 g) of butter, and cook over medium heat until the butter is foamy. Carefully tip the skillet and, using a large spoon, baste the chicken repeatedly with the melted butter just until cooked through, about 5 minutes. Transfer the chicken and brown butter mixture to a platter and let rest for 5 minutes.

4.

Transfer the chicken breasts to a cutting board, remove the toothpicks, and halve the breasts lengthwise. Spoon the turnips and carrots onto plates, lean the breasts on top, and drizzle with the brown butter. Season with fleur de sel and pepper and serve.

chicken breast *with* chard, beets *&* sorrel

Four Servings

—

1 pound (500 g) medium red beets, scrubbed

2 cups (500 ml) bottled beet juice

½ cup (125 ml) ruby port

¼ cup (60 ml) red wine vinegar

½ star anise pod

½ cinnamon stick

Fleur de sel and freshly ground pepper

Four 5-ounce (150-g) skinless boneless chicken breast halves, pounded ¼ inch (6 mm) thick (see Note)

12 or more small sorrel leaves, thick stems and center veins removed

Swiss chard or ramp leaves, thick stems and center veins removed, for wrapping

Extra-virgin olive oil, for brushing

Crème fraîche or sour cream, for serving

—

Note
Pounding the chicken breast halves helps them cook evenly and quickly. To prepare them, place each chicken breast half between 2 sheets of plastic wrap. Using a rolling pin or heavy skillet, pound the chicken until about ¼ inch (6 mm) thick.

Make Ahead
The recipe can be prepared through Step 3 and refrigerated overnight.

To play off her light, steamed chicken rolls, Haï Kaï chef Amélie Darvas simmers beets with ruby port, star anise, and cinnamon until tender. The cooking liquid is reduced to make a concentrated, sweetly spiced sauce. It also works sympathetically with luscious braising cuts of beef, like short rib, brisket, and chuck.

—

1.
In a medium saucepan, combine the beets with the beet juice, port, vinegar, star anise, and cinnamon. Bring to a simmer and cook over medium heat, partially covered, until the beets are tender, 50 to 60 minutes. Using a spider or slotted spoon, transfer the beets to a cutting board and let cool slightly. Peel the beets and cut crosswise into slices ¼ inch (6 mm) thick.

2.
Meanwhile, bring the cooking liquid to a simmer and cook over medium-high heat until syrupy, 12 to 15 minutes. Discard the star anise and cinnamon. Season with fleur de sel and pepper. Gently reheat before serving.

3.
Lay each chicken breast on a piece of plastic wrap and season all over with fleur de sel and pepper. Cover with sorrel leaves and, starting with a long side, roll up the chicken; wrap in the plastic to seal.

4.
In a steamer, cook the chicken, covered, for 3 minutes. Remove the plastic, wrap the rolls in the chard leaves, and brush with oil. Return the rolls to the steamer and cook until still a little pink in the center, about 2 minutes; the chicken will continue to cook.

5.
Arrange 3 or 4 beet slices on each plate. Drizzle the beet-port sauce around the plates. Cut the ends off the chicken rolls to neaten them, then cut in half on the diagonal and lean on the beets. Season with fleur de sel and pepper, dollop crème fraîche on the plates, and serve.

cashew-stuffed guinea hen
with cauliflower steaks

Four Servings

—

5 tablespoons (80 g) unsalted butter, 2 tablespoons (30 g) softened

2 tablespoons mixed chopped herbs, such as parsley, chives, tarragon, dill, and summer savory

1 tablespoon (10 g) finely chopped cashews, plus more for sprinkling

1 tablespoon (10 g) almond meal

1 teaspoon finely grated ginger

Fleur de sel and freshly ground pepper

Two 8-ounce (250-g) skin-on boneless guinea hen breasts (see Note) or chicken breasts

1 small cauliflower, with tender green ribs and leaves attached

2 tablespoons grapeseed oil

1½ cups (375 ml) dry white wine

1 shallot, finely chopped

1½ cups (375 ml) chicken stock

—

Note
Guinea hen can be ordered from dartagnan.com.

Make Ahead
The stuffed breasts can be refrigerated overnight.

Le Servan chef Tatiana Levha uses one skillet—that's it—to prepare her guinea hen breasts, browned sautéed cauliflower, and a simple pan sauce. She spreads an aromatic blend of chopped cashews, herbs, grated ginger, and softened butter under the skin of the breasts before searing them until richly browned. Another inspired move: Levha leaves the tender green leaves and ribs attached to the cauliflower steaks for color and texture. Why did we ever trim them off?

—

1.
In a small bowl, mash the 2 tablespoons (30 g) of softened butter with the herbs, cashews, almond meal, and ginger. Season the stuffing with fleur de sel and pepper.

2.
Gently run your fingers under the skin of each breast to form a pocket. Carefully spread half of the stuffing under the skin of each breast. Smooth the skin over the stuffing to form an even layer. Season all over with fleur de sel and pepper. Cover and refrigerate.

3.
Cut the cauliflower from top to bottom into two ½-inch-thick (1-cm) steaks. Reserve the remaining cauliflower for another use. Set a medium cast-iron or other heavy skillet over high heat until very hot. Reduce the heat to medium-high and add 1 tablespoon of the oil. Add the cauliflower in a single layer, season with fleur de sel and pepper, and cook until browned on the bottom, 2 to 3 minutes. Carefully turn the steaks and cook until browned, 2 to 3 minutes. Add ½ cup (125 ml) of the wine and cook until it is nearly evaporated and the

cauliflower is easily pierced with a knife, 3 to 5 minutes. Transfer the steaks to a cutting board and slice each in half through the core.

4.
In the same skillet, heat the remaining 1 tablespoon of oil until shimmering. Add the guinea hen breasts skin-side down and cook over medium-high heat until richly browned, about 5 minutes. Turn the breasts and cook over medium heat just until cooked through, 5 to 7 minutes. Transfer the breasts to a cutting board and let rest for 5 minutes.

5.
In the same skillet, melt 1 tablespoon (15 g) of the butter. Add the shallot and cook over medium heat, stirring occasionally, until the shallot is softened but not browned, 2 to 3 minutes. Add the remaining 1 cup (250 ml) of wine and cook over medium-high heat, scraping up the browned bits on the bottom of the skillet, until nearly evaporated, about 5 minutes. Add the stock and cook until reduced to ½ cup (125 ml), 10 to 12 minutes. Remove the skillet from the heat and stir in the remaining 2 tablespoons (30 g) of butter until it melts creamily. Strain the sauce into a small saucepan, pressing hard on the shallot with the back of a spoon, and season with fleur de sel and pepper.

6.
Halve the breasts lengthwise. Spoon some of the sauce onto each plate. Set one cauliflower steak half on top and lean a breast half on top. Season with fleur de sel and pepper, sprinkle with cashews, and serve.

spice-crusted duck breast *with* creamy polenta

Four Servings

—

½ teaspoon cardamom seeds

½ teaspoon cumin seeds

½ teaspoon juniper berries

½ teaspoon Madras curry powder

Two 12-ounce (350-g) magret duck breasts, fat side lightly scored in a crosshatch pattern

Fleur de sel and freshly ground pepper

2 cups (500 ml) chicken stock

½ cup (80 g) instant polenta

⅓ cup (80 ml) heavy cream

½ cup (50 g) shredded Gruyère cheese

2 tablespoons (30 g) unsalted butter

Piment d'Espelette

—

Make Ahead
The duck breasts can be rubbed with the spice mix and refrigerated overnight.

The spicy juices from burnished duck breast soak into superbly rich polenta from La Cantine du Troquet chef Christian Etchebest. Cooking the meat to your preferred doneness is easy; insert an instant-read thermometer horizontally into the breast until it reaches the desired temperature: 125°F (50°C) for rare and 135°F (55°C) for medium-rare.

—

1.
In a small dry skillet, toast the cardamom, cumin, and juniper over medium heat, shaking the skillet occasionally, until fragrant, 2 to 3 minutes. Transfer to a spice mill and let cool, then grind to a powder. Transfer the spice mix to a small bowl and stir in the curry powder.

2.
Season the duck breasts with fleur de sel and pepper and rub all over with the spice mix. In a medium skillet, cook the duck breasts fat-side down over medium-low heat until the fat has rendered and the skin is richly browned, 15 to 20 minutes. Turn the breasts over and cook until an instant-read thermometer inserted horizontally into the center of the meat registers 135°F (55°C) for medium-rare, about 5 minutes. Transfer to a cutting board and let rest for 5 minutes.

3.
In a medium saucepan, bring the stock to a boil. Gradually stir in the polenta and return to a boil. Cook over medium-low heat, stirring often, until thickened, about 3 minutes. Remove the pan from the heat and stir in the cream, cheese, and butter. Season with fleur de sel and pepper.

4.
Slice the duck breasts crosswise ¼ inch (6 mm) thick. Spoon the polenta onto plates and top with the duck slices. Season with fleur de sel and piment d'Espelette and serve.

duck breast *with* grilled spring onions *&* shallot puree

Four Servings

—

2 tablespoons (30 g) unsalted butter

3 tablespoons plus 1 teaspoon extra-virgin olive oil, plus more for brushing

4 ounces (125 g) large shallots, finely chopped, plus 1 teaspoon finely chopped shallots

Sea salt and freshly ground pepper

½ cup (125 ml) red wine or ruby port

1 tablespoon plus 1 teaspoon Banyuls or sherry vinegar

1 tablespoon veal and duck demi-glace (see Note), meat juices, or extra-virgin olive oil

1 teaspoon Dijon mustard

Fleur de sel

½ cup (40 g) hardwood chips, such as applewood

Two 12-ounce (350-g) magret duck breasts, fat side lightly scored in a crosshatch pattern

4 large spring onions, white part only, halved lengthwise

Small lettuce leaves, thick central veins removed, for garnish

—

Note
Veal and duck demi-glace (as well as magret duck breast) is available at specialty food shops and from dartagnan.com.

Make Ahead
The recipe can be prepared through Step 3 and refrigerated overnight.

In conceiving this dish, Septime chef Bertrand Grébaut drew on garniture grandmère (a garnish of bacon and onions straight out of Auguste Escoffier's *Le Guide Culinaire)* as well as the bistro staple steak and salad. The bacon and steak elements come together in Grébaut's version as beefy, house-smoked duck magret. The onions appear grilled (more smoke) and as shallot puree instead of glazed.

—

1.
In a small saucepan, melt the butter in 2 tablespoons of the oil. Add 4 ounces (125 g) of the shallots and season with salt and pepper. Cover and cook over low heat, stirring occasionally, until soft, 15 to 20 minutes. Add the wine and cook over medium-high heat until nearly evaporated, about 5 minutes. Using an immersion blender, puree the shallots.

2.
Meanwhile, in a small bowl, whisk 1 tablespoon of the vinegar with the demi-glace, 1 tablespoon of the oil, the mustard, and the remaining 1 teaspoon of shallots. Season the vinaigrette with fleur de sel and pepper.

3.
Line the inside of a wok and its lid with foil, leaving about 2 inches (5 cm) of overhang. Add the wood chips to the wok and set a small cake rack on top. Cover and heat the chips over medium-high heat until the edges are slightly burned and smoke starts billowing out, 8 to 10 minutes. Set the duck breasts on the rack and quickly cover with the lid. Smoke the duck over medium heat for 10 minutes. Transfer the duck to a work surface.

4.
Season the duck breasts with fleur de sel and pepper. In a medium skillet, cook the duck breasts, fat-side down, over medium-low heat until the fat has rendered and the skin is richly browned, 15 to 20 minutes. Turn the breasts over and cook until an instant-read thermometer inserted horizontally into the center of the meat registers 135°F (55°C) for medium-rare, about 5 minutes. Transfer to a cutting board and season with fleur de sel and pepper.

5.
Meanwhile, heat a grill or grill pan. Brush the onions with oil and grill over medium-high heat until lightly charred on both sides and crisp-tender, about 4 minutes per side. Season with fleur de sel and pepper.

6.
Halve each duck breast lengthwise. In a medium bowl, combine the remaining 1 teaspoon of oil and remaining 1 teaspoon of vinegar and season lightly with fleur de sel and pepper. Add the lettuce and gently toss to coat. Spoon 1 tablespoon of the vinaigrette on each plate. Set a duck breast half in the center and arrange 2 onion halves around it. Set a quenelle or spoonful of the shallot puree on each plate. Top with the lettuce and serve.

—

Variation
Try the dish without smoking the duck breast. It's still fantastic.

SHAUN KELLY

braised rabbit *with* radishes & mustard

Four Servings

—

3 cups (750 ml) water

Sea salt

4 whole rabbit legs (see Notes) or skin-on whole chicken legs

Freshly ground pepper

½ cup (125 ml) pickle juice from a jar

2 tablespoons yellow mustard seeds

2 tablespoons extra-virgin olive oil

4 small shallots, peeled

2 cups (500 ml) rabbit or chicken stock

2 thyme sprigs

2 tablespoons heavy cream

1 tablespoon Dijon mustard

4 whole scallions

12 round red radishes with greens (see Notes)

Fresh lemon juice, for serving

Fleur de sel and freshly ground pepper, for serving

—

Notes
Rabbit is available at butcher shops and farmers' markets and from dartagnan.com.

Shaun Kelly brines his rabbit overnight because it tends to be dry.

Wash the radishes really well to make sure there's no grit.

Make Ahead
Start this recipe a day before you plan to serve it. The rabbit must be brined and the mustard seeds pickled overnight.

Shaun Kelly's mustard appears in two forms. One is sharp Dijon mustard stirred into the delicious braising liquid along with cream just before serving. The other is the pop and brine of homemade pickled mustard seeds spooned on the rabbit. And the way Kelly cooks his radishes—he steams them just until crisp-tender and still spicy—should probably count as another.

—

1.

In a medium saucepan, combine 1 cup (250 ml) of the water and 2 tablespoons plus 1 teaspoon (38 g) of salt and simmer, swirling the pan to dissolve the salt. Remove the pan from the heat, stir in the remaining 2 cups (500 ml) of cold water, and let the brine cool to room temperature, stirring occasionally, about 30 minutes. In a large resealable plastic bag, combine the rabbit legs with the brine and a generous pinch of pepper. Seal the bag, pressing out any air, and refrigerate overnight.

2.
In a small jar, combine the pickle juice and mustard seeds. Seal and refrigerate overnight. Drain before using.

3.
Heat the oven to 425°F (220°C). In a large ovenproof skillet, heat the oil until shimmering. Drain the rabbit and pat dry. Add the rabbit and shallots to the skillet and cook over medium-high heat, turning once, until nicely browned, 5 to 8 minutes. Add the stock and thyme and bring to a simmer. Transfer the skillet to the oven and braise the rabbit, uncovered, until cooked through, 30 to 35 minutes. Transfer the rabbit and shallots to a platter; discard the thyme. Whisk the cream and mustard into the cooking liquid in the skillet.

4.
Meanwhile, in a large steamer, cook the scallions, covered, for 3 minutes. Add the radishes with their greens and cook until still bright red and crisp-tender, about 2 minutes.

5.
Spoon the sauce into shallow bowls. Add the rabbit, shallots, radishes, and scallions. Season the radishes with lemon juice, fleur de sel, and pepper. Garnish the rabbit with the pickled mustard seeds and serve.

Shaun Kelly

—

SHAUN KELLY was studying for an art degree when he decided to switch career paths. "As soon as I started cooking, it totally consumed my life," said the Brisbane native. Kelly's food epiphany began with Thai cuisine at Spirit House in Queensland and evolved into an odyssey, including two years at St. John in London, which turned him into a whole-animal, scratch-cooking convert. "I dig all the old stuff," he said. "Ideally, I do everything in-house." Kelly traveled to France to expand his skill set with stages in pastry and cheese making and ended up cheffing at Au Passage, then, briefly, at Yard, where I caught up with him. The fact of being in Paris has given Kelly's ingredient-driven Commonwealth food a French accent, like finessing braised rabbit with mustard (pictured here). But he hasn't entirely forgotten his art school days. "Color is a big thing for me," he told me. "It's a good starting point for creating a dish. It always seems to work."

red wine–braised beef cheeks *with* smoked sunchoke puree

Four Servings

—

4 tablespoons (60 ml) grapeseed oil

2 pounds (1 kg) boneless beef cheek or chuck, cut into 2-inch (5-cm) pieces (see Note)

Sea salt

¼ cup (30 g) all-purpose flour

1 large onion, finely chopped

2 carrots, finely chopped

3 thyme sprigs

1½ bottles red wine or a mix of wine and beef stock

1½ pounds (750 g) sunchokes (Jerusalem artichokes), scrubbed, sliced 1 inch (2.5 cm) thick

½ cup (40 g) hardwood chips

2 tablespoons (30 g) unsalted butter, diced

Freshly ground pepper

Fleur de sel

Fresh horseradish root, peeled, for grating

Chickweed sprigs (see page 141) or baby arugula, for garnish

—

Note
Franck Baranger simmers beef cheeks to make his dark and savory stew. If you have a butcher who will source and clean beef cheeks for you, try the recipe with this fantastic braising cut.

Make Ahead
The stew can be prepared through Step 2 and refrigerated for up to 2 days. Remove the surface fat and gently reheat before continuing. The smoked sunchoke puree can be refrigerated for up to 2 days.

Franck Baranger applies the habits of generations of French cooks to the long-cooked beef at Le Pantruche. But as a modern chef, instead of serving it with the usual potato puree, he spoons the tender meat and wine-y sauce over an untraditional sunchoke puree, which absorbs surprising flavor in a (makeshift) stovetop smoker.

—

1.
Heat the oven to 325°F (165°C). In a large enameled cast-iron casserole, heat 2 tablespoons of the oil until shimmering. Season the beef with salt. Spread the flour in a shallow bowl and dredge the beef in the flour; pat off the excess. Working in batches, add the beef to the pot and cook over medium heat until browned on all sides, about 10 minutes per batch; transfer to a large bowl. Discard the fat in the pot.

2.
Add the onion, carrots, thyme, and remaining 2 tablespoons of oil to the pot and season with salt. Cook over medium heat, stirring occasionally, until the vegetables are lightly browned, 8 to 10 minutes. Add the beef and beef juices and wine, cover, and bring to a simmer. Transfer the pot to the oven and cook until the beef is very tender, 1½ to 2 hours.

3.
Meanwhile, in a large saucepan, cover the sunchokes with water. Bring to a boil and simmer over medium-high heat until the sunchokes are very tender, about 30 minutes; drain. In a food processor, puree the sunchokes until very smooth. Spread the puree in a medium gratin dish.

4.
Line the inside of a wok and its lid with foil, leaving about 2 inches (5 cm) of overhang. Add the wood chips to the wok and set a small cake rack on top. Cover and heat the chips over medium-high heat until the edges are slightly burned and smoke starts billowing out, 8 to 10 minutes. Set the gratin dish on the rack and quickly cover with the lid. Smoke the puree over medium heat for about 10 minutes. Remove the dish from the wok. Stir in the butter and season with salt.

5.
Remove the pot from the oven and transfer the beef to a bowl. Simmer the braising liquid over medium-high heat until slightly thickened, about 10 minutes. Return the beef to the pot to heat through. Season with salt and pepper. Dollop the sunchoke puree into shallow bowls. Spoon the beef and sauce on top and sprinkle with fleur de sel. Finely grate the horseradish over the top, garnish with the chickweed, and serve.

hanger steak *with* arugula puree *&* shoestring potatoes

Four Servings

—

2 tablespoons (30 g) unsalted butter, diced

6 ounces (180 g) baby arugula

Sea salt and freshly ground pepper

4 ounces (125 g) russet (baking) potato, peeled and cut into fine julienne strips

1 tablespoon grapeseed oil, plus more for shallow frying

1½ pounds (750 g) hanger or skirt steak (see Note)

1 tablespoon fresh lemon juice

Fleur de sel

Fresh horseradish root, peeled, for grating

Watercress sprouts, tiny watercress sprigs, or baby arugula, for garnish

—

Note
Hanger, flatiron, and skirt steaks are all favorite bistro cuts. Some other inexpensive alternatives to rib-eye, strip, and porterhouse also include beef culotte, the sirloin cap; tri-tip, which is another section of sirloin; and the fork-tender teres major, from the shoulder.

Make Ahead
The recipe can be prepared through Step 3 up to 4 hours ahead.

You might be tempted to drop Caillebotte sous chef Thibault Eurin's fried potatoes. Or at the very least, to skip blanching the potatoes before frying them. Blanching turns out to help keep them crisp. When you taste the steak dragged through the nutty arugula puree (Eurin blends in brown butter), you realize the dish would not be complete without the fried potatoes.

—

1.
In a small saucepan, melt the butter over medium-high heat, then cook, swirling the pan occasionally, until the milk solids brown, 3 to 4 minutes. Remove the pan from the heat.

2.
In a large saucepan of boiling water, blanch the arugula, stirring gently with a spider or slotted spoon, for 2 minutes. Using the spider or slotted spoon, transfer the arugula to a colander and rinse under cold water. Transfer the arugula, still dripping wet, to a food processor. Add the brown butter and puree until very smooth. Season with salt and pepper. Keep the water boiling.

3.
In the same saucepan, blanch the potato for 1 minute. Drain and pat dry with paper towels.

4.
In a medium skillet, heat ¼ inch (6 mm) of oil until very hot. Add the potatoes and fry over medium-high heat, stirring occasionally, until crisp and golden, 2 to 4 minutes. Using a spider or slotted spoon, transfer the fried potatoes to paper towels to drain. Season with salt.

5.
Set a large cast-iron or other heavy skillet over high heat until very hot. Season the steak with salt. Reduce the heat to medium-high and add the 1 tablespoon of oil. Add the hanger steak and cook for 4 to 5 minutes per side for medium-rare; cook skirt steak 2 to 3 minutes per side. Transfer the steak to a cutting board and let rest for 5 minutes.

6.
Cut the steak against the grain on a diagonal into 4 pieces. Spoon the arugula puree onto plates and season with the lemon juice. Set a piece of steak alongside the puree and season with fleur de sel and pepper. Top the steak with the shoestring potatoes and finely grate the horseradish over the steak. Garnish with the watercress and serve.

onion-and-garlic rib eye
with peas & carrots

Four Servings

—

½ cup (60 g) chopped yellow onion

7 garlic cloves: 3 crushed with skin, 4 halved lengthwise and thinly sliced

Sea salt and freshly ground pepper

Two 1¼-pound (625-g) bone-in rib-eye steaks

1 pound (500 g) green peas in the pod, shelled (1 cup/250 g), or 8 ounces (250 g) thawed frozen baby peas

4 large carrots, peeled, 2 carrots sliced on the diagonal ⅛ inch (3 mm) thick on a mandoline

5 tablespoons (80 g) unsalted butter

½ small red onion, halved and very thinly sliced, 1 tablespoon reserved for garnish

½ small celery rib, thinly sliced

½ baby leek, white and pale green parts only, halved lengthwise and thinly sliced

¾ cup (185 ml) chicken stock

Snipped chives, for sprinkling

1 tablespoon grapeseed oil

4 thyme sprigs

—

Make Ahead
The dehydrated onion and garlic can be refrigerated in an airtight container for up to 1 week.

Dried onion and garlic sounds jokey until you taste it at L'Ami Jean. Stéphane Jégo dehydrates his own crunchy chips, which turns out to be simple to do in a microwave oven. To go with his crusty steak, Jégo serves carrots prepared like risotto. He sweats aromatics in butter first, then stirs in the carrots and gradually adds chicken stock, cooking until the liquid nearly evaporates with each addition.

—

1.
Spread the yellow onion on a microwave-safe plate. Microwave, uncovered, at high power, stirring occasionally, until dehydrated but still plump, 6 to 8 minutes. Transfer the onion to another plate to cool. On the same microwave-safe plate, spread the sliced garlic. Microwave, uncovered, at high power, stirring occasionally, until dehydrated but still plump, about 4 minutes. Transfer to the plate with the onion and season with salt and pepper.

2.
In a large gratin dish, season the rib-eye steaks with salt and pepper. Let stand at room temperature for 30 minutes.

3.
Meanwhile, in a small saucepan of boiling salted water, cook the peas until tender, 1 to 3 minutes. Drain and rinse in cold water. Drain again and pat dry with paper towels; refrigerate.

4.
Slice a ¼-inch (6-mm) piece from a whole carrot on the diagonal. Roll the carrot until the cut side faces up and slice another ¼-inch (6-mm) piece on the diagonal. Continue rolling and slicing the carrot. Repeat with the remaining whole carrot.

5.
In a medium saucepan, melt 1 tablespoon (15 g) of the butter. Add the red onion, celery, and leek and cook over medium heat, stirring occasionally, until softened, about 5 minutes. Add all the carrots and season with salt. Add 2 tablespoons of the stock and bring to a simmer. Cook over medium-high heat until nearly evaporated. Continue adding the stock, 2 tablespoons at a time, and cook until nearly evaporated and the carrots are just tender, about 10 minutes total. Just before serving, stir in the peas and gently reheat. Transfer to a serving bowl and sprinkle with chives and the reserved red onion.

6.
Set a large cast-iron or other heavy skillet over high heat until very hot. Reduce the heat to medium-high and add the oil. Add the steaks and cook until crusty on the bottom, about 5 minutes. Turn the steaks and add the remaining 4 tablespoons (60 g) of butter, the thyme, and crushed garlic to the skillet. Cook, basting the steaks with the melted butter, garlic, and herbs, until the steaks are medium-rare, 5 to 7 minutes longer. Transfer the steaks to a cutting board and let rest for 10 minutes.

7.
Cut the steaks off the bone, then slice the meat across the grain. Transfer the steak slices to a platter and sprinkle with the dried onion and garlic. Spoon the brown butter in the skillet around the meat. Serve with the peas and carrots.

—

Serve With
To make this a meat-and-three, chef Stéphane Jégo sets out a bowl of silky potato puree for sharing.

hanger steak *with* pickled pepper potato salad

Four Servings

—

½ cup (125 ml) apple cider vinegar

¼ cup (60 ml) water

Sea salt

4 jalapeños or other mildly hot peppers with seeds, halved or quartered lengthwise

4 tablespoons (60 g) unsalted butter, diced

One 4- to 6-inch (10- to 15-cm) dried kombu seaweed strip

1 thick slice of onion

2 garlic cloves, crushed

2 bay leaves

12 small new or red potatoes, scrubbed (12 ounces/350 g total)

¼ cup (8 g) mixed chopped tender herbs, such as tarragon, carrot tops, and parsley

2 tablespoons finely chopped shallots

1 tablespoon small capers

2 teaspoons Dijon mustard

Freshly ground pepper

1½ pounds (750 g) hanger, strip, or skirt steak

1 tablespoon grapeseed oil

Fleur de sel

—

Make Ahead
The pickled peppers can be refrigerated in a sealed jar for up to 1 week.

Rich meat needs acid, which Au Passage chef Edward Delling-Williams delivers here in the form of potato salad. The potatoes have the appeal of a warm, vinegar-and-bacon-fat dressing, but are actually made with brown butter and the vinegar from homemade chile pepper pickles.

—

1.
In a small nonreactive saucepan, combine the vinegar, water, and ½ tablespoon of salt and bring to a simmer over medium heat, swirling the pan occasionally, until the salt dissolves. Layer the jalapeños in a heatproof 2-cup (500-ml) jar. Pour the pickling liquid into the jar and let stand at room temperature, pushing the peppers into the brine occasionally, for 2 hours.

2.
In the same saucepan, melt the butter over medium-high heat, then cook, swirling the pan occasionally, until the milk solids brown, 3 to 4 minutes. Remove the pan from the heat.

3.
Bring a medium saucepan of salted water to a boil with the kombu, onion, garlic, and bay leaves. Using a spider or slotted spoon, remove the kombu from the boiling water. Add the potatoes and cook over medium-high heat until tender, 15 to 20 minutes. Drain and cut the potatoes in half.

4.
Meanwhile, in a large bowl, whisk 2 tablespoons of the pickling liquid with the herbs, shallots, capers, and mustard. Whisk in the brown butter until emulsified. Season with salt and pepper. Add the warm potatoes and pickled peppers and gently toss to coat.

5.
Set a large cast-iron or other heavy skillet over high heat until very hot. Season the steak with salt. Reduce the heat to medium-high and add the oil. Add the hanger or strip steak and cook for 4 to 5 minutes per side for medium-rare; cook skirt steak 2 to 3 minutes per side. Transfer the steak to a cutting board and let rest for 5 minutes.

6.
Slice the steak across the grain on a diagonal. Fan the steak slices on one side of each plate and mound the potato salad alongside. Season with fleur de sel and pepper and serve.

—

Variation
Delling-Williams adds whole pickled talon-like guindillas, green peppers from the Basque country, to the potato salad, but any mildly hot chile can be used.

pork chops *with* salt-roasted carrot puree

Four Servings

—

Sea salt

1 pound (500 g) carrots (about 4 large), scrubbed

5 tablespoons (80 g) unsalted butter

2 tablespoons water

Freshly ground pepper

1 tablespoon grapeseed oil

Four 8-ounce (250-g) rib pork chops

2 garlic cloves, crushed with skin

2 large thyme sprigs

Fleur de sel

Micro green mustard leaves or arugula, for garnish

—

Make Ahead
The carrot puree can be prepared up to 4 hours ahead. Gently reheat the puree before serving.

Le 6 Paul Bert chef Louis-Philippe Riel breaks down whole, rugged carrots into an ethereal puree, first softening them in the oven buried in a tray of sea salt, then slicing and sweating them in a saucepan.

—

1.
Heat the oven to 425°F (220°C). Spread ¼ inch (6 mm) of salt in a gratin dish. Nestle the carrots in the salt and roast, turning them occasionally, until tender, 45 minutes to 1 hour. Let the carrots cool slightly, then thinly slice. Leave the oven on.

2.
In a medium saucepan, combine the carrots with 2 tablespoons (30 g) of the butter and the water. Cover with a parchment paper round and cook over low heat, stirring occasionally, until very soft, about 10 minutes. Transfer the carrots to a food processor and puree until smooth. Season with pepper.

3.
In a large ovenproof skillet, heat the oil until shimmering. Season the chops with salt and pepper and cook over medium-high heat until browned on both sides, about 3 minutes. Transfer the skillet to the oven and roast the chops until an instant-read thermometer inserted horizontally into the center of the meat registers 135°F (55°C), 3 to 5 minutes.

4.
Set the skillet with the pork over medium heat. Add the remaining 3 tablespoons of butter, the garlic, and thyme and cook until the butter is foamy. Carefully tip the skillet and, using a large spoon, baste the chops repeatedly until the butter is browned and smells nutty, 2 to 3 minutes.

5.
Mound the carrot puree on plates, lean the pork chops on top, and drizzle with the garlic butter in the skillet. Season with fleur de sel. Garnish with the mustard greens and serve.

thyme-basted pork tenderloin
with oyster mushrooms

Four Servings

—

1 tablespoon grapeseed oil

One 1¼-pound (625-g) pork tenderloin

Sea salt and freshly ground pepper

4 tablespoons (60 g) unsalted butter

2 tablespoons extra-virgin olive oil

1½ pounds (750 g) oyster mushrooms, torn

4 garlic cloves: 2 finely chopped, 2 crushed with skin

2 tablespoons chopped parsley

2 large thyme sprigs

Fleur de sel

Chopped toasted walnuts (for toasting, see page 105, Step 1), for serving

Finely chopped shallots, for serving

Snipped chives, for serving

Les Enfants Rouges chef Daï Shinozuka first sears pork tenderloin on top of the stove, then roasts it in a moderate oven to keep it moist and create a golden crust. That's classic French technique. Here's the genius touch: Shinozuka sets out small bowls of toasted walnuts, minced shallots, and snipped chives—intense shots of flavor—which he showers on dishes as they leave the kitchen.

—

1.
Heat the oven to 350°F (175°C). In a medium ovenproof skillet, heat the grapeseed oil until shimmering. Season the pork with salt and pepper. Add the pork to the skillet and cook over medium-high heat until browned all over, about 5 minutes. Transfer the skillet to the oven and roast the pork, turning twice, until an instant-read thermometer inserted into the thickest part of the meat registers 135°F (55°C), 18 to 20 minutes.

2.
Meanwhile, in a large skillet, melt 1 tablespoon (15 g) of the butter in the olive oil. Add the mushrooms, season with salt and pepper, and cook over medium-high heat, stirring occasionally, until golden, 10 to 12 minutes. Add the chopped garlic and parsley and cook, stirring, until the garlic is fragrant, about 30 seconds. Remove the skillet from the heat.

3.
Set the skillet with the pork over medium heat. Add the remaining 3 tablespoons (45 g) of butter, the crushed garlic cloves, and the thyme and cook until the butter is foamy. Carefully tip the skillet and, using a large spoon, baste the meat repeatedly until the butter is browned and smells nutty, 2 to 3 minutes.

4.
Transfer the pork to a cutting board and cut into 8 equal wedges, slicing on the diagonal. Spoon the mushrooms onto plates, top with the pork, and drizzle with the brown butter in the skillet. Sprinkle with fleur de sel, walnuts, shallots, and chives and serve.

pork belly *with* darphin potatoes *&* tamarind jus

Four Servings

—

Pork Belly

3 tablespoons grapeseed oil

2 pounds (1 kg) fresh (unsalted) skin-on pork belly

Sea salt

1 large carrot, coarsely chopped

1 large celery rib, coarsely chopped

1 large onion, coarsely chopped

½ head of garlic (from 1 garlic head cut in half horizontally)

3 thyme sprigs

3 parsley sprigs

2 bay leaves

1 cup (250 ml) dry white wine

4 cups (1 L) chicken stock

Freshly ground pepper

2 tablespoons (30 g) unsalted butter, diced

2 teaspoons tamarind paste

Fleur de sel

Septime chef Bertrand Grébaut balances fantastically rich pork belly with sour, tropical tamarind. But the most provocative food on the plate is a wedge of pommes darphin (not to be confused with pommes dauphine, potato puffs). The provocation lies in serving an outdated side dish that hasn't been seen on a buzzy table since the '80s. Similar to American hash browns, the golden cake is made by pressing shredded potatoes into a cast-iron skillet and frying it so it's crisp on the outside and soft on the inside.

—

1. Pork Belly

Heat the oven to 325°F (165°C). In a medium enameled cast-iron casserole, heat 1 tablespoon of the oil until shimmering. Season the pork with salt. Add the pork to the pot and cook over medium heat until browned on all sides, about 10 minutes; transfer to a plate. Discard the fat in the pot.

2.

Add the carrot, celery, onion, garlic, thyme, parsley, bay leaves, and 2 tablespoons of the oil to the pot and season with salt. Cook over medium heat, stirring occasionally, until the vegetables are lightly browned, 8 to 10 minutes.

3.

Add the wine to the pot, bring to a boil over medium-high heat, and cook until nearly evaporated, 5 to 8 minutes. Add the pork, pork juices, and stock, cover, and bring to a simmer. Transfer the pot to the oven and cook, turning the meat once, until a metal skewer slides easily into the meat, about 2½ hours. Remove the pot from the oven and let the pork cool completely in the cooking liquid. Refrigerate overnight; 2 days is even better.

4.

Gently reheat the pork in the cooking liquid. Carefully transfer the pork to a large plate and pat dry with paper towels. Season with salt and pepper. Wrap tightly in plastic wrap, set another plate on top of the pork, and weight down with a heavy can. Refrigerate overnight to make the meat more compact. Strain the cooking liquid; cover and refrigerate separately overnight. Remove the fat before continuing in Step 7.

Darphin Potatoes

1½ pounds (750 g) russet (baking) potatoes, scrubbed

Sea salt

½ teaspoon freshly ground pepper

Pinch of freshly grated nutmeg

4 tablespoons (60 ml) grapeseed oil

—

Note
Pressing the grated potatoes in the skillet helps them stick together so the cake doesn't fall apart when it's flipped.

Make Ahead
The pork belly requires 2 days of preparation, so plan accordingly.

5. Darphin Potatoes

Bring a large saucepan of water to a boil. Add the potatoes and cook until starting to soften but still almost raw in the middle, about 10 minutes. Drain and rinse in cold water. Working with one potato at a time, peel the potatoes, then shred on the large holes of a box grater, transferring them to a large bowl as they're shredded. Season with 1 teaspoon of salt, the pepper, and nutmeg, and toss well to mix.

6.

Heat a 9-inch (23-cm) cast-iron skillet until very hot. Add 2 tablespoons of the oil and the potatoes, spreading them to the edge. Fry over medium heat, pressing the potatoes into the pan occasionally, until crisp and browned on the bottom, 5 to 8 minutes. Carefully invert the potato cake onto a large plate. Add the remaining 2 tablespoons of oil to the skillet, slide the potato cake back in, and fry until crisp and browned on the bottom, 5 to 8 minutes.

7.

In a small saucepan, melt the butter over medium-high heat, then cook, swirling the pan occasionally, until the milk solids brown, 3 to 4 minutes. In a small skillet, simmer the reserved pork cooking liquid over medium-high heat until syrupy, about 5 minutes. Remove the skillet from the heat and whisk in the brown butter and tamarind paste. Season the jus with salt and pepper.

8.

In a large skillet, heat the remaining 1 tablespoon of oil. Unwrap the pork and cut it into 4 equal rectangles. Add the pork to the skillet skin-side down and cook over medium heat until browned on the bottom, about 3 minutes. Turn the pork over and remove the pan from the heat. Spoon the jus onto plates. Set the pork on one side of each plate and arrange a wedge of the potato cake next to it. Season with fleur de sel and pepper and serve.

Bertrand Grébaut

—

BERTRAND GRÉBAUT ranks as one of the world's most respected kitchen auteurs. His restaurant Septime has a Michelin star, plus it has consistently made the World's 50 Best Restaurants list for brainy creations such as "chlorophyll meringue" (pictured on page 185). Grébaut absorbed a perfectionist's mentality at La Table de Joël Robuchon. At three-star Arpège, he developed an artist's sensibility, which is evident in everything from his meticulous plating to his restaurant's warehouse-chic design, with Paola Navone bistro chairs, reclaimed-wood tables, and handmade stoneware from French ceramics legend Jars. The chef is as obsessed with seasonal ingredients as he is with the modernist toolbox—his includes a PacoJet, a Thermomix, a blowtorch, a sous vide machine, and a Big Green Egg barbecue. Like Septime, Grébaut's newest outlets, Clamato, a no-reservations seafood bar, and eat-in wine shop Septime La Cave, mix past and future. What's changed with his growing success? "It's even harder to get a table," he said. "And we're more rigorous in the kitchen than ever."

pork belly *with* heirloom beans *&* piquillo peppers

Four Servings

—

3 tablespoons extra-virgin olive oil

2 shallots, chopped

1 teaspoon juniper berries

1 teaspoon whole black peppercorns

1 teaspoon coriander seeds

1 star anise pod

One 1-inch (2.5-cm) piece of ginger

2 carrots, coarsely chopped

2 large celery ribs, coarsely chopped

2 large onions, coarsely chopped

1 cup (250 ml) dry white wine

2 pounds (1 kg) fresh (unsalted) pork belly, skin removed (fat intact)

½ head of garlic (from 1 garlic head cut in half horizontally), plus 2 garlic cloves, crushed

5 thyme sprigs

5 parsley sprigs

3 bay leaves

4 cups (1 L) chicken stock

Sea salt and freshly ground pepper

1 tablespoon tomato paste

1 cup (200 g) dried white heirloom beans (see Note), soaked overnight and drained

Chef Daï Shinozuka slow-braises pork belly (fresh bacon) at Les Enfants Rouges until it melts in the mouth and cuts like butter. But this is not a stew. Shinozuka first presses the meat overnight until it's firm and then sears it like steak. Haricots maïs, white heirloom beans from southwest France, are served alongside, but Tarbais (cassoulet) or cannellini beans are also excellent here.

—

1.
Heat the oven to 325°F (165°C). In a medium enameled cast-iron casserole, heat 2 tablespoons of the oil until shimmering. Add the shallots, juniper berries, peppercorns, coriander seeds, star anise, ginger, half the chopped carrots, half the chopped celery ribs, and half the chopped onions and cook over medium heat, stirring occasionally, until the vegetables are lightly browned, 8 to 10 minutes.

2.
Add the wine to the pot, bring to a boil over medium-high heat, and cook until nearly evaporated, 5 to 8 minutes. Add the pork, ½ head of garlic, 3 thyme sprigs, 3 parsley sprigs, 2 bay leaves, and the stock. Cover and bring to a simmer. Transfer the pot to the oven and cook, turning the meat once, until a metal skewer slides easily into the meat, about 2½ hours. Remove the pot from the oven and let the pork cool completely in the cooking liquid. Refrigerate overnight; 2 days is even better.

3.
Gently reheat the pork in the cooking liquid. Carefully transfer the pork to a large plate and pat dry with paper towels. Season with salt and pepper. Wrap tightly in plastic wrap, set another plate on top, and weight down with a heavy can. Refrigerate overnight to make the meat more compact. Strain the pork cooking liquid and refrigerate overnight. Remove the fat before continuing.

4.
Tie the remaining chopped carrot, chopped celery rib, chopped onion, 2 garlic cloves, 2 thyme sprigs, 2 parsley sprigs, and 1 bay leaf in a cheesecloth bundle. In a large saucepan, cook the tomato paste over medium heat, stirring, until the color deepens, about 1 minute. Gradually pour in the reserved pork cooking liquid, whisking to dissolve the tomato paste. Add the beans and herb bundle. Add water, if needed, to cover the beans. Bring to a boil and simmer over medium-low heat, partially covered, until the beans are tender, 1 to 1½ hours, depending on the age of the beans. Remove and discard the herb bundle.

2 tablespoons (30 g) unsalted butter, diced

¼ cup (60 ml) jarred piquillo peppers, cut into thin strips

2 teaspoons sherry vinegar

Toasted chopped walnuts (for toasting, see page 105, Step 1), finely chopped shallots, and snipped chives, for garnish

—

Note
Tarbais (cassoulet) or cannellini beans are available at Whole Foods and from ranchogordo.com.

Make Ahead
The pork belly requires 2 days of preparation, so plan accordingly.

5.
Meanwhile, in a small saucepan, melt the butter over medium-high heat, then cook, swirling the pan occasionally, until the milk solids brown, 3 to 4 minutes. Remove the pan from the heat and let the brown butter cool.

6.
Strain the bean cooking liquid into a small skillet and return the beans to the pan. Stir the piquillo peppers into the beans and season with salt and pepper. Simmer the bean cooking liquid over medium-high heat until syrupy, about 5 minutes. Remove the skillet from the heat and whisk in the brown butter and vinegar. Season the jus with salt and pepper.

7.
In a large skillet, heat the remaining 1 tablespoon of oil. Unwrap the pork and cut it into 4 equal rectangles. Add the pork to the skillet skinned-side down and cook over medium heat until browned on the bottom, about 3 minutes. Turn the pork over and remove the pan from the heat. Mound the beans on plates, lean the pork browned-side up on top, and drizzle the jus around the plate. Garnish with the walnuts, shallots, and chives and serve.

—

Variation
Finding fresh pork belly can be a hassle for home cooks. Instead, try 2 pounds (1 kg) of boneless country-style pork ribs, which, coincidentally, look similar to rectangles of pork belly but require a fraction of the time to cook. Braise the pork ribs for 1 to 1½ hours and omit refrigerating and wrapping the meat overnight.

navarin d'agneau printanier

Four Servings

—

8 tablespoons (125 g) unsalted butter, sliced

1 bay leaf

4 garlic cloves, crushed with skin

4 thyme sprigs

8 small red potatoes, scrubbed (about 8 ounces/250 g total)

Sea salt

8 baby carrots, peeled, tops trimmed to ½ inch (1 cm)

8 baby turnips, peeled, tops trimmed to ½ inch (1 cm)

1 small zucchini, cut into ½-inch (1-cm) chunks on the diagonal

1 small summer squash, cut into ½-inch (1-cm) chunks on the diagonal

2½ ounces (80 g) shelled fresh peas or thawed frozen baby peas (⅓ cup/80 ml)

1 tablespoon grapeseed oil

2 pounds (1 kg) boneless leg of lamb, cut into 1½-inch (4-cm) cubes

Freshly ground pepper

1 shallot, finely chopped

1 cup (250 ml) dry white wine

1½ cups (375 ml) chicken stock

Fleur de sel

Micro parsley sprigs or chopped parsley, for garnish

—

Make Ahead
The blanched vegetables in Step 2 can be refrigerated for up to 4 hours.

The difference between this navarin and the Escoffier-variety spring lamb stew comes down to cut of meat and cooking time. The original is long-simmered and prepared with lamb shoulder. Le Bistrot d'à Côté chef Nicolas Beaumann lightens it by briefly sautéing cubes of tender boneless lamb leg until just pink and, for a sauce, he simply deglazes the browned bits stuck to the bottom of the skillet with white wine and stock. The traditional garnish of tender garden vegetables remains the same.

—

1.
In a medium saucepan, melt the butter. Stir in the bay leaf, 2 garlic cloves, and 2 thyme sprigs. Add the potatoes and season with salt. Cover and cook over medium-low heat, swirling the pan occasionally, until the potatoes are tender, 15 to 20 minutes. Reduce the heat if the butter starts to brown. Drain, reserving the butter. Discard the herbs.

2.
Meanwhile, line a baking sheet with a thick kitchen towel. In a medium saucepan of boiling salted water, cook the carrots and turnips until tender, about 5 minutes. Using a spider or slotted spoon, transfer them to the towel-lined baking sheet and pat dry. Add the zucchini and summer squash to the boiling water and cook until crisp-tender, about 2 minutes. Using a spider or slotted spoon, transfer the zucchini and summer squash to a colander and rinse in cold water. Drain well, spread on the baking sheet, and pat dry. Add the peas to the boiling water and cook for 1 minute. Drain and rinse in cold water. Drain again, spread on the baking sheet, and pat dry.

3.
In a large skillet, heat the oil until shimmering. Add the lamb, season with salt and pepper, and cook over medium-high heat until browned on all sides, 2 to 3 minutes. Reduce the heat to medium. Add 3 tablespoons of the reserved butter and the remaining 2 garlic cloves and 2 thyme sprigs. Cook the lamb, tilting the pan and basting it repeatedly with the butter, until medium-rare, about 2 minutes more. Using a spider or slotted spoon, transfer the meat to a cake rack set over a plate.

4.
Add 1 tablespoon of the reserved butter to the skillet with the shallot and cook, stirring occasionally, until the shallot is softened but not browned, 2 to 3 minutes. Add the wine and cook over medium-high heat, scraping up the browned bits on the bottom of the skillet, until nearly evaporated, about 5 minutes. Add the stock and cook until reduced to ½ cup (125 ml), 10 to 12 minutes. Stir in 1 tablespoon of the reserved butter. Strain the sauce into a small saucepan, pressing hard on the shallot with the back of a spoon, and season with salt and pepper.

5.
Return the lamb, vegetables, and sauce to the skillet and gently reheat. Spoon the sauce onto plates and top with the lamb and vegetables. Season with fleur de sel and pepper, garnish with the parsley, and serve.

rack of lamb *with* chickpea puree *&* red onion relish

Four Servings

—

One 5-ounce (150-g) red onion, finely chopped

2 tablespoons sherry or Banyuls vinegar

Sea salt

½ cup (15 g) finely chopped mixed herbs, such as parsley, mint, and thyme

6 tablespoons (100 ml) extra-virgin olive oil

2 garlic cloves, thinly sliced

One 15-ounce (425-g) can chickpeas with their liquid

1 tablespoon fresh lemon juice

Freshly ground pepper

One 1¼- to 1½-pound (625- to 750-g) frenched rack of lamb with 8 ribs

2 tablespoons (30 g) unsalted butter

1 large shallot, finely chopped

½ cup (125 ml) dry red wine

½ cup (125 ml) veal demi-glace (see Note)

Fleur de sel

—

Note
Veal demi-glace is made from reduced stock. D'Artagnan makes an excellent demi-glace that is available at many specialty food shops and from dartagnan.com and amazon.com.

Make Ahead
The onion relish and chickpea puree can be refrigerated overnight. Gently reheat the puree before serving.

To eat this dish from Daniel Rose at Spring, cut a piece of pink lamb chop, smear it with the chickpea puree, and then drag it through the meat jus. It's at once creamy, earthy, and rich—with a hit of zippy onion right when you need it.

—

1.
In a small bowl, toss the red onion with the vinegar and 1 teaspoon of salt and let stand for 5 minutes. Stir in the herbs and 2 tablespoons of the oil.

2.
In a medium skillet, heat 1 tablespoon of the oil until shimmering. Add the garlic and cook over medium heat until fragrant, about 30 seconds. Stir in the chickpeas and liquid and simmer over high heat until the liquid is reduced by half, about 4 minutes. Using a spider or slotted spoon, transfer the chickpeas to a food processor. Add the lemon juice and 2 tablespoons of the oil and process until very smooth. Add the chickpea cooking liquid by tablespoons if needed to loosen the texture. Season with salt and pepper and scrape the puree into a bowl.

3.
Heat the oven to 400°F (200°C). Set a medium cast-iron or other heavy ovenproof skillet over high heat until very hot. Season the lamb rack with salt. Reduce the heat to medium-high and add the remaining 1 tablespoon of oil. Add the lamb, fat-side down, and cook until richly browned, about 3 minutes. Turn the lamb fat-side up and cook for 2 minutes. Transfer the skillet to the oven and roast the lamb until an instant-read thermometer inserted into the thickest part of the meat registers 125° to 130°F (50° to

55°C) for rare to medium-rare, 15 to 20 minutes. Remove the skillet from the oven. Transfer the lamb to a cutting board.

4.
Spoon off any fat in the skillet. Set the skillet over medium heat, add 1 tablespoon (15 g) of the butter and the shallot, and cook until just beginning to brown, about 3 minutes. Add the wine and cook over medium-high heat, scraping up the browned bits on the bottom of the skillet, until nearly evaporated, about 5 minutes. Stir in the demi-glace and bring to a boil. Strain the sauce through a fine sieve into a small saucepan, pressing hard on the shallot with the back of a spoon. Season the jus with salt and pepper and swirl in the remaining 1 tablespoon (15 g) of butter until it melts creamily.

5.
Slice between the lamb ribs into double chops. Spoon some of the jus onto plates and arrange the lamb chops on one side. Set a large quenelle or generous spoonful of chickpea puree across from the lamb. Sprinkle the lamb with fleur de sel and pepper. Spoon some of the onion relish on the chickpea puree and lamb and serve, passing the remaining jus and onion relish separately.

—

Variation
The red onion relish is also great with boiled or roasted beef, ham, and sausages, hot or cold, as well as with boiled or steamed vegetables, such as asparagus.

0 1 23 120

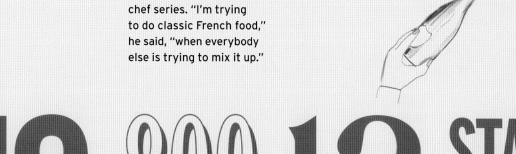

STATS
—
spring -OR- -IN-

0 PRINTED MENUS
Servers ask guests if they'd like to know what's on the night's prix fixe or be surprised. "There is no menu," said Daniel Rose. "We just make dinner."

1 COOKBOOK
Rose self-published his first book—illustrated with his own drawings—available at the restaurant and online at springparis.fr. His inspiration comes from traditional cookbooks, like French publisher Robert Laffont's nouvelle cuisine chef series. "I'm trying to do classic French food," he said, "when everybody else is trying to mix it up."

23 TIMES A NIGHT,
Chicago-born chef-owner Daniel Rose slices open a Champagne bottle with a saber at his Paris restaurant, Spring, near the Louvre.

120 MISSES
Number of Champagne bottles broken.

19 YEARS
Spring executive chef Gilles Chesneau worked with Michelin-three-star chef Guy Savoy for almost two decades at restaurant Guy Savoy in Paris. "Why do I hire guys with so much experience?" Rose asked. "So I can learn something."

800 COVERS
Argentine-born maître d', Guillermo Campos, oversaw dining rooms in Paris palace hotels turning out dinners for 800. Now at Spring, he smiles all the time.

1.2 TONS
of chicken wings were purchased to make chicken stock in the first year Spring reopened near the Louvre.

STAFF BY THE NUMBERS

17 STAFF
make Spring run smoothly.

28 YEARS OLD
Median age of Spring employees.

9 BABIES
Spring staffers have a happy family life.

5 EXES
First you have to find the right partner. Being with someone who works in the restaurant business helps.

Rooting Section

1 2 3 4 5 6 7 8 9 10 11 12

Root vegetables have always been a mainstay of French home cooking yet virtually nonexistent on ambitious restaurant menus. But as a logical extension of the bigger green movement and as a creative antidote to butter-laden potato puree, these humble roots—and bulbs and tubers—are now the darlings of hip bistro chefs. What's more, as any properly frugal cook knows, many of the vegetables give doubly, because the leaves are often as delicious as the roots. From radishes and rutabaga to parsley root and sunchokes, singly or in combination, there's no way you'll get bored with these vegetables.

1
BEETS
Cooks love beetroots for their candy sweetness, dramatic colors (red, golden, striped!), and earthy flavor. Le Servan chef Tatiana Levha steams small ones in a mere 20 minutes. Daniel Rose, the chef at Spring, tops boiled beet slices with smoked fish and crème fraîche for a tasty two-bite appetizer (page 52).

2
CARROTS
A workhorse vegetable, carrots have long been diced with onions and celery in mirepoix, grated in carottes râpées, and glazed in butter. But adventurous chefs like Louis-Philippe Riel at Le 6 Paul Bert roast them in salt, then sweat them in butter to make an outstanding puree (page 157). Spring carrots in jewel colors are best lightly cooked or served raw in salads.

3
CELERY ROOT
This gnarly root needs to be thickly peeled with a knife. Quarter it first, so it's easier to handle before preparing soup, puree, céléri rémoulade (page 75), or as a topping (with or without potatoes) for hachis parmentier (shepherd's pie). Squeeze lemon juice over the top to keep the flesh ivory white.

4
CROSNES
Give these small, crunchy tubers (pronounced "krone") a quick scrub and prepare them in ways that preserve their squiggly shape and artichoke-like flavor. (They're also called Chinese or Japanese artichokes.)

5
HORSERADISH ROOT
Chef Franck Baranger grates a snowdrift of this heady root over his fall-apart beef stew (page 152) and over juicy hanger steak (page 153).

6
PARSLEY ROOT
Yes, the tender herb is edible from leaf to root (just like chervil). Cook this mild vegetable like celery root.

7
PARSNIPS
This supermarket veg is served fried like chips, pureed, and roasted. Or simmer the underrated parsnip to make a velvety soup (page 39). Some have woody cores, which you'll want to cut away before cooking.

8
RADISHES
Chefs slice raw radishes into paper-thin rounds to add a crisp, spicy, and colorful (the green and watermelon varieties are especially pretty) element to dishes. They're also superlative lightly steamed as a flourish twirled across braised rabbit with mustard (pictured on page 151).

9
RUTABAGAS
Though on the sweeter side and less starchy, rutabagas are heavenly prepared in all the same ways as potatoes—i.e., with lots of butter and cream.

10
SALSIFY
Think of salsify as cold weather white asparagus. The (cocoa-colored) skin needs to be peeled down to the white flesh. (Add the peeled stalks to lemon water to discourage browning.) It turns silky and sweet as it cooks. And its subtle flavor works beautifully in unctuous dishes (the creamy, buttery, cheesy kind) and with seafood, chicken, veal, and ham.

11
SUNCHOKES
Spring chef Daniel Rose leaves the thin skin on these knobby-looking tubers, a.k.a. Jerusalem artichokes, when using them in a suave soup (page 38). So does Franck Baranger at Le Pantruche, where he smokes a puree of the nutty tubers as an accompaniment to braised beef (page 152). When I couldn't find sunchokes at my supermarket, I ordered them through the produce department.

12
TURNIPS
In spring, turnips add spice and crunch to salads and as pickles. In summer, the roots and greens need only minutes to become tender (page 166). In wintertime, they're slow-cooked into mellowness yet maintain their shape.

rolled lamb shoulder *with* fresh apricots, lemon verbena & almonds

Four Servings

—

5 tablespoons (80 ml) grapeseed oil, plus more for frying

2 pounds (1 kg) boneless lamb shoulder, rolled and tied (see Note)

Sea salt

2 onions, cut into ¼-inch (6-mm) dice

2 carrots, cut into ¼-inch (6-mm) dice

3 thyme sprigs

2 bay leaves

1 cup (250 ml) dry white wine

3 cups (750 ml) water

Freshly ground pepper

12 lemon verbena leaves, rinsed and patted dry with paper towels

3 tablespoons (45 g) unsalted butter

10 ounces (300 g) chanterelle mushrooms, halved if large

Fleur de sel

4 apricots, cut lengthwise into thin wedges

2 tablespoons (20 g) green almonds (see page 60) or blanched almonds, halved from top to bottom

—

Note
Have your butcher prepare the rolled and tied boneless lamb shoulder for you.

Make Ahead
Start this a day before you plan to serve it. The rolled lamb must be refrigerated for at least 1 (and up to 2) days before putting the finished dish together.

Pirouette chef Tomy Gousset accessorizes glossy slices of braised lamb with raw apricot in place of the expected dried fruit (pictured on page 172). He also finishes the plate with shatteringly crisp, fried lemon verbena leaves (instead of parsley) and, during their too-brief early summer season, green almonds.

—

1.
Heat the oven to 325°F (165°C). In a medium enameled cast-iron casserole, heat 1 tablespoon of the oil until shimmering. Season the lamb with salt. Add the lamb to the pot and cook over medium heat until browned on all sides, about 10 minutes; transfer the lamb to a plate. Discard the fat in the pot.

2.
Add the onions, carrots, thyme, bay leaves, and 2 tablespoons of the oil to the pot and season with salt. Cook over medium heat, stirring occasionally, until lightly browned, 8 to 10 minutes. Add the wine to the pot, bring to a boil over medium-high heat, and cook until nearly evaporated, 5 to 8 minutes. Add the lamb, lamb juices, and water, cover, and bring to a simmer. Transfer the pot to the oven and cook, turning the meat once, until a metal skewer slides easily into the meat, 1½ to 2 hours. Remove the pot from the oven and let the meat cool completely in the cooking liquid.

3.
Carefully transfer the meat to a large plate and pat dry with paper towels. Season with salt and pepper. Wrap tightly in plastic wrap and refrigerate overnight to make the meat more compact. Strain the lamb cooking liquid and refrigerate overnight. Remove the fat before continuing in Step 6.

4.
In a small skillet, heat ¼ inch (6 mm) of oil until shimmering. Add the lemon verbena leaves and fry over medium heat until crisp, about 10 seconds. Using a spider or slotted spoon, transfer the lemon verbena leaves to paper towels to drain.

5.
In a medium skillet, melt 1 tablespoon (15 g) of the butter in 1 tablespoon of the oil. Add the mushrooms, season with salt and pepper, and cook over medium-high heat, stirring occasionally, until golden, 10 to 12 minutes.

6.
In a small saucepan, melt the remaining 2 tablespoons (30 g) of butter over medium-high heat, then cook, swirling the pan occasionally, until the milk solids brown, 3 to 4 minutes. Remove from the heat. In a small skillet, simmer the reserved lamb cooking liquid until syrupy, about 5 minutes. Remove the skillet from the heat and whisk in the brown butter. Season the jus with salt and pepper.

7.
In a large skillet, heat the remaining 1 tablespoon of oil. Unwrap the lamb and slice it ½ inch (1 cm) thick, discarding the string. Carefully add the lamb to the skillet and cook over medium heat until lightly browned on the bottom, about 3 minutes. Turn the lamb over and remove the pan from the heat. Transfer the lamb slices to plates, season with fleur de sel and pepper, and spoon the jus over the top. Garnish with the apricots, almonds, and fried verbena leaves and serve.

Tomy Gousset
PIROUETTE

—

TOMY GOUSSET'S cooking brings elegant subtlety to the ultratouristy former market neighborhood of Les Halles, now a mix of futurist park and shopping mall. The Cambodian-French chef, who honed his skills at Le Meurice and at Restaurant Daniel in New York, takes what he's learned about French cuisine and revisits it. For instance, he lightens a traditionally hearty stew of lamb and dried apricots by swapping in fresh fruit and adding delicate green almonds (pictured opposite). Despite the technical mastery on display, Gousset's food is entirely approachable, especially in Pirouette's relaxed, airy dining room, with a traveling blackboard menu, open shelves of wine bottles, and 1960s-era Baumann bistro chairs. On sunny days, the waitstaff set tables in the courtyard just outside the front door. The vibe is casual enough for Gousset to hang out with his family between lunch and dinner. What does the award-winning Gousset consider his biggest achievement? "This is my best recipe," said the first-time father, holding his son, Hugo.

slow-cooked lamb *with* rutabaga mash

Four Servings

—

4 tablespoons (60 ml) grapeseed oil

2 pounds (1 kg) boneless lamb shoulder, cut into 1½-inch (4-cm) pieces

Sea salt

1 large onion, halved and thinly sliced

1 celery rib, chopped

1 carrot, chopped

2 shallots, chopped

2 garlic cloves, thinly sliced

3 thyme sprigs

2 bay leaves

1 star anise pod

1 cinnamon stick

⅓ cup (80 ml) walnut or malt vinegar, plus more for serving

3 cups (750 ml) lamb or chicken stock

½ cup (125 ml) tomato passata (puree)

1½ pounds (750 g) rutabaga, peeled and cut into 1-inch (2.5-cm) pieces

4 tablespoons (60 g) unsalted butter

Freshly ground pepper

Fleur de sel

Chopped parsley or snipped chives, for sprinkling

—

Make Ahead
The stew can be prepared through Step 2 and refrigerated for up to 2 days. Remove the surface fat and gently reheat before continuing. The mashed rutabaga can be refrigerated for up to 2 days. Gently reheat before serving.

You try to figure out what the tastes are in this deep and focused stew from Au Passage; there's star anise, cinnamon, and walnut vinegar in the background. The rutabaga side dish is fantastic boiled and mashed with a bit of butter, but chef Edward Delling-Williams's original version is infinitely richer. He cooks the rutabaga in a mix of half water and half butter, then drains it before mashing it with fresh butter, "more than you can possibly imagine," he says.

—

1.
Heat the oven to 325°F (165°C). In a large enameled cast-iron casserole, heat 2 tablespoons of the oil until shimmering. Season the lamb with salt. Working in batches, add the lamb to the pot and cook over medium heat until browned on all sides, about 10 minutes per batch; transfer the lamb to a large bowl. Discard the fat in the pot.

2.
Add the onion, celery, carrot, shallots, garlic, thyme, bay leaves, star anise, cinnamon, and remaining 2 tablespoons of oil to the pot and season with salt. Cover and cook over low heat, stirring occasionally, until the vegetables are softened, 8 to 10 minutes. Add the vinegar and simmer, scraping up any browned bits on the bottom. Add the lamb and lamb juices, stock, and tomato passata. Cover and bring to a simmer. Transfer the pot to the oven and cook until the lamb is very tender, 1½ to 2 hours.

3.
Meanwhile, in a large saucepan, cover the rutabaga with water. Bring to a boil and simmer over medium heat until the rutabaga is very tender, about 30 minutes; drain. Add the butter and, using an immersion blender or potato masher, puree the rutabaga until coarsely smooth. Season with salt and pepper.

4.
Remove the pot from the oven and transfer the lamb to a bowl. Simmer the braising liquid in the pot over medium-high heat until slightly thickened, about 10 minutes. Return the lamb to the pot to heat through. Season with salt, pepper, and a splash of vinegar. Spoon the stew into shallow bowls and sprinkle with fleur de sel. Dollop the rutabaga on top, sprinkle with parsley, and serve.

—

Variations
When you prepare restaurant quantities of this dish, as Edward Delling-Williams does, you can braise a mix of cuts, including the neck (for the meaty bones), the breast (for richness), and shank (for the meaty flavor).

If you're at the supermarket and can find only lamb shoulder chops, they work beautifully, too. Simply cut the meat off the bones before browning it in Step 1.

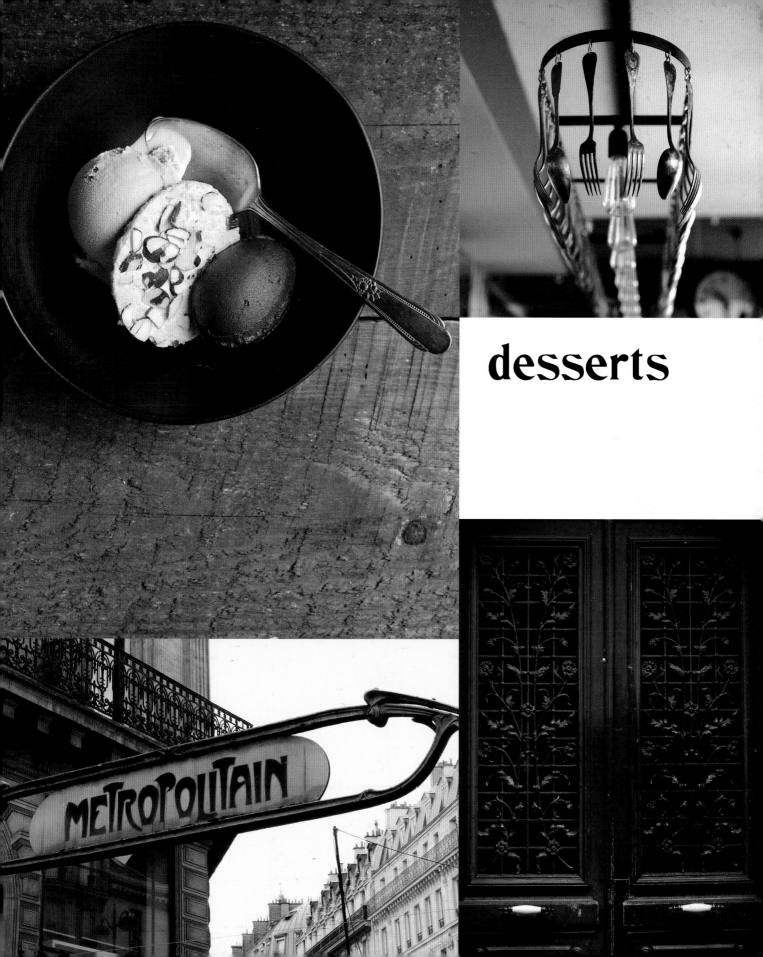

desserts

SHAUN KELLY

cherry & beetroot pavlova

Six Servings

—

French Meringue

4 large egg whites,
at room temperature

1 cup (200 g) granulated sugar

1 teaspoon fresh lemon juice

½ teaspoon cornstarch

¼ teaspoon coarsely
ground pepper

¼ teaspoon cream of tartar

Pinch of fine sea salt

Beet Puree, Syrup, and Chips

2 small red beets (about
4 ounces/125 g each), scrubbed

½ cup (125 ml) water

½ cup (100 g) granulated sugar

½ cup (125 ml) bottled beet juice

Confectioners' sugar,
for dusting

Whipped Cream and Cherries

1 cup (250 ml) heavy cream

1 tablespoon (15 g) granulated
sugar

Finely grated zest of ½ lemon

1 vanilla bean, split lengthwise
and seeds scraped, or
1 teaspoon pure vanilla extract

1 pound (500 g) Bing cherries
with stems

—

Make Ahead
The recipe can be prepared
through Step 5 up to 1 day
ahead. Store the meringue and
beet chips separately in airtight
containers in a cool, dry place.
Refrigerate the beet puree and
beet syrup separately.

Although Pavlova is from Oz (as is chef Shaun Kelly), the lighthearted meringue fits perfectly into the Paris dessert landscape of airy egg whites and whipped cream. The beets make this Pavlova doubly Australian: "I always had a slice of beetroot and an egg on my burger growing up," says Kelly, a Brisbane native. Here, they're disguised as puree, syrup, and chips. Alongside Bing cherries, they're easily mistaken for red fruit.

—

1. French Meringue
Heat the oven to 300°F (150°C). Trace a 9-inch (23-cm) circle on a sheet of parchment paper and invert it onto a baking sheet. In a large bowl, whip the egg whites at medium-high speed until foamy. Whip in the granulated sugar, 2 tablespoons (25 g) at a time, at high speed until the whites hold a soft peak. Add the lemon juice, cornstarch, pepper, cream of tartar, and salt and whip until the meringue is firm and glossy.

2.
Using an offset spatula, spread the meringue inside the 9-inch (23-cm) circle on the parchment to fill completely, about ¾ inch (2 cm) thick in the center and 1½ inches (4 cm) thick at the edges, creating a well for the filling. Transfer to the oven and bake, rotating the sheet halfway through, until the surface is dry with just a wisp of color and the center is still a bit soft, about 1 hour and 15 minutes. Transfer the meringue to a rack and let cool completely on the baking sheet, about 30 minutes.

3. Beet Puree, Syrup, and Chips
Peel one of the beets and cut it into ½-inch (1-cm) dice. In a small saucepan, combine the beet dice with the water and ¼ cup (50 g) of the granulated sugar. Bring to a simmer and cook, partially covered, until the beets are very tender, about 20 minutes. Transfer the beets with their cooking liquid to a food processor and puree until smooth. Let cool completely.

4.
Meanwhile, in another small saucepan, simmer the beet juice and the remaining ¼ cup (50 g) of granulated sugar over medium-high heat, swirling the pan occasionally, until syrupy, about 4 minutes. Let cool completely.

5.
Peel the remaining beet and slice it ¹⁄₁₆ inch (1.5 mm) thick on a mandoline. Dust a microwave-safe plate with confectioners' sugar. Spread as many beet slices as will fit on the plate without overlapping and dust with more confectioners' sugar. Microwave at high power, uncovered, turning the beet slices every 2 minutes, until they are dehydrated but still plump, 6 to 8 minutes total.

6. Whipped Cream and Cherries
In a medium bowl, whip the cream with the sugar, lemon zest, and vanilla seeds until the cream holds a medium peak. Carefully transfer the meringue to a serving platter. Fill with the whipped cream, spoon the beet puree over the cream, and drizzle with the beet syrup. Arrange the cherries on top, decorate with the beet chips, and serve.

vanilla cream *with* sautéed cherries

Four Servings

—

½ cup (100 g) sugar

¼ cup (60 ml) water

2 large egg whites, at room temperature

1 vanilla bean, split lengthwise and seeds scraped, or 1 teaspoon pure vanilla extract

1 cup (250 ml) heavy cream

1 cup (250 ml) fromage blanc, Greek yogurt, fresh ricotta, or a mix

2 tablespoons (30 g) unsalted butter

2 tablespoons red currant jelly

¼ cup (60 ml) dry white wine

1 pound (500 g) Bing cherries with stems

Crumbled spice cookies, for garnish

Toasted almond slices, for garnish

Finely grated lime zest, for garnish

—

Make Ahead
Begin making this recipe a day before you plan to serve it. The vanilla cream needs to chill overnight (or for up 2 days).

Daï Shinozuka's version of crémet d'Anjou is equal parts whipped cream, Italian meringue, and fromage blanc, which are gently folded together and left to drain in a sieve to firm up overnight. The Les Enfants Rouges chef serves the vanilla cream with cherries quickly sautéed in butter and red currant jelly. "Leave the stems on," he says, "because they're pretty and then you can eat the cherries with your fingers."

—

1.
In a small saucepan, heat the sugar with the water over medium heat, swirling the pan, until the sugar dissolves. Bring to a boil and simmer without stirring until the syrup reaches 248°F (120°C). Meanwhile, in a medium bowl, whip the egg whites until stiff. Gradually pour the hot syrup down the side of the bowl, whipping continuously, until the meringue is completely cool. Beat in the vanilla seeds. Cover and refrigerate.

2.
Line a large sieve or colander with dampened cheesecloth, leaving about 1 inch (2.5 cm) of overhang, and set it in a medium bowl. In another medium bowl, whip the cream until it holds a soft peak. In a small bowl, whisk the fromage blanc until smooth. Gently fold the whipped cream and fromage blanc into the meringue. Scrape the mixture into the prepared sieve, cover with plastic wrap, and refrigerate overnight.

3.
In a medium skillet, cook the butter with the jelly and wine over medium-high heat, stirring, until melted. Add the cherries and cook, shaking the pan, just until juicy, about 1 minute. Scoop the vanilla cream into bowls. Arrange the cherries with the stems up around the cream and drizzle the juices over the cherries. Sprinkle the cookie crumbs, almonds, and lime zest over the top and serve.

—

Variations
Cherry season is short; peaches, cut into thin wedges, or halved Empress plums (Italian prune plums) can stand in for the cherries. Or simply serve the vanilla cream with fresh berries.

MER*Magic*INGUE

BISTRO CHEFS HAVE hit on brilliantly simple meringue as a way of adding complexity to the usual roster of homey desserts without having to buy big-deal equipment or hire a pastry cook.

Just by beating air into egg whites and sugar and baking the bubbly mixture (French meringue), Tatiana Levha of Le Servan creates a crunchy flourish for fromage blanc and berries (pictured on page 183). Le Pantruche chef Franck Baranger folds in almond meal to a make a chewy, crumbly dacquoise (nut meringue) contrast for smooth chocolate ganache (pictured on page 204).

Lots of chefs are riffing on traditional meringue. At Septime, Bertrand Grébaut blends in parsley to produce "chlorophyll" meringue shards for fruit salad (pictured on page 185). Similarly, Shaun Kelly spices up the meringue base of his Pavlova with ground pepper as a punchy foil for cherries (pictured on page 179).

Some chefs are whipping up egg whites with hot sugar syrup to make Italian meringue, a softer, more stable mixture than French meringue, which is prepared with uncooked sugar. Daï Shinozuka, the chef of Les Enfants Rouges, stirs Italian meringue with whipped cream and fromage blanc to make an airy cold dessert (opposite). James Henry of Bones blasts Italian meringue with a blowtorch for a Baked Alaska–type dessert that looks like a snow cave (pictured on page 187).

It's hard to mess up meringue. Though it feels mysterious, the sweet foam simply doesn't require the kind of precision and expertise that goes into most pâtisserie. Still, if you want to geek out on meringue, here's how.

WHIPPING EGG WHITES

◯ Whip egg whites at room temperature. They increase more in volume than cold whites.

◯ Fish out any specks of egg yolk in your whites. The fat in the yolks discourages perfect whipping.

◯ Clean and dry your mixing bowl just before using.

◯ For the gold standard of fluffy egg whites, beat them in a copper bowl. Before using a copper bowl, always clean the inside by rubbing it with 1 to 2 tablespoons of salt and 1 to 2 tablespoons of vinegar. Rinse and dry the bowl thoroughly.

◯ For better-than-good frothy egg whites, use a stainless steel bowl or, secondarily, a glass one. Avoid other kinds of bowls, like plastic and pottery.

◯ If you want to whip egg whites by hand, use a wire balloon whisk. Electric beaters and stand mixers incorporate less air but certainly make beating easier. A stand mixer is eminently useful for making Italian meringue, because you can pour in the hot sugar syrup without having to hold the beater at the same time.

◯ If you're using a whisk or electric beater, lay a folded kitchen towel under the mixing bowl for stability.

◯ Choose either granulated sugar or superfine sugar to make meringue. Superfine sugar melts a little more easily when you're making French meringue. Avoid brown sugar, because its impurities make the meringue crystallize.

◯ You can help the egg whites hold more air by adding a little lemon juice, cream of tartar, or salt.

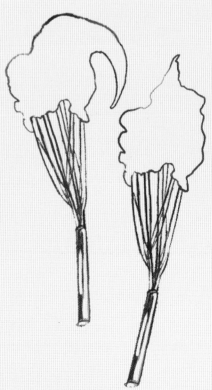

MERINGUE MAGIC
continued

FOLDING

Folding is the method of gently blending an ingredient into whipped egg whites or whipped cream while turning the mixing bowl counterclockwise with one hand so as not to deflate the whipped component. You cut down into the center of the bowl, scoop under the contents, and turn them bottom to top in a rolling motion. While folding, turn the bowl in the opposite direction with the other hand.

○ Choose a large flexible spatula for folding so you can incorporate the batter from the sides of the mixing bowl and scrape up any dry ingredients that fall to the bottom of the bowl.

○ Sometimes a little whipped egg white is beaten into a denser mixture to lighten it and make it easier to blend with the remaining egg whites.

○ You want to continue folding just until no clumps of egg white remain. Be careful not to overfold or your egg whites will deflate.

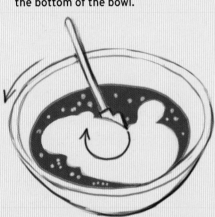 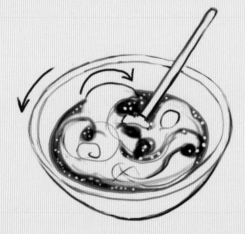

COOKING SUGAR

For Italian meringue, in which sugar syrup is cooked to 248°F (120°C), a candy thermometer that clips to the side of your saucepan is helpful but not essential. An instant-read thermometer available at any supermarket works just as well.

BAKING MERINGUE

○ To prevent meringue from sticking to the baking sheet, line it with parchment paper or a silicone mat.

○ Use heavy baking sheets that won't warp in the oven.

○ Avoid baking meringue on humid days or the meringue will soften.

STORING MERINGUE

○ Store baked French meringue in an airtight container at room temperature. Meringue stored in the refrigerator or freezer absorbs moisture and becomes soggy.

○ Italian meringue can be kept in a covered container in the refrigerator for up to 1 week.

○ If baked meringue gets soggy, it can be crisped in a 225°F (105°C) oven.

○ Freeze leftover whites from, say, making vanilla custard sauce (page 198), in ice cube trays, one to a cup. That way you know how many whites you have without having to measure them. And you can defrost only as many as you need.

whipped fromage blanc *with* crushed meringue *&* berries

Four Servings

—

French Meringue

2 large egg whites, at room temperature

4 tablespoons (50 g) granulated sugar

⅓ cup (50 g) confectioners' sugar

Fromage Blanc and Berries

1½ cups (375 ml) fromage blanc, Greek yogurt, or fresh ricotta

4 tablespoons (50 g) granulated sugar

½ cup (125 ml) heavy cream

8 ounces (250 g) mixed berries, such as raspberries, small sliced strawberries, blackberries, and red currants

—

Make Ahead
The meringue can be stored in an airtight container for up to 1 week. The fromage blanc mixture can be refrigerated for up to 2 hours.

This simple confection from Le Servan's Tatiana Levha is the alpha of the cream-fruit-meringue genre. It's the purest, the one I order again and again in Paris bistros just to taste light, lactic fromage blanc. It can be further streamlined—you can whisk in crème fraîche instead of the whipped cream or skip the cream, meringue, and berries altogether and stir in a bit of grainy sugar instead, which is what French schoolchildren do. It's all good.

—

1. French Meringue
Heat the oven to 225°F (105°C). Line a baking sheet with parchment paper. In a small bowl, whip the egg whites with 2 tablespoons (25 g) of the granulated sugar at high speed until they hold a medium peak. Whip in the remaining 2 tablespoons (25 g) of granulated sugar until firm and glossy. Using a flexible spatula, gently fold in the confectioners' sugar.

2.
Using an offset spatula, spread the meringue on the prepared baking sheet in a layer about 1 inch (2.5 cm) thick. Bake until firm and dry, about 1 hour. Turn off the oven; leave the meringue in the oven for at least 4 hours or overnight. Crush the meringue into bite-size pieces.

3. Fromage Blanc and Berries
In a small bowl, whisk the fromage blanc with 2 tablespoons (25 g) of the granulated sugar. In a medium bowl, whip the cream with the remaining 2 tablespoons (25 g) of granulated sugar until the cream holds a medium peak. Fold the whipped cream into the fromage blanc. Mound the fromage blanc cream in bowls. Spoon the berries on top, sprinkle with the crushed meringue, and serve.

—

Variation
Try pink grapefruit or blood orange segments or diced pineapple or mango when berries are not in season.

strawberries & pink grapefruit *with* fennel

Four Servings

—

½ cup (15 g) parsley leaves

½ cup plus 2 tablespoons (125 g) sugar

2 large egg whites, at room temperature

Pinch of fine sea salt

¼ cup (60 ml) fromage blanc or Greek yogurt

½ cup (125 ml) heavy cream

1 pink grapefruit

8 ounces (250 g) small strawberries, hulled, sliced crosswise

1 pint (150 g) mint or vanilla ice cream

Fennel fronds, for garnish

—

Note
If your strawberries are not local, you may want to toss them with sugar to soften and sweeten them before serving.

Make Ahead
The meringue can be stored in an airtight container for up to 1 week. The whipped cream can be refrigerated for up to 2 hours.

Bertrand Grébaut of Septime knows how to build a fruit salad, mixing in totally unexpected fennel fronds and shards of what he calls "chlorophyll meringue" (flavored with parsley). His mix of strawberries and grapefruit reflects the fleeting period between winter and spring, but try it also with gorgeous summer peaches, plums, or apricots.

—

1.
Heat the oven to 225°F (105°C). Line a baking sheet with parchment paper. In a food processor, combine the parsley and 2 tablespoons (25 g) of the sugar.

2.
In a medium bowl, whip the egg whites with the salt at low speed until foamy, then whip at high speed until they hold a soft peak. Whip in 6 tablespoons (80 g) of the sugar, 2 tablespoons (25 g) at a time, whipping well between additions. Process the parsley until finely chopped, then whip into the meringue until firm and glossy.

3.
Using an offset spatula, spread the meringue on the prepared baking sheet in a thin layer about ⅛ inch (3 mm) thick. Bake until firm and dry, about 1 hour. Turn off the oven; leave the meringue in the oven for at least 4 hours or overnight. Peel the meringue off the paper, breaking the meringue into large shards.

4.
In a small bowl, whisk the fromage blanc with 1 tablespoon of the sugar. In a medium bowl, whip the cream with the remaining 1 tablespoon of sugar until the cream holds a medium peak. Fold in the fromage blanc; cover and refrigerate the whipped cream.

5.
Using a sharp knife, cut the skin and all of the bitter white pith off the grapefruit. Working over a small bowl, cut in between the membranes to release the segments. Squeeze the juice from the membranes into the bowl. Spoon the grapefruit, grapefruit juice, and strawberries into shallow bowls. Top with the whipped cream and scoops of ice cream. Garnish with the meringue and fennel fronds and serve.

red berries & lovage granité *with* torched meringue

Four Servings

—

Granité

½ cup (125 ml) water

½ cup (100 g) sugar

2 cups (60 g) packed lovage or basil leaves

Italian Meringue and Berries

½ cup (100 g) sugar

¼ cup (60 ml) water

2 large egg whites, at room temperature

8 ounces (250 g) mixed berries, such as raspberries, small sliced strawberries, blackberries, and red currants

Wood sorrel, lovage, or celery leaves, for garnish

—

Note
Italian meringue, egg whites beaten with cooked sugar, is an extremely stable mixture that doesn't deflate when you remove the whisk or beaters. Its texture is somewhat finer and softer than French meringue (egg whites beaten with uncooked sugar).

Make Ahead
Before it's scraped, the lovage granité can be frozen for up to 1 week. The Italian meringue can be refrigerated overnight.

Bones chef James Henry revisits Baked Alaska with a naturalist take—icy shards of lovage stand in for the usual ice cream. The lovage tastes grassy on its own but it balances the sweet meringue and berries. Henry smears the meringue on the inside of pottery bowls and then browns it with a blowtorch. Eating this dessert feels like gathering wild berries and herbs in a meringue cave.

—

1. Granité
In a small saucepan, combine the water and sugar and cook over medium heat, swirling the pan occasionally, until the sugar melts. Let cool slightly. Transfer the sugar syrup to a food processor. Add the lovage and puree until coarsely smooth. Scrape into a loaf pan, cover with plastic wrap, and freeze until solid. About 30 minutes before serving, transfer the granité to the refrigerator and let soften slightly. Using the tines of a fork, scrape the granité until slushy. Cover tightly and return to the freezer.

2. Italian Meringue
In a small saucepan, heat the sugar with the water over low heat, swirling the pan, until the sugar dissolves. Bring to a boil and simmer without stirring until the syrup reaches 248°F (120°C). Meanwhile, in a medium bowl, whip the egg whites until stiff. Gradually pour in the hot syrup down the side of the bowl, whipping continuously, until the meringue is completely cool. Cover and refrigerate.

3.
Using a flexible spatula, spread the meringue on one half of the inside of heatproof bowls. Using a kitchen blowtorch, caramelize the meringue. Mound the berries in the bowls. Set a tablespoon of the granité on top, garnish with the wood sorrel, and serve immediately.

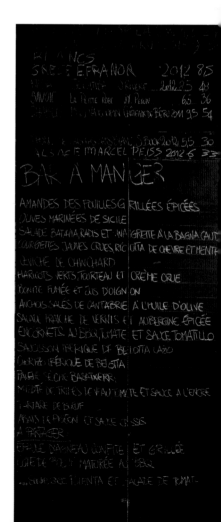

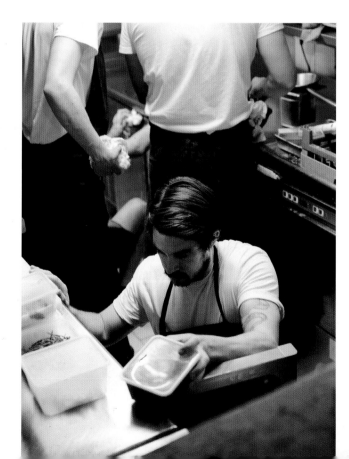

James Henry

BONES

—

CANBERRA-BORN James Henry didn't apprentice in a great kitchen. He hasn't been to cooking school. He's a free spirit mixing top-notch ingredients in never-before-seen ways (berries with lovage granité, pictured on page 187) and letting nothing go to waste. I watched him break down sea bass into fillets for crudo, the fat roe salted for bottarga, and scraps confited for fish rillettes. Henry experiments in-house with staples most chefs would outsource, like bread and yogurt. His split-level restaurant, Bones, has a four-course prix fixe dining room, plus a bar thronged two and three deep for nose-to-tail snacking. It's hard to separate the food's louche sexiness from that of Henry's hipster customers and the excavated-brick décor, with a concrete banquette and hand-thrown ceramics by Amsterdam-based pottery studio J.C. Herman. Still, even his well-traveled patrons can be squeamish when it comes to the funkier options. "It breaks your heart to see half a pigeon come back untouched," Henry said.

empress plum crumble

Eight Servings

—

¾ cup (100 g) all-purpose flour

¾ cup (100 g) finely ground walnuts or almond meal

½ cup (100 g) granulated sugar

¼ teaspoon fine sea salt

7 tablespoons (100 g) unsalted butter, diced

3 pounds (1.5 kg) Empress plums (Italian prune plums), pitted and quartered

2 tablespoons (30 g) light brown sugar

2 tablespoons (20 g) cornstarch

2 tablespoons fresh lemon juice

Whipped cream, crème fraîche, or vanilla ice cream, for serving

—

Note
The secret to making a crisp, coarse topping is to chill the crumble dough until it's firm, then break it into largish pieces rather than fine crumbs.

Make Ahead
The crumble dough can be refrigerated for up to 2 days or frozen for up to 1 month. The dish can be assembled and refrigerated up to 4 hours before baking.

Beginning a few years ago and quick to gain momentum, the English crumble has invaded bistro menus. As French chefs have embraced this homey dessert, they've also made it their own, incorporating local ingredients like quetsches (Empress plums) and quinces. At La Pointe du Grouin, chef Thierry Breton is super-generous with the crunchy, buttery topping.

—

1.
In a large bowl, squeeze the flour, walnuts, granulated sugar, and salt with the butter until the ingredients form a dough. Press into a disk, wrap in plastic, and freeze until firm, about 30 minutes.

2.
Heat the oven to 350°F (175°C). In a medium gratin dish, toss the plums with the brown sugar, cornstarch, and lemon juice. Spread the plums in a layer in the gratin dish. Break the cold dough into large clumps evenly over the top. Transfer the dish to the oven and bake, rotating the dish halfway through, until golden on top and the fruit is bubbling, about 1 hour. Let cool at least 15 minutes before serving with the whipped cream.

—

Variations
Late summer purple Empress plums are excellent baking fruit because they keep their shape and they're easy to pit. Earlier in the year, use other stone fruit (peaches, nectarines, and apricots) cut into wedges, berries (strawberries, raspberries, blackberries), or a mix.

tea-poached apricots *with* caramelized pine nuts

Four Servings

—

1 cup (125 g) all-purpose flour

7 tablespoons (100 g) unsalted butter

⅓ cup (65 g) light brown sugar

Pinch of fine sea salt

½ cup (50 g) toasted pine nuts

¾ cup (150 g) plus 2 tablespoons granulated sugar

2 cups (500 ml) plus 2 tablespoons water

8 firm ripe apricots, halved and pitted, pits reserved

2 tablespoons hojicha tea or another green tea

1 pint (150 g) vanilla ice cream

Chickweed sprigs or small mint or basil leaves, for garnish

—

Make Ahead
Each component of the recipe can be prepared up to 4 hours ahead. Assemble the dessert just before serving.

You probably think poached fruit is pleasant but not super-delicious. I am here to say, you are wrong. At least when that fruit is an apricot (or plum) and it's simmered in hojicha—a roasted green tea from Japan. That combination from chef Sota Atsumi at Clown Bar is good enough to stop right there, but it's exceptional topped with vanilla ice cream, sugared pine nuts, and buttery crumbs.

—

1.
In a large bowl, squeeze the flour with the butter, brown sugar, and salt until the ingredients form a dough. Press into a disk, wrap in plastic, and freeze until firm, about 30 minutes.

2.
Heat the oven to 350°F (175°C). Break the cold dough into large crumbs on a baking sheet. Transfer to the oven and bake, stirring occasionally, until golden and slightly dry, 8 to 10 minutes. Let cool.

3.
Line a plate with parchment paper. In a small skillet, stir the pine nuts with 2 tablespoons (25 g) of the granulated sugar and 2 tablespoons of the water. Bring to a simmer and cook over high heat, shaking the pan occasionally, until the nuts have caramelized and all the liquid has evaporated, about 4 minutes. Transfer the nuts to the plate to cool, spreading them in a single layer.

4.
In a small saucepan, combine the remaining 2 cups (500 ml) of water, ¾ cup (150 g) of granulated sugar, and the reserved apricots pits. Bring to a boil, swirling the pan occasionally, to dissolve the sugar. Add the tea and cover, then remove from the heat and let stand for 3 minutes.

5.
Strain the tea into a medium skillet. Bring to a simmer, add the apricot halves, and poach over medium heat, turning a few times, just until tender, 5 to 8 minutes. Remove from the heat and let the fruit cool to room temperature in the tea poaching liquid.

6.
Spoon the apricots into bowls with some of the poaching liquid. Sprinkle the crumble over one third of each bowl and the caramelized pine nuts next to it over another third. Set a scoop of ice cream alongside, garnish with the chickweed, and serve.

—

Variation
This recipe can also be prepared with Empress plums halves (Italian prune plums) or wedges of peach or nectarine.

oven-poached rhubarb crumble

Four Servings

—

Rhubarb

1 pound (500 g) rhubarb, cut crosswise into 2½-inch (6-cm) pieces

¼ cup (50 g) granulated sugar

¼ cup (60 g) light brown sugar

¼ cup (60 ml) rosé wine

1 tablespoon fresh lemon juice

½ teaspoon rose water

Finely grated zest of 1 orange

Finely grated zest of 1 lemon

Crumble

1 cup (125 g) all-purpose flour

7 tablespoons (100 g) unsalted butter

⅓ cup (65 g) light brown sugar

Pinch of fine sea salt

Garnish

Sweetened whipped cream

Extra-virgin olive oil (optional)

—

Make Ahead
The baked crumble can be stored in an airtight container for up to 3 days.

Shaun Kelly keeps his crumble topping extra-crisp by baking it separately from the fruit. The puckery rhubarb gets a floral, aromatic sweetness from poaching in a syrup of rose water, rosé wine, and citrus juice and zest. The rhubarb needs to marinate overnight before poaching, so plan accordingly.

—

1. Rhubarb
In a large gratin dish, toss the rhubarb with the granulated and brown sugars. Spread the rhubarb in a layer in the gratin dish. Cover and refrigerate overnight.

2.
Heat the oven to 350°F (175°C). Sprinkle the wine, lemon juice, rose water, and orange and lemon zests over the rhubarb. Transfer to the oven and bake until the rhubarb is tender but still keeps its shape, 10 to 20 minutes. Leave the oven on.

3. Crumble
Meanwhile, in a large bowl, squeeze the flour with the butter, brown sugar, and salt until the ingredients form a dough. Press into a disk, wrap in plastic, and freeze until firm, about 30 minutes.

4.
Break the cold dough into large crumbs on a baking sheet. Transfer to the oven and bake, stirring occasionally, until golden and slightly dry, 8 to 10 minutes. Let cool.

5.
Stack the rhubarb on plates and moisten with the cooking juices. Sprinkle with the crumble and spoon the whipped cream on top. Drizzle with oil, if using, and serve.

fresh pineapple *with* basil syrup

Four Servings

—

½ cup (125 ml) water

½ cup (100 g) sugar

2 cups (60 g) packed basil leaves

1 pineapple, peeled, cored, and cut into ¼-inch (6-mm) dice

Crème fraîche, sour cream, or Greek yogurt, for serving

Sugar cookies, for serving

—

Make Ahead
The basil syrup can be refrigerated for up to 2 days.

Le Comptoir chef Yves Camdeborde cuts honey-sweet pineapple into tiny dice, which elevates this simple, cooling dessert. Somehow, using a spoon instead of cutting the fruit as you eat makes it feel more refined. The emerald-green syrup would also be refreshing with juicy peaches or plums. Whatever the fruit and its size, crème fraîche (or sour cream) is essential; it adds both tang and creaminess.

—

1.
In a small saucepan, combine the water and sugar and cook over medium heat, swirling the pan occasionally, until the sugar melts. Let cool slightly. Transfer the sugar syrup to a blender. Add the basil and puree until very smooth. Refrigerate the basil syrup until chilled.

2.
Spoon the pineapple dice into bowls and pour in the syrup. Set a quenelle or spoonful of crème fraîche and a cookie on top and serve.

—

Variation
I've tried making the syrup with baby arugula, too, which doesn't involve picking any leaves off stems. It's remarkably good.

NADIA IGUÉ

coconut panna cotta *with* honeyed mango

Four Servings

—

2 sheets of leaf gelatin (see Note)

1 cup (250 ml) heavy cream

½ cup (125 ml) milk

½ cup (125 ml) unsweetened coconut milk

3 tablespoons (35 g) sugar

1 tablespoon acacia honey

1 ripe mango, peeled, seeded, and cut into ½-inch (1-cm) dice

Juice of ½ lime

—

Note
Leaf (or sheet) gelatin is available in the baking section of specialty markets.

Make Ahead
The panna cottas can be refrigerated for up to 2 days.

"With each menu every day, I try to travel a little bit," says chef Nadia Igué. This simple, creamy dessert makes stops in Italy and Asia. Mixing and matching cuisines is in keeping with Igué's background: she's Benin born, Dijon raised, and Providence, Rhode Island, educated.

—

1.
Fill a medium bowl with cold water. Add the gelatin sheets and let soak until softened, 2 to 3 minutes. Drain the gelatin and squeeze out as much water as possible.

2.
In a small saucepan, heat the cream, milk, coconut milk, and sugar over medium-high heat, stirring occasionally, until bubbles appear around the edge. Remove the pan from the heat, add the gelatin, and stir until dissolved.

3.
Strain the coconut cream into pretty 8-ounce (250-ml) glasses or jelly jars and cover with plastic wrap. Set the glasses in a small gratin dish and refrigerate until set, at least 3 hours.

4.
Meanwhile, in a medium nonstick skillet, warm the honey over medium-high heat. Add the mango, squeeze the lime juice through a sieve over the fruit, and cook, stirring occasionally, until the mango is coated in the honey, about 2 minutes. Let cool completely.

5.
Remove the plastic wrap from the glasses, spoon the mango on the panna cotta, and serve.

—

Variation
This panna cotta is also great with Empress plums (Italian prune plums), nectarines, or apricots instead of the mango.

grand marnier soufflés *with* salted caramel

Four Servings

—

Caramel Sauce

2 tablespoons light corn syrup

¼ cup (50 g) granulated sugar

3 tablespoons (45 g) unsalted butter, diced

3 tablespoons heavy cream

¼ teaspoon fine sea salt

Soufflés

Unsalted butter, softened, for brushing

4 tablespoons (50 g) granulated sugar, plus more for coating

1 cup (250 ml) whole milk

½ vanilla bean, split lengthwise and seeds scraped

3 tablespoons (25 g) cornstarch

3 large egg yolks

¼ cup (60 ml) Grand Marnier liqueur

5 large egg whites

Pinch of fine sea salt

Confectioners' sugar, for dusting

—

Note
If the caramel is too thick to pour, warm it in a microwave at 10-second intervals.

Make Ahead
The sauce and soufflés can be prepared through Step 4 and refrigerated for up to 4 hours.

Folding whipped egg whites into flavored pastry cream to make a soufflé rise never loses its wizardry. Le Pantruche chef Franck Baranger's extra magic: breaking the puffy surface with a spoon and pouring in salty-sweet caramel.

—

1. Caramel Sauce
In a medium saucepan, heat the corn syrup. Stir in the granulated sugar and cook over medium-high heat, swirling the pan occasionally, until a light amber caramel forms, 4 to 6 minutes. Remove the pan from the heat and carefully stir in the butter using a wooden spoon. Stir in the cream in a thin stream. Stir in the salt. Pour the caramel into a small heatproof pitcher.

2. Soufflés
Heat the oven to 425°F (220°C). Generously brush four 1-cup (8-ounce/250-ml) ramekins, including the rims, with the butter. Add 1 tablespoon of granulated sugar to each ramekin and turn to coat the bottoms and sides, tapping out any excess. Transfer to a baking sheet and refrigerate.

3.
In a small saucepan, bring the milk and 1 tablespoon of the granulated sugar just to a simmer over medium-high heat. Add the vanilla bean pod and seeds. Remove the pan from the heat, cover, and let stand for 15 minutes. Strain the milk into a heatproof measuring cup; reserve the vanilla bean for another use.

4.
In a medium bowl, whisk the cornstarch with 1 tablespoon of the granulated sugar. Whisk in the egg yolks until smooth. Gradually whisk in the hot milk. Pour the mixture back into the saucepan and cook over medium heat, whisking continuously, until the pastry cream is very thick, 3 to 4 minutes. Remove the pan from the heat and whisk in the liqueur.

5.
In a large bowl, whip the egg whites with the salt at low speed until foamy, then whip at high speed until the whites hold a firm peak. Add the remaining 2 tablespoons (25 g) of granulated sugar and whip until glossy. Beat one-fourth of the whipped whites into the pastry cream. Gently fold this lightened mixture into the remaining whipped whites.

6.
Scrape the soufflé mixture into the prepared ramekins and smooth the tops. Bake until the soufflés are puffed and browned, 12 to 15 minutes.

7.
Dust the tops of the soufflés with confectioners' sugar and serve with the caramel sauce.

lemon curd *with* fresh goat cheese

Four Servings

—

6 tablespoons (80 g) sugar

Finely grated zest of 1½ lemons

2 large egg yolks plus 1 large whole egg

⅓ cup (85 ml) fresh lemon juice

5 tablespoons (80 g) unsalted butter, diced

4 ounces (125 g) soft fresh goat cheese, crumbled

4 Salted Chocolate Shortbread Cookies (page 220) or other crisp cookies, crumbled

—

Make Ahead
The lemon curd can be refrigerated for up to 3 days.

At Au Passage, Edward Delling-Williams reinterprets the classic pairing of lemon and cream, swapping tangy chèvre for the sweet cream. Crumbled chocolate cookies add color and crunch.

—

1.
In a small bowl, rub the sugar with the lemon zest.

2.
In a small saucepan, whisk the lemon sugar with the egg yolks and whole egg. Gradually whisk in the lemon juice. Set the pan over medium heat and heat, whisking occasionally, until a bubble or two breaks the surface, then cook, whisking continuously, until the mixture thickens slightly, about 3 minutes. Remove the pan from the heat and gradually whisk in the butter. Using a flexible spatula, work the curd through a fine strainer into a small bowl. Press a piece of plastic directly onto the surface of the curd and refrigerate until chilled, at least 2 hours.

3.
Spoon the lemon curd into shallow bowls and sprinkle the goat cheese and cookies on top; serve.

—

Variation
Swap in oranges for the lemons to make orange curd.

unbelievably creamy rice pudding

Eight Servings

—

Rice Pudding

1 cup (200 g) arborio rice

4 cups (1 L) milk

1 cup (200 g) granulated sugar

Vanilla Custard Sauce

¾ cup (185 ml) whole milk

¼ cup (60 ml) heavy cream

½ vanilla bean, split lengthwise and seeds scraped

2 large egg yolks

1½ tablespoons (20 g) granulated sugar

Whipped Cream

1 cup (250 ml) heavy cream

1 tablespoon granulated sugar

Caramelized Nuts

½ cup (50 g) sliced almonds

Confectioners' sugar, for dusting

½ cup (50 g) toasted skinned hazelnuts, walnut halves, or pistachios or a mix (for toasting, see page 105, Step 1)

2 tablespoons (25 g) granulated sugar

2 tablespoons water

What makes this pudding unbelievable is what Stéphane Jégo does to the rice after cooking it with milk and sugar, which is where most recipes stop. L'Ami Jean's chef folds in crème anglaise and whipped cream. The add-ons are equally critical. Jégo serves caramelized nuts; actually, a mix of toasted and caramelized nuts. Caramelized nuts alone aren't as texturally complex, you know. Plus, he delivers a bowl of salted-caramel cream to the table. Help yourself.

—

1. Rice Pudding

In a medium saucepan, combine the rice and milk and bring to a simmer. Cook over low heat, stirring occasionally, until the liquid is absorbed and the rice is tender, 1½ to 2 hours. Add the granulated sugar and stir until dissolved. Scrape the rice into a large bowl and let stand until stodgy.

2. Vanilla Custard Sauce

Meanwhile, in a small saucepan, bring the milk, cream, and vanilla bean pod and seeds to a simmer over medium-high heat. In a small bowl, whisk the egg yolks with the granulated sugar just until the sugar dissolves. Slowly whisk one-third of the warm milk mixture into the egg yolks, then whisk this mixture back into the remaining warm mixture in the saucepan. Cook the sauce over medium heat, stirring continuously with a wooden spoon, until it registers 175°F (80°C) on an instant-read thermometer and lightly coats the back of a spoon, 2 to 3 minutes. Strain the sauce into a pitcher and refrigerate until cold. Reserve the vanilla bean for another use. Working in batches, fold the cold vanilla custard sauce into the rice. Cover and refrigerate until absorbed and set.

3. Whipped Cream

In a small bowl, whip the cream with the granulated sugar until it holds a medium peak. Fold the whipped cream into the rice. Refrigerate until absorbed and set.

4. Caramelized Nuts

Heat the oven to 350°F (175°C). Spread the almonds on a rimmed baking sheet and dust generously with the confectioners' sugar. Toast in the oven until golden, 8 to 10 minutes. Transfer to a small bowl.

Salted-Caramel Cream

½ cup (100 g) granulated sugar

2 tablespoons water

½ teaspoon fine sea salt

1 cup (250 ml) heavy cream

—

Make Ahead
The caramelized nuts can be stored in an airtight container for up to 5 days. The rice pudding can be refrigerated for up to 2 days. The salted-caramel cream can be refrigerated overnight before whipping, or frozen for up to 1 month. Bring to room temperature before serving.

5.
Line a plate with parchment paper. In a medium skillet stir the hazelnuts with the granulated sugar and water. Bring to a simmer and cook over high heat, shaking the pan occasionally, until the nuts have caramelized and all the liquid has evaporated, about 4 minutes. Transfer the nuts to the prepared plate to cool, spreading them in a single layer. Coarsely chop the caramelized nuts and toss with the toasted almonds.

6. Salted-Caramel Cream
In a medium saucepan, heat the granulated sugar, water, and salt over medium heat, swirling the pan occasionally, until the sugar dissolves. Bring to a simmer over medium-high heat and cook, swirling the pan occasionally, until a deep amber color forms, 5 to 6 minutes. Remove the pan from the heat and gradually add the cream—the mixture will bubble like crazy. Whisk over medium heat until the caramel melts smoothly, about 2 minutes. Scrape the caramel cream into a medium bowl. Cover the bowl and refrigerate until very cold, at least 1 hour. Whip the caramel cream until it holds a firm peak. Cover and refrigerate.

7.
Serve the rice pudding and pass the nuts and caramel cream separately.

Stéphane Jégo
L'AMI JEAN
—

I GOT TO KNOW Stéphane Jégo at a giant chefs' picnic in Queens, New York, organized by the irreverent French restaurant guide *Le Fooding*. Funny, unshaven, self-deprecating, and prone to breaking into a goofy grin, Jégo displayed none of the hauteur you'd expect from such a brilliant cook. After spending twelve years with the enormously influential chef Yves Camdeborde, Jégo went out on his own at L'Ami Jean, a rollicking, cartoon-plastered Basque pub. Jégo, who's Breton, is admired by the general public but he's also a chef's chef. (Venerated Michelin-three-star chef Pierre Gagnaire comes to visit.) In his hands, the peas and carrots served with a slab of dry-aged beef (pictured on page 155) receive the same ardent concentration usually reserved for truffles. Half the carrots are sliced thin and the rest are cut into small wedges to create complexity and sophistication. "We're a Deux Chevaux with a Ferrari engine," said Jégo.

chocolate terrine *with* caramelized hazelnuts

Eight to Ten Servings

—

Chocolate Terrine

4 large eggs, separated

4 tablespoons (50 g) sugar

8 tablespoons (125 g) unsalted butter, sliced

8 ounces (250 g) bittersweet chocolate chips (60 to 70 percent cocoa)

Pinch of fine sea salt

Caramelized Hazelnuts

½ cup (50 g) toasted skinned hazelnuts (for toasting, see page 105, Step 1)

2 tablespoons (25 g) sugar

2 tablespoons water

Unsweetened cocoa powder, for dusting

Vanilla custard sauce (page 198), for serving

—

Notes
Please note that the eggs in this recipe are not cooked.

To make neat slices, warm your knife in hot water and wipe it dry before slicing the terrine in Step 4.

Make Ahead
The terrine can be served once it's set, after 2 or 3 hours, but it's more delicious left to chill overnight and can be refrigerated for up to 2 days.

Prepared ahead and simple enough for rookie cooks, this dense, decadent mousse from Les Enfants Rouges chef Daï Shinozuka is perfect for entertaining. Note: The egg-rich vanilla custard sauce plays a crucial supporting role; it balances the bittersweet chocolate.

—

1. Chocolate Terrine
Dampen a 4-cup (1-L) terrine mold with water and line the bottom and sides with plastic wrap, leaving a 1-inch (2.5-cm) overhang on the long sides. In a medium bowl, whisk the egg yolks with 2 tablespoons (25 g) of the sugar just until the sugar dissolves. In a large saucepan, melt the butter over high heat. Remove the pan from the heat and add the chocolate chips; let stand until melted, about 2 minutes. Whisk the butter with the chocolate until smooth. Whisk in the egg mixture.

2.
In a large bowl, whip the egg whites with the salt at low speed until foamy, then whip at high speed until they hold a medium peak. Add the remaining 2 tablespoons (25 g) of sugar and whip until glossy. Beat one-fourth of the whites into the chocolate mixture to lighten the mixture. Gently fold in the remaining whites. Scrape the chocolate mixture into the prepared terrine. Smooth the top. Refrigerate the terrine for 24 hours.

3. Caramelized Hazelnuts
Line a plate with parchment paper. In a medium skillet, stir the hazelnuts with the sugar and water. Bring to a simmer and cook over high heat, shaking the pan occasionally, until the nuts have caramelized and all the liquid has evaporated, about 4 minutes. Transfer the nuts to the prepared plate to cool, spreading them in a single layer. Very coarsely chop.

4.
Dust dessert plates with the cocoa powder. Turn out the terrine onto a cutting board and remove the plastic. Slice the terrine crosswise and arrange the chocolate slices on the plates. Sprinkle with the caramelized hazelnuts and serve with the vanilla custard sauce.

chocolate ganache & coffee ice cream with almond meringue

Four Servings

—

Ganache

4 ounces (125 g) bittersweet chocolate chips (60 to 70 percent cocoa)

1 large egg yolk

2½ tablespoons (30 g) sugar

½ cup (125 ml) heavy cream

½ cup (125 ml) milk

Almond Meringue

3 large egg whites, at room temperature

½ cup (100 g) sugar

1 cup (120 g) almond meal

½ cup (50 g) sliced almonds

For Serving

1 pint (150 g) coffee ice cream

Sweetened whipped cream

—

Make Ahead
The ganache can be refrigerated for up to 2 days. The almond meringue can be stored in an airtight container for up to 3 days.

In Franck Baranger's reimagined ice cream sundae at Le Pantruche, intense chocolate ganache that's firm enough to stand a spoon in replaces the typical velvety hot fudge. (In fact, the "ganache" is prepared more like chocolate pudding; you make a crème anglaise—vanilla custard sauce—and stir it into melted bittersweet chocolate, then chill it until set.) It's the coffee ice cream that creates a creamy sauce as it melts. For crunch, Baranger adds a disk of almond meringue (a.k.a. dacquoise, a baked nut meringue) to the bowl.

—

1. Ganache
Place the chocolate in a medium bowl. Set over a saucepan filled with 1 inch (2.5 cm) of barely simmering water, making sure the bottom of the bowl does not touch the water. Let the chocolate melt, stirring occasionally until smooth. Remove the bowl from the heat.

2.
In another medium bowl, whisk the egg yolk with the sugar just until the sugar dissolves. In a small saucepan, bring the cream and milk to a simmer. Gradually pour the hot cream into the egg yolk mixture and whisk until smooth. Return the custard to the pan and cook over medium heat, stirring continuously with a wooden spoon, until it registers 175°F (80°C) on an instant-read thermometer and lightly coats the back of a spoon, 2 to 3 minutes. Pour one-third of the custard over the melted chocolate and stir until smooth. Stir in the remaining custard. Pour the ganache into a small bowl; cover and refrigerate until set, at least 2 hours.

3. Almond Meringue
Heat the oven to 350°F (175°C). Line a baking sheet with parchment paper. In a large bowl, whip the egg whites with a little sugar at high speed until they hold a soft peak. Whip in the remaining sugar, 2 tablespoons (25 g) at a time, beating well between additions, until firm and glossy. Using a flexible spatula, gently fold in the almond meal until smooth.

4.
Using an offset spatula, spread the meringue on the prepared baking sheet in a layer ⅛ inch (3 mm) thick and sprinkle with the sliced almonds. Transfer to the oven and bake, rotating the sheet halfway through, until the meringue is lightly browned, 15 to 20 minutes. Transfer the meringue on the parchment paper to a rack and let cool. Using the rim of a glass, cut out meringue rounds.

5.
Set a quenelle or spoonful of ganache and a scoop of ice cream into each bowl. Decorate with a meringue round and serve with the whipped cream.

—

Variations
Swap in mint ice cream or raspberry, passion fruit, or mango sorbet for the coffee ice cream.

pastry

beet & ginger brownies

Makes 20 Brownies

—

Brownies

1 pound (500 g) red beets, scrubbed

7 tablespoons (100 g) unsalted butter, sliced

7 ounces (200 g) bittersweet chocolate chips (60 to 70 percent cocoa)

1 tablespoon finely chopped candied ginger

1 vanilla bean, split lengthwise and seeds scraped, or 1 teaspoon pure vanilla extract

¾ cup (100 g) all-purpose flour

5 tablespoons (25 g) unsweetened cocoa powder

½ teaspoon fine sea salt

3 large eggs

1¼ cups (250 g) sugar

Vanilla Custard Sauce

1½ cups (375 ml) whole milk

½ cup (125 ml) heavy cream

½ vanilla bean, split lengthwise and seeds scraped, or ½ teaspoon pure vanilla extract

3 large egg yolks

3 tablespoons (35 g) sugar

—

Notes
Delling-Williams eliminates any bubbles in the batter in Step 4 by quickly passing over the surface with a kitchen blowtorch.

To speed up chilling the vanilla sauce, you can set the pitcher in a bowl of ice water and whisk often until chilled, about 5 minutes.

You don't expect an English chef to be baking ginger-accented brownies for the French in Paris. What's more, this version from Edward Delling-Williams at Au Passage is reminiscent of fine-textured red velvet cake, with red beets in lieu of food coloring and, instead of cream cheese frosting, vanilla custard sauce passed at the table.

—

1. Brownies
In a medium saucepan, cover the beets with 2 inches (5 cm) of water. Bring to a simmer and cook until the beets are very tender, about 1 hour. Drain and let cool slightly. Peel the beets and cut into 1-inch (2.5-cm) pieces. Transfer the beets to a food processor and puree until smooth.

2.
Heat the oven to 350°F (175°C). Line a 9 x 13-inch (23 x 33-cm) baking pan with foil, pressing it into the corners and leaving overhang on 2 sides.

3.
In a medium saucepan, melt the butter over high heat. Remove the pan from the heat and add the chocolate; let stand until melted, about 2 minutes. Whisk the butter with the chocolate until smooth. Whisk in the pureed beets, candied ginger, and vanilla seeds.

4.
In a small bowl, whisk the flour with the cocoa powder and salt. In a large bowl, using an electric mixer, beat the eggs with the sugar until tripled in volume, 3 to 5 minutes. Beat in the chocolate-beet mixture. Add the flour mixture and beat to combine, scraping down the sides of the bowl. Scrape the batter into the prepared pan and bake until a toothpick inserted in the center comes out with a few moist crumbs attached, 30 to 35 minutes. Let the brownie cool completely in the pan on a rack.

5. Vanilla Custard Sauce
Meanwhile, in a small saucepan, bring the milk, cream, and vanilla bean pod and seeds to a simmer over medium-high heat. In a small bowl, whisk the egg yolks with the sugar just until the sugar dissolves. Slowly whisk one-third of the warm milk mixture into the egg yolks, then whisk this mixture back into the remaining warm milk mixture in the saucepan. Cook the sauce over medium heat, stirring continuously with a wooden spoon, until it registers 175°F (80°C) on an instant-read thermometer and lightly coats the back of a spoon, 2 to 3 minutes. Strain the sauce into a pitcher and refrigerate until cold. Reserve the vanilla bean for another use.

6.
Lift the brownie out of the pan and peel off the foil. Cut into 20 rectangles and serve with the vanilla custard sauce.

brown sugar–walnut cake *with* poached quince

Four Servings

—

8 tablespoons (125 g) unsalted butter, sliced, plus more, softened, for brushing

2 cups (250 g) chopped walnuts

1½ cups (300 g) light brown sugar

1 teaspoon (3 g) baking powder

Fine sea salt

4 large eggs, separated

2 cups fresh orange juice

2 quinces, peeled

Crème fraîche, Greek yogurt, or whipped cream, for serving

—

Note
"Quinces start out very, very hard," says Shinozuka. "Then they fall apart very quickly." It's easier to cook them properly when you poach them whole.

Make Ahead
The whole poached quinces can be refrigerated overnight in the orange juice before it's reduced. The cake can also be refrigerated overnight before serving.

At Les Enfants Rouges, Daï Shinozuka dresses up this dense, supremely moist cake with rosy quinces that have been poached in orange juice and with a pleasantly tart syrup made from the poaching liquid. But a plain slice dusted with confectioners' sugar is phenomenally good with a cup of tea.

—

1.
Heat the oven to 350°F (175°C). Brush the bottom and sides of a 9-inch (23-cm) round cake pan with butter. Line the bottom of the pan with a parchment paper round and brush with butter.

2.
In a food processor, finely grind the walnuts with ¼ cup (50 g) of the brown sugar, the baking powder, and ¼ teaspoon of salt.

3.
In a medium saucepan, melt the butter. Remove the pan from the heat and stir in the remaining 1¼ cups (250 g) of brown sugar. Using a wooden spoon, beat in the egg yolks, one at a time. Stir in the ground walnut mixture.

4.
In a large bowl, whip the egg whites with a pinch of salt at low speed until foamy, then whip at high speed until they hold a firm peak. Beat one-fourth of the whites into the walnut mixture to loosen it. Gently fold the lightened mixture into the remaining whites. Scrape the batter into the prepared pan.

5.
Bake until a toothpick inserted in the center comes out with a few moist crumbs attached, about 40 minutes. Transfer to a rack and let cool for 10 minutes in the pan. Run a knife around the side of the pan and turn the cake out onto a serving plate to cool completely. Peel off the parchment paper.

6.
Meanwhile, in a medium saucepan, combine the orange juice and quinces. Set a small heatproof plate on top to keep the quinces submerged. Bring to a simmer, cover partially, and cook over low heat until tender, about 2 hours. Remove the quinces using a spider or slotted spoon. Boil the orange juice until syrupy, about 25 minutes. Cut each quince into 8 wedges and discard the core. Return the quinces to the syrup.

7.
Slice the cake into wedges and transfer to plates. Spoon the quinces next to the cake and drizzle with the syrup. Dollop with the crème fraîche and serve.

—

Variations
Firm fruit such as Bosc pears or Golden Delicious apples can be used instead; poach them for 20 to 30 minutes. Try the cake also with vanilla custard sauce (opposite).

orange pound cake crumble *with* strawberries *&* oranges

Six Servings

—

3 oranges

8 tablespoons (125 g) unsalted butter, diced, plus more, softened, for brushing

1 cup (125 g) all-purpose flour

1 teaspoon (3 g) baking powder

3 large eggs, separated

¾ cup (150 g) sugar

Pinch of fine sea salt

1½ pounds (750 g) strawberries, quartered lengthwise

1 pint (150 g) strawberry sorbet

—

Make Ahead
The cake can stand at room temperature wrapped in plastic for up to 3 days. After that, it's delicious toasted.

Pierre Sang Boyer's version of cake and ice cream does involve making a cake, but then it's pulsed to bits in a food processor. The *Top Chef* finalist of Pierre Sang in Oberkamp and Pierre Sang on Gambey also layers in ripe fruit.

—

1.
In a medium bowl, combine one of the oranges with enough water to reach halfway up the orange. Cover with plastic wrap, leaving a corner open. Microwave on high until very soft, turning the orange every 2 minutes, about 6 minutes total; drain. Quarter the orange. In a food processor, pulse the orange quarters until finely chopped.

2.
Meanwhile, heat the oven to 350°F (175°C). Brush the bottom and sides of an 8-inch (20-cm) round cake pan with butter. Line the bottom of the pan with a parchment paper round and brush with butter. In a small saucepan, melt the butter over medium heat and let cool.

3.
In a medium bowl, whisk the flour with the baking powder. In a large bowl, beat the egg yolks with ½ cup plus 2 tablespoons (125 g) of the sugar until thick and pale, about 2 minutes. Beat in the melted butter and 2 tablespoons (30 g) of the orange puree, then the flour mixture.

4.
In another large bowl, whip the egg whites with the salt at low speed until foamy, then whip at high speed until they hold a soft peak. Add the remaining 2 tablespoons (25 g) of sugar and whip until firm and glossy. Using a flexible spatula, beat one-fourth of the whites into the orange mixture to loosen it. Gently fold in the remaining whites. Scrape the batter into the prepared pan, transfer to the oven, and bake until a knife inserted in the center comes out clean, 20 to 25 minutes. Transfer the pan to a rack and let the cake cool for 10 minutes. Run a knife around the edge of the pan and turn it out on a rack. Peel off the paper and let the cake cool completely. Cut the cake into large cubes. In a food processor, pulse the cake into large crumbs.

5.
Using a small sharp knife, cut the skin and all of the bitter white pith off the remaining 2 oranges. Working over a small bowl, cut in between the membranes to release the segments. Squeeze the juice from the membranes into the bowl.

6.
Spoon the oranges, juice, and strawberries into shallow bowls. Sprinkle with some of the crumbled cake, set scoops of sorbet on top, and serve.

—

Variation
Cut the cake into wedges, dust it with confectioners' sugar, and serve with the fruit and sorbet.

honey-almond madeleines

Makes 12 Madeleines

—

7 tablespoons (100 g) unsalted butter, sliced, plus more, softened, for brushing

½ cup (65 g) almond meal

¼ cup plus 2 tablespoons (55 g) all-purpose flour

¾ teaspoon baking powder

⅛ teaspoon fine sea salt

2 tablespoons (25 g) granulated sugar

Finely grated zest of 2 lemons

2 large eggs

¼ cup (80 g) clover honey

Confectioners' sugar, for dusting (optional)

—

Make Ahead
The batter can be refrigerated overnight. The madeleines can be stored in an airtight container overnight.

These little lemony cakes, a recipe from Bones restaurant, have all the romance of Proust's scallop-shaped madeleines, but they're moist (from the almond meal and honey) and delightful even the next day with a cup of tea.

—

1.
In a small saucepan, melt the butter over medium-high heat, then cook, swirling the pan occasionally, until the milk solids brown, about 5 minutes.

2.
In a medium bowl, whisk the almond meal with the flour, baking powder, and salt.

3.
In a large bowl, rub the granulated sugar with the lemon zest. Using an electric mixer, beat in the eggs and honey at medium speed for 2 minutes. Using a flexible spatula, fold in the almond-flour mixture, then the butter, scraping up any browned butter solids from the bottom of the pan. Cover the bowl with plastic wrap and refrigerate until the batter is firm, at least 1 hour.

4.
Heat the oven to 400°F (200°C). Set a madeleine pan on a baking sheet and brush the cups with butter. Spoon the firm batter into the cups. Don't worry about smoothing the tops; the batter will fill the cups evenly when baked. Transfer the baking sheet to the oven and bake, rotating the sheet halfway through, until the madeleine edges are golden and a toothpick comes out clean, about 10 minutes.

5.
Let the madeleines cool in the pan for 2 minutes, then transfer the cakes to a rack to cool slightly. Dust with the confectioners' sugar and serve.

almond-coconut orange cake

12 Servings

—

3 blood oranges or navel oranges, scrubbed

Unsalted butter, softened, for brushing

6 large eggs

2¾ cups (550 g) sugar

2¾ cups (275 g) almond meal

3 cups (275 g) unsweetened shredded coconut

1 teaspoon (3 g) baking powder

½ cup (50 g) sliced almonds

2 cups (500 ml) heavy cream

¼ cup (60 ml) blood orange curd (see Notes)

¼ cup (75 g) apricot jam

1 teaspoon water

—

Notes
Follow the directions for lemon curd on page 197, replacing the lemons with blood oranges. Or—even easier—fold ¼ cup (60 ml) of the remaining orange puree into the whipped cream.

Instead of boiling the oranges until soft, which takes forever, you can cook them quickly in a microwave oven; for directions, see Orange Pound Cake Crumble with Strawberries and Oranges, page 210, Step 1.

Make Ahead
The cake can be refrigerated for up to 2 days.

Beating pureed, boiled oranges into the batter makes this flourless cake taste like it's been soaked in citrus syrup. Alice Quillet and Anna Trattles of Le Bal Café first learned the recipe from Rose Bakery owner Rose Carrarini but have since made it their own, subbing shredded coconut for half the almond meal and flavoring the whipped cream with orange curd to match the cake.

—

1.
In a large saucepan, combine the oranges with water to cover by 2 inches (5 cm) and weight down with a small pan lid. Bring the water to a boil and simmer the oranges over medium heat until very soft, about 2 hours. Top off with boiling water as needed to keep the oranges covered. Drain. Quarter the oranges.

2.
Heat the oven to 350°F (175°C). Brush the bottom and sides of a 10-inch (25-cm) springform pan with butter. Line the bottom of the pan with a parchment paper round and brush with butter.

3.
In a food processor, puree the orange quarters until smooth. In a large bowl, beat the eggs with the sugar to mix. Beat in 1½ cups (340 g) of the orange puree. Fold in the almond meal, coconut, and baking powder. Scrape the mixture into the prepared pan and smooth the top using an offset spatula. Sprinkle the sliced almonds evenly over the top.

Transfer to the oven and bake until a wooden skewer inserted in the center comes out with a few moist crumbs attached, 45 minutes to 1 hour.

4.
Meanwhile, in a large bowl, whip the cream until it holds a medium peak. Gently fold in the blood orange curd. Cover and refrigerate.

5.
Transfer the springform pan to a rack and let the cake cool slightly. In a small bowl, warm the jam with the water in a microwave oven until melted. Brush the jam over the top of the warm cake. Let the cake cool to room temperature in the pan.

6.
Run a knife around the side of the cake; remove the side of the springform pan. Turn out the cake onto a cooling rack and remove the parchment paper. Invert the cake onto a serving plate. Cut the cake into wedges and serve with the citrus whipped cream.

—

Variations
The cake can be prepared with other citrus fruit, such as lemons or tangerines. Or use only almond meal (use weight, not volume) instead of half almond meal and half coconut.

Anna Trattles & Alice Quillet

LE BAL CAFÉ

—

ALICE QUILLET (left in photo here) and Anna Trattles chummily share duties at two establishments: Le Bal Café, in a 1920s dance-hall-turned-photographic-arts-center, and Ten Belles, their coffee shop near the Canal Saint-Martin. (The exceptionally good beans at both come from Quillet's husband, Anselme Blayney, of Belleville Brûlerie.) The self-taught Anglo-French Quillet and British expat Trattles met at the very English, quirky-for-Paris Rose Bakery (now an international brand) and helped introduce the French to crumbles and scones. At Le Bal Café the pair experiment with a mix of modern British cooking and fresh French produce, like Cold Fennel Soup with Chervil (pictured on page 34). Their food is hugely influenced by Fergus Henderson's homemade-everything ethic—Trattles is a veteran of his restaurant St. John Bread and Wine—so there's always meat curing, stews marinating, poultry brining, lemons pickling. "We need a lot of fridge space," said Quillet.

calvados babas *with* apple-ginger compote

Eight Servings

—

Apple Compote

2 pounds (1 kg) McIntosh apples, peeled, cored, and cut into eighths

1 cup (250 ml) water

One 1-inch (2.5-cm) piece of ginger, peeled and sliced

Syrup

4 cups (1 L) water

2⅔ cups (500 g) sugar

Thinly peeled zest of 1 orange

Thinly peeled zest of 1 lemon

¼ cup (60 ml) Calvados, plus more for drizzling

Vanilla Whipped Cream

2 cups (500 ml) heavy cream

2 tablespoons (25 g) sugar

1 vanilla bean, split lengthwise and seeds scraped, or 1 teaspoon pure vanilla extract

Cakes

1 teaspoon active dry yeast

1½ tablespoons (20 g) sugar

¼ cup (60 ml) lukewarm water

1¾ cups (225 g) all-purpose flour

Pinch of fine sea salt

3 large eggs

4 tablespoons (60 g) unsalted butter, softened, plus more for brushing

—

Make Ahead
The compote, syrup, and whipped cream can all be refrigerated separately overnight. The cakes can be refrigerated in the syrup overnight. Bring the compote and cakes to room temperature before serving.

These golden, yeasty, syrup-infused cakes are a low-stress (do-ahead) showstopper. At Le Pantruche, Franck Baranger rejuvenates the boozy relic by swapping in Calvados for the usual rum and adding gingery apple compote to the bowl. (Babas are basically a delivery system for spirits.) Many people have never tasted a baba—or Calvados, the truly memorable cider brandy from Normandy—so think about it for a ta-da! dinner party finale.

—

1. Apple Compote
In a large saucepan, combine the apples, water, and ginger and bring to a boil. Cover and cook over medium-high heat, stirring occasionally, until the apples are soft, 30 to 40 minutes. Whisk until a compote forms. Remove and discard the ginger.

2. Syrup
In another large saucepan, bring the water and sugar to a boil with the orange and lemon zests, stirring, until the sugar dissolves. Remove from the heat and let steep.

3. Vanilla Whipped Cream
Whip the cream with the sugar and vanilla seeds until the cream holds a medium peak. Cover and refrigerate.

4. Cakes
In a small bowl, sprinkle the yeast and sugar over the water and let stand until foamy, about 5 minutes. In a medium bowl, whisk the flour with the salt and make a well in the center. Pour the yeast mixture into the well. Crack 2 of the eggs into the well and, using a fork, beat the yeast mixture with the eggs. Using a wooden spoon, gradually stir the flour into the yeast mixture, then beat the dough

until smooth and fairly firm. Add the remaining egg and beat until the dough is soft but elastic, 2 to 3 minutes. Add the 4 tablespoons (60 g) of softened butter and beat until smooth, 2 to 3 minutes. Cover the bowl with plastic wrap; let the dough rise at room temperature until almost doubled in volume, about 30 minutes.

5.
Brush 8 cups in a 12-cup muffin pan with butter. Spoon about ¼ cup (65 g) of the dough into each buttered cup. Dip a finger in water and smooth the tops. Let rise in the pan, uncovered, until almost doubled in volume, about 30 minutes.

6.
Heat the oven to 350°F (175°C). Transfer the muffin pan to the oven and bake, rotating the pan halfway through, until the cakes are golden, about 20 minutes. Run a table knife around the cups to loosen the cakes if needed. Turn the cakes out onto a rack and let cool for 5 minutes.

7.
Return the syrup in the pan to the stove and heat until it reaches 130°F (55°C). Strain into a large gratin dish and add the Calvados. Add the cakes and turn to soak. Transfer the cakes to a rack set over a baking sheet to drain for at least 10 minutes. Just before serving, return the cakes to the syrup and turn to soak.

8.
Spoon the apple compote into shallow bowls. Gently tear or slice the cakes lengthwise in half and set on the compote. Drizzle the cakes with Calvados. Dollop the centers with whipped cream and serve. Pass the remaining whipped cream and Calvados separately.

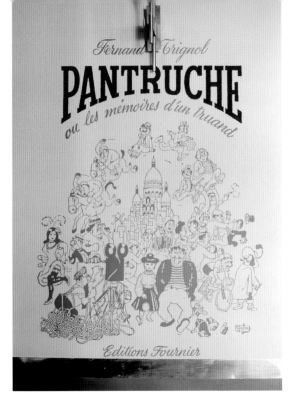

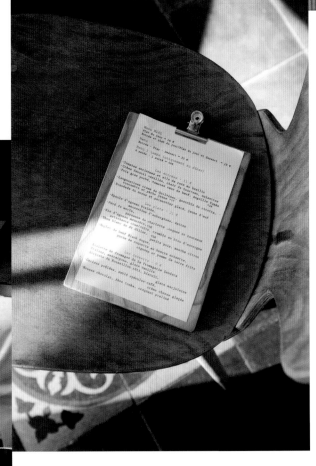

Franck Baranger

LE PANTRUCHE
CAILLEBOTTE

—

ON MY FIRST visit to Le Pantruche, Franck Baranger's perfectly intact 1930s bistro in Pigalle, it was a brave, super-cool outpost in a functioning red light district. (I lived just down the hill when I was at cooking school. Don't tell my mother.) Baranger (second from right in photo here) applied the rigorous technique he had learned in high-end kitchens (Le Bristol, Le Violon d'Ingres) to the organic vegetables grown by his father-in-law. By the time his second restaurant, Caillebotte, debuted four years later, the neighborhood had gentrified to the point where it was rechristened "SoPi" (South Pigalle). I shuffled between the two kitchens to get a sense of each's qualities. In both, Baranger reworks classic French cooking in a much more inspired style, like smoking sunchoke puree over smoldering hay in a makeshift stovetop contraption to go with wine-braised beef (page 152). Customers, however, are persuaded Caillebotte is more trailblazing, perhaps because of its minimalist decor and open kitchen. "It's the same food," Baranger told me. "We just put it on a different plate."

salted chocolate shortbread cookies

Makes About 30 Cookies

—

13 tablespoons (190 g) unsalted butter, softened

½ cup (100 g) granulated sugar

¾ teaspoon (5 g) fine sea salt

1¾ cups (225 g) all-purpose flour

¼ cup (20 g) unsweetened cocoa powder, sifted

½ cup (100 g) decorating sugar

1 small egg, beaten to mix

—

Make Ahead
The cookie dough can be prepared through Step 2 and refrigerated for up to 3 days or frozen for up to 1 month. If baking from frozen, slice the frozen dough and bake the cookies for a couple minutes longer. The cookies can be stored in an airtight container for up to 3 days.

Le Comptoir chef Yves Camdeborde's slice-and-bake cocoa sablés are wonderfully simple. The centers are buttery and tender, and the edges have a nice crunch from being rolled in decorating sugar. Plus, he adds just the right amount of sea salt.

—

1.
In a large bowl, using an electric mixer, beat the butter until smooth. Add the granulated sugar and salt and beat until fluffy, about 2 minutes. In a medium bowl, whisk the flour with the cocoa powder. Add the cocoa flour to the butter mixture in two additions, beating at low speed just until incorporated; the dough will be fairly crumbly and barely hold together when squeezed.

2.
On a work surface, shape the dough into two logs 1½ inches (4 cm) wide and wrap in plastic. Refrigerate until very firm, at least 2 hours.

3.
Position racks in the upper and lower thirds of the oven and heat the oven to 350°F (175°C). Line 2 baking sheets with silicone mats or parchment paper. Spread the decorating sugar in a shallow pan. Unwrap one cookie log and brush it with the beaten egg. Roll the log in the decorating sugar to coat. Using a sharp knife, cut the log into ⅜-inch (1-cm) slices. Arrange on the prepared baking sheet about ¾ inch (2 cm) apart. Repeat with the second log.

4.
Transfer the baking sheets to the oven and bake, shifting the pans from top to bottom and front to back halfway through, until the cookies are firm, 16 to 18 minutes. Transfer the baking sheets to racks and let the cookies cool for 5 minutes. Transfer the cookies to the racks to cool completely.

—

Variation
To make chocolate chocolate chip cookies, knead 1 cup (5 ounces/150 g) of mini bittersweet chocolate chips into the dough in Step 1.

peach tart *with* toasted pecan frangipane

Eight Servings

—

Pâte Brisée

2 cups (250 g) all-purpose flour, plus more for dusting

9 tablespoons (150 g) cold unsalted butter, cut into ¼-inch (6-mm) dice, plus more, softened, for brushing

5 tablespoons (60 g) sugar

¼ teaspoon fine sea salt

1 large egg, beaten to mix with 1 ice cube

½ vanilla bean, split lengthwise and seeds scraped, or ½ teaspoon pure vanilla extract

Frangipane and Peaches

¾ cup (100 g) chopped pecans

½ cup (100 g) sugar

7 tablespoons (100 g) unsalted butter, softened

3 large egg yolks

½ vanilla bean, split lengthwise and seeds scraped, or ½ teaspoon pure vanilla extract

Pinch of fine sea salt

3 firm ripe skin-on yellow peaches, cut into thin wedges

Sweetened whipped cream, for serving

—

Make Ahead
The wrapped dough and frangipane can be refrigerated for up to 3 days.

Le Bal Café chefs Alice Quillet and Anna Trattles—who are Anglo-French—give ingredients from the American South a French treatment in this irresistible tart (pictured on page 206). Go ahead, beat a little bourbon whiskey into the whipped cream accompaniment; the quintessentially American spirit ultimately gets its name from the French Bourbon dynasty.

—

1. Pâte Brisée
In a food processor, blend the flour with 5 tablespoons (75 g) of the butter, the sugar, and salt until the mixture resembles cornmeal. Scrape the mixture into a large bowl. Add the beaten egg, vanilla seeds, and remaining 4 tablespoons (60 g) of butter and, using a fork, quickly toss the dough until evenly dampened. Gently knead the dough until it just comes together. Pat into a disk, wrap in plastic, and refrigerate until firm, at least 1 hour.

2.
Roll out the dough between 2 silicone mats or sheets of parchment paper into a 13-inch (32-cm) round. Transfer, still covered and flat, to a baking sheet and freeze until firm, about 5 minutes.

3.
Brush the bottom and sides of a 10-inch (25-cm) fluted tart pan with a removable bottom with butter and dust it with flour. Peel the top mat off the dough, invert the round onto the prepared tart pan, and remove the second mat. Gently press the dough into the pan. Trim or fold in the dough around the pan to make an even edge. Prick the base of the tart all over with a fork and freeze for at least 30 minutes.

4.
Heat the oven to 350°F (175°C). Set the tart pan on a baking sheet and bake, rotating the baking sheet halfway through, until the tart shell is firm and lightly browned, 15 to 20 minutes. Transfer the tart pan to a rack and let cool. Leave the oven on.

5. Frangipane and Peaches
Meanwhile, spread the pecans in a rimmed baking sheet and toast in the oven, stirring occasionally, until golden, 8 to 10 minutes. Pour the nuts into a pan and let cool completely. In a food processor, finely grind the pecans with ¼ cup (50 g) of the sugar.

6.
In a medium bowl, beat the butter and remaining ¼ cup (50 g) of sugar with a wooden spoon until soft and fluffy. Beat in the egg yolks and vanilla seeds. Add the ground pecans and salt and stir until smooth.

7.
Spread the frangipane in the tart shell. Arrange the peach wedges in concentric circles in the tart shell. Set the tart pan on a baking sheet and bake, rotating the baking sheet halfway through, until the frangipane is set and browned, 50 to 60 minutes. Transfer the tart to a rack to cool to room temperature. Remove the tart ring and transfer the tart to a plate. Cut into wedges and serve with the whipped cream.

rhubarb meringue tart
with frozen yogurt

Six Servings

—

Meringue

2 large egg whites, at room temperature

4 tablespoons (50 g) granulated sugar

⅓ cup (50 g) confectioners' sugar

Pâte Sablée

7 tablespoons (100 g) unsalted butter, softened, plus more for brushing

½ cup (100 g) granulated sugar

2 large egg yolks

1 cup (125 g) all-purpose flour, plus more for dusting

2 tablespoons (15 g) almond meal

¼ teaspoon fine sea salt

At Le Bistrot d'à Côté, chef Nicolas Beaumann replaces the usual topping of pillowy meringue with shards of crisp baked meringue. He adds house-made fromage blanc sorbet to the plate, too; frozen yogurt also gives the tart extra tang (and creaminess).

—

1. Meringue
Heat the oven to 225°F (105°C). Line a baking sheet with parchment paper. In a medium bowl, whip the egg whites with 2 tablespoons (25 g) of the granulated sugar at high speed until they hold a medium peak. Whip in the remaining 2 tablespoons (25 g) of granulated sugar until firm and glossy. Using a flexible spatula, gently fold in the confectioners' sugar.

2.
Using an offset spatula, spread the meringue on the prepared baking sheet in a thin layer about ⅛ inch (3 mm) thick. Bake until firm and dry, about 1 hour. Turn off the oven; leave the meringue in the oven at least 4 hours or overnight. Peel the meringue off the paper, breaking the meringue into large shards.

3. Pâte Sablée
In a medium bowl, using a wooden spoon, beat the butter with the granulated sugar until creamy. Beat in the egg yolks. Add the flour, almond meal, and salt and stir just until a very soft dough forms. Pat into a disk, wrap in plastic, and refrigerate until firm, at least 1 hour.

4.
Roll out the dough between 2 silicone mats or sheets of parchment paper into a 12-inch (30-cm) round. Transfer, still covered and flat, to a baking sheet and freeze until firm, about 5 minutes.

5.
Brush the bottom and sides of a 9-inch (23-cm) fluted tart pan with a removable bottom with butter and dust with flour. Peel the top mat off the dough, invert the round onto the prepared tart pan, and remove the second mat. Gently press the dough into the pan. Trim or fold in the dough around the pan to make an even edge. Prick the base of the tart all over with a fork and freeze for at least 30 minutes.

6.
Heat the oven to 350°F (175°C). Set the tart pan on a baking sheet and bake, rotating the baking sheet halfway through, until the tart shell is firm and lightly browned, 15 to 20 minutes. Transfer the tart pan to a rack and let cool. Leave the oven on.

Filling

1 pound (500 g) trimmed rhubarb, cut into 1-inch (2.5-cm) pieces

4 tablespoons (50 g) granulated sugar

2 tablespoons water

¾ cup (185 ml) half-and-half

2 large eggs

1 vanilla bean, split lengthwise and seeds scraped, or 1 teaspoon pure vanilla extract

1 pint (150 g) vanilla frozen yogurt

—

Notes
Rhubarb goes from firm to falling apart in an instant, so watch carefully when cooking it in Step 7. Remove the pieces of rhubarb as they're done; they cook at different rates.

You might want to remove the meringue shards before slicing the tart, which makes cutting easier, then replace the meringue.

Make Ahead
The meringue can be stored in an airtight container for up to 1 week. The dough can be wrapped in plastic and refrigerated for up to 3 days.

7. Filling
Meanwhile, in a medium skillet, combine the rhubarb, 2 tablespoons (25 g) of the granulated sugar, and the water. Bring to a simmer and cook over medium heat until the rhubarb is tender but still intact, 2 to 3 minutes; drain. Arrange the pieces of rhubarb as they're done in the tart shell.

8.
In a medium bowl, whisk the half-and-half with the eggs, vanilla seeds, and remaining 2 tablespoons (25 g) of granulated sugar. Pour the custard over the rhubarb in the tart shell. Transfer the tart to a baking sheet and bake in the lower third of the oven, rotating the sheet halfway through, until the custard is set, 35 to 45 minutes. Transfer the tart to a rack to cool completely.

9.
Remove the tart ring and transfer the tart to a plate. Decorate with the meringue shards, standing them on their edges between the pieces of rhubarb. Cut the tart into wedges and serve with scoops of the frozen yogurt.

jammy strawberry tart *with* hazelnut cream

Six Servings

—

Pâte Sucrée

7 tablespoons (100 g) unsalted butter, softened, plus more for brushing

½ cup (70 g) sifted confectioners' sugar

1 large egg

¼ teaspoon fine sea salt

3 tablespoons (25 g) ground skinned hazelnuts

1¼ cups (165 g) all-purpose flour, plus more for dusting

Hazelnut Cream and Strawberries

5 tablespoons (80 g) unsalted butter, softened

6 tablespoons (80 g) granulated sugar

1 large egg

½ vanilla bean, split lengthwise and seeds scraped or ½ teaspoon pure vanilla extract

⅔ cup (80 g) ground skinned hazelnuts

1 tablespoon cornstarch

Pinch of fine sea salt

1½ pounds (750 g) small strawberries, hulled and halved lengthwise (see Note)

Confectioners' sugar, for dusting

Crème fraîche or sour cream, for serving

—

Note
If you're not using local strawberries, sprinkle brown sugar over the tart before baking.

Make Ahead
The wrapped dough and hazelnut cream can be refrigerated for up to 3 days.

Neo-bistro chefs love to fill tart shells with fruit and frangipane (a blend of ground nuts, sugar, butter, and eggs), slide them into the oven until browned, and serve them dusted with confectioners' sugar. They're everywhere in endless variations, garnished with firm, ripe apricots, peaches, nectarines, figs, or plums. The nuts change, too—hazelnuts, almonds, walnuts, even pecans—and they can be raw or toasted. Frenchie chef Greg Marchand's inspiration is to top the tart with fragile strawberries, which break down slightly in baking and create a jammy, or confit, effect.

—

1. Pâte Sucrée
In a large bowl, using an electric mixer, beat the butter with the confectioners' sugar at high speed until light and fluffy, about 1 minute. Beat in the egg at medium speed. Beat in the salt, then the ground hazelnuts. Add the flour and beat just until mixed. Pat the dough into a disk, wrap in plastic, and refrigerate until firm, at least 1 hour.

2.
Roll out the dough between 2 silicone mats or sheets of parchment paper into a 12-inch (30-cm) round. Transfer, still covered and flat, to a baking sheet and freeze until firm, about 5 minutes.

3.
Brush the bottom and sides of a 9-inch (23-cm) fluted tart pan with a removable bottom with butter and dust it with flour. Peel the top mat off the dough, invert the round onto the prepared tart pan, and remove the second mat. Gently press the dough into the pan. Trim or fold in the dough around the pan to make an even edge. Prick the base of the tart all over with a fork and freeze for at least 30 minutes.

4.
Heat the oven to 350°F (175°C). Set the tart pan on a baking sheet and bake, rotating the baking sheet halfway through, until the tart shell is firm and lightly browned, 15 to 20 minutes. Transfer the tart pan to a rack and let cool. Leave the oven on.

5. Hazelnut Cream
Meanwhile, in a medium bowl, beat the butter and granulated sugar with a wooden spoon until soft and fluffy. Beat in the egg and vanilla seeds. Add the ground hazelnuts, cornstarch, and salt and stir until smooth.

6.
Spread the hazelnut cream in the tart shell. Arrange the strawberry halves, tips up, in tight concentric circles in the tart shell. Reserve the remaining strawberries for garnish. Transfer the tart pan to a baking sheet and bake, rotating the sheet halfway through, until the hazelnut cream is set and the strawberries are slightly jammy, 50 to 60 minutes. Transfer the tart to a rack to cool to room temperature. Dust with confectioners' sugar. Remove the tart ring and transfer the tart to a plate. Cut into wedges and serve with the remaining strawberries and crème fraîche.

CLOWN BAR

42 Grove Stre
28 Rue Henry Mo
ilovebuvette

ants
ges

Beauce
aris
8 87 80 61

chatomat

6 rue Victor Leralle Paris 20ᵉ
- du mercredi au dimanche le soir
01 47 97 25 77

Bones

abri
92 Rue du Faubourg-Poissonnière
75010 Paris
☎ 01.83.97.00.00

Le Servan
32 RUE St MAUR
75011 PARIS
01.55.28.51.82
06 13 82 23 19

BLE D'EUGEN

restaurant

l'Office
RESTAURANT

RICHER ◊ 75009 PARIS ◊ 01 47 70 67 31

l'e
café-bi
cuisine
168 rue d'A
75014 PARI
01 48 42 64
ouvert tous

ant
oi

PARIS
11

80 Rue de CHARONNE

RESTAURANT
01 43 67 3

AUX DEUX AMIS

L'Office

SEPTIME
LA CAVE

A ÉG
NSERV

75009 PARIS   01 47 70

SPRING

l Rose
@springparis.fr

aurant
e Bailleul
001, Paris
45.96.05.72

boutique
52 rue de l'Arbre Sec
75001, Paris
01.58.62.44.30

LE
PARIO
RESTAURANT
PARIS XVᵉ

CAFÉ

RANT

Au Passa

onge

54, avenue Emile Zola - Paris XVᵉ
01 45 77 28 82 - Fax : 01 45 75 09 3
otlepario@gmail.com - ww

2, RUE RICHER
75009 PARIS

RESTA
FREN

5-6

selected guide

For travelers to Paris, this directory lists all the addresses of the restaurants profiled in the book, plus some additional favorites.

1ST ARRONDISSEMENT

L'ARDOISE (Pierre Jay)
28 rue du Mont-Thabor
33/1 42-96-28-18
lardoise-paris.com

ELLSWORTH (Braden Perkins)
34 rue de Richelieu
33/1 42-60-59-66
ellsworthparis.com

HEIMAT (Pierre Jancou)
37 rue de Montpensier
33/1 40-26-78-25
heimatparis.com

PIROUETTE (Tomy Gousset)
5 rue Mondétour
33/1 40-26-47-81

RACINES 2
(Alexandre Navarro)
39 rue de l'Arbre-Sec
33/1 42-60-77-34
racinesparis.com

**LA RÉGALADE
SAINT-HONORÉ**
(Bruno Doucet)
123 rue Saint-Honoré
33/1 42-21-92-40

SPRING (Daniel Rose)
6 rue Bailleul
33/1 45-96-05-72
springparis.fr

VERJUS (Braden Perkins)
52 rue de Richelieu
33/1 42-97-54-40
verjusparis.com

VERJUS WINE BAR
(Laura Adrian)
47 rue Montpensier
33/1 42-97-54-40
verjusparis.com

YAM'TCHA
(Adeline Grattard)
121 rue Saint-Honoré
33/1 40-26-08-07
yamtcha.com

2ND ARRONDISSEMENT

FRENCHIE
(Greg Marchand)
5-6 rue du Nil
33/1 40-39-96-19
frenchie-restaurant.com

FRENCHIE BAR À VINS
(Greg Marchand)
5-6 rue du Nil
no phone

A NOSTE (Julien Duboué)
6 bis, rue du Quatre Septembre
33/1 47-03-91-91

RACINES (Renaud Marcille)
8 passage des Panoramas
33/1 40-13-06-41
racinesparis.com

SATURNE (Sven Chartier)
17 rue Notre-Dame des Victoires
33/1 42-60-31-90
saturne-paris.fr

TERROIR PARISIEN
(Yannick Alléno)
Palais Brongniart
28 place de la Bourse
33/1 83-92-20-30
yannick-alleno.com

3RD ARRONDISSEMENT

LES ENFANTS ROUGES
(Daï Shinozuka)
9 rue de Beauce
33/1 48-87-80-61
les-enfants-rouges.com

5TH ARRONDISSEMENT

ITINÉRAIRES (Sylvain Sendra)
5 rue de Pontoise
33/1 46-33-60-11

LES PAPILLES
(Bertrand Bluy)
30 rue Gay-Lussac
33/1 43-25-20-79
lespapillesparis.fr

TERROIR PARISIEN
(Yannick Alléno)
20 rue Saint-Victor
33/1 44-31-54-54
yannick-alleno.com

AUX VERRES DE CONTACT
(Guillaume Delage)
52 boulevard Saint-Germain
33/1 46-34-58-02
auxverresdecontact.com

6TH ARRONDISSEMENT

L'AVANT COMPTOIR
(Yves Camdeborde)
9 carrefour de l'Odéon
no phone; hotel-paris-relais-
saint-germain.com

LE COMPTOIR DU RELAIS
(Yves Camdeborde)
9 carrefour de l'Odéon
33/1 44-27-07-97; hotel-paris-
relais-saint-germain.com

RESTAURANT AG
(Alan Geaam), 2 rue Clément
33/1 43-25-77-66
ag-restaurant.fr

SEMILLA (Éric Trochon)
54 rue de Seine
33/1 43-54-34-50

7TH ARRONDISSEMENT

L'AMI JEAN
(Stéphane Jégo)
27 rue Malar
33/1 47-05-86-89
lamijean.fr

BISTROT BELHARA
(Thierry Dufroux)
23 rue Duvivier
33/1 45-51-41-77
bistrobelhara.com

CAFÉ CONSTANT
(Christian Constant)
139 rue Saint-Dominique
33/1 47-53-73-34
maisonconstant.com

CLOVER
(Jean-François Piège)
5 rue Perronet
33/1 75-50-00-05
jeanfrancoispiege.com

LES COCOTTES
(Christian Constant)
135 rue Saint-Dominique
no phone; maisonconstant.com

LA TABLE D'AKI
(Akihiro Horikoshi)
49 rue Vaneau
33/1 45-44-43-48

8TH ARRONDISSEMENT

NEVA CUISINE
(Beatriz Gonzales)
2 rue de Berne
33/1 45-22-18-91

9TH ARRONDISSEMENT

BUVETTE (Jody Williams)
28 rue Henry Monnier
33/1 44-63-41-71
paris.ilovebuvette.com

CAILLEBOTTE
(Franck Baranger)
8 rue Hippolyte-Lebas
33/1 53-20-88-70

COMPTOIR CANAILLES
(Nicolas Pando)
47 rue Rodier
33/1 53-20-95-56; restaurant-
comptoircanailles.com

L'OFFICE (Konrad Keglowski)
3 rue Richer
33/1 47-70-67-31

LE PANTRUCHE
(Franck Baranger)
3 rue Victor Massé
33/1 48-78-55-60
lepantruche.com

**LA RÉGALADE
CONSERVATOIRE**
(Bruno Doucet)
7-9 rue du Conservatoire
33/1 44-83-83-60

RICHER (Adrien Bouchaud
and Romain Lamon)
2 rue Richer
no phone

10TH ARRONDISSEMENT

52 FAUBOURG SAINT-DENIS
(Adrien Bouchaud and
Romain Lamon)
52 rue du Faubourg Saint-Denis
no phone

ABRI (Katsuaki Okiyama)
92 rue du Faubourg-
Poissonnière
33/1 83-97-00-00

ALBION (Matt Ong)
80 rue du Faubourg-
Poissonière
33/1 42-46-02-44

BISTRO BELLET
(François Chenel)
84 rue du Faubourg Saint-Denis
33/1 45-23-42-06

LA CAVE À MICHEL
(Romain Tischenko)
36 rue Sainte-Marthe
33/1 42-45-94-47

CHEZ CASIMIR (Thierry Breton)
6 rue de Belzunce
33/1 48-78-28-80

CHEZ MICHEL (Thierry Breton)
10 rue de Belzunce
33/1 44-53-06-20

LE GALOPIN
(Romain Tischenko)
34 rue Sainte-Marthe
33/1 42-06-05-03
le-galopin.com

HAÏ KAÏ (Amélie Darvas)
104 quai de Jemmapes
33/9 81 99 98 88
haikai.fr

PARADIS (Nicolas Gaudin)
14 rue de Paradis
33/1 45-23-57-98
restaurant-paradis.com

LA POINTE DU GROUIN
(Thierry Breton)
8 rue de Belzuce, no phone

TEN BELLES (Alice Quillet
and Anna Trattles)
10 rue de la Grange aux Belles
33/1 42-40-90-78
tenbelles.com

LE VERRE VOLÉ
(Cyril Bordarier)
67 rue de Lancry
33/1 48-03-17-34
leverrevole.fr

11TH ARRONDISSEMENT

LE 6 PAUL BERT
(Louis-Philippe Riel)
6 rue Paul Bert
33/1 43-79-14-32

AU PASSAGE
(Edward Delling-Williams)
1 bis passage Saint-Sébastien
33/1 43-55-07-52
restaurant-aupassage.fr

BONES (James Henry)
43 rue Godefroy Cavaignac
33/9 80-75-32-08
bonesparis.fr

LA BUVETTE
(Camille Fourmont)
67 rue Saint-Maur
33/9 83-56-94-11

LE CHATEAUBRIAND
(Inaki Aizpitarte)
129 avenue Parmentier
33/1 43-57-45-95

CLOWN BAR
(Sota Atsumi)
114 rue Amelot
33/1 43-55-87-35
clown-bar-paris.fr

LE DAUPHIN
(Inaki Aizpitarte)
131 avenue Parmentier
33/1 55-28-78-88

LES DÉSERTEURS
(Daniel Baratier)
46 rue Trousseau
33/1 48-06-95-85

AUX DEUX AMIS
(David Loyola)
45 rue Oberkempf
33/1 58-30-38-13

L'ORILLON BAR
(Thomas Chevrier)
35 rue de l'Orillon
33/1 42-00-00-00

MARTIN
(Edward Delling-Williams)
24 boulevard du Temple
33/1 43-57-82-37
bar-martin.fr

PIERRE SANG IN OBERKAMPF
(Pierre Sang Boyer)
55 rue Oberkampf, no phone
pierresangboyer.com

PIERRE SANG ON GAMBEY
(Pierre Sang Boyer)
8 rue Gambey, no phone

6036 (Haruka Casters)
82 rue Jean-Pierre Timbaud
33/1 73-71-38-12

LE SERVAN (Tatiana Levha)
32 rue Saint-Maur
33/1 55-28-51-82
leservan.com

SEPTIME (Bertrand Grébaut)
80 rue de Charonne
33/1 43-67-38-29
septime-charonne.fr

LE SOT L'Y LAISSE
(Eiji Doihara)
70 rue Alexandre Dumas
33/1 40-09-79-20

YARD (Nye Smith)
6 rue de Mont-Louis
33/1 40-09-70-30

12TH ARRONDISSEMENT

WILL (William Pradeleix)
75 rue Crozatier
33/1-53-17-02-44

13TH ARRONDISSEMENT

L'AVANT-GOUT
(Christophe Beaufront)
26 rue Bobillot
33/1 53-80-24-00
lavantgout.com

L'OURCINE
(Sylvain Danière)
92 rue Broca
33/1 47-07-13-65
restaurant-lourcine.fr

14TH ARRONDISSEMENT

LA CANTINE DU TROQUET
(Christian Etchebest)
101 rue de l'Ouest
33/1 45-40-04-98

LA CERISAIE
(Cyril Lalanne)
70 boulevard Edgar-Quinet
33/1 43-20-98-98

LE CORNICHON
(Matthieu Nadjar)
34 rue Gassendi
33/1 43-20-40-19
lecornichon.fr

AUX ENFANTS GÂTÉS
(Frédéric Bidault)
4 rue Danville
33/1 40-47-56-81
auxenfantsgates.fr

LE JEU DE QUILLES
(Benoît Reix)
45 rue Boulard
33/1 53-90-76-22
jdequilles.fr

LA RÉGALADE
(Bruno Doucet)
14 avenue Jean-Moulin
33/1 45-45-68-58

15TH ARRONDISSEMENT

BEURRE NOISETTE
(Thierry Blanqui)
68 rue Vasco de Gama
33/1 48-56-82-49

LA CANTINE DU TROQUET DUPLEIX
(Christian Etchebest)
53 boulevard de Grenelle
33/1 45-75-98-00

LE CASSE NOIX
(Pierre-Olivier Lenormand)
56 rue de la Fédération
33/1 45-66-09-01
le-cassenoix.fr

L'ÉPICURISTE
(Sébastian Segurola)
41 boulevard Pasteur
33/1 47-34-15-50

LE GRAND PAN
(Benoît Gauthier)
20 rue Rosenwald
33/1 42-50-02-50
legrandpan.fr

JADIS (Guillaume Delage)
208 rue de la Croix Nivert
33/1 45-57-73-20
bistrotjadisparis.com

LE PARIO
(Eduardo Jacinto)
54 avenue Emile Zola
33/1 45-77-28-82
lepario.fr

17TH ARRONDISSEMENT

**LE BISTROT
D'À CÔTÉ FLAUBERT**
(Michel Rostang)
10 rue Gustave Flaubert
33/1 42-67-05-81
bistrotflaubert.com

CORETTA (Beatriz Gonzales)
151 bis rue Cardinet
33/1 42-26-55-55

GARE AU GORILLE
(Marc Cordonnier)
68 rue des Dames
33/1 42-94-24-02

18TH ARRONDISSEMENT

L'ATELIER RAMEY
(Nicolas Boissière)
23 rue Ramey
33/1 42-51-04-78

LE BAL CAFÉ
(Alice Quillet and
Anna Trattles)
16 impasse de la Défense
33/1 44-70-75-51
le-bal.com

LA CANTINE DE LA CIGALE
(Christian Etchebest)
124 rue de la Rochechouart
33/1 55-79-10-10

LA RALLONGE
(Marine Thomas)
16 rue Eugène Sue
33/1 42-59-43-24
larallonge.fr

19TH ARRONDISSEMENT

Ô DIVIN (Mathieu Moity)
35 rue des Annelets
33/1 40-40-79-41
odivin.fr

20TH ARRONDISSEMENT

CHATOMAT
(Alice Di Cagno and
Victor Gaillard)
6 rue Victor-Letalle
33/1 47-97-25-77

LES PÈRES POPULAIRES
(Elsa Marie)
46 rue de Buzenval
33/1 43-48-49-22

ROSEVAL (Simone Tondo)
1 rue d'Eupatoria
33/9 53-56-24-14

acknowledgments

PARIS

The chefs profiled here (and many more) let me hang out in their kitchens, disrupt meal service, and move tables and chairs around dining rooms. They also pulled cups of espresso for me, answered tedious questions, and handed over their kitchen notebooks. Fredrika Stjärne, *Food & Wine's* intensely curious and unstoppable creative director, used vacation time to meet me in Paris and tell the bistronomy story in pictures. Then she dedicated a long (fun) weekend in her upstate New York studio to photographing plated dishes. Photo assistant Romain Diani gamely hauled equipment up and down stairs, scrambled across rooftops, and in every other way freed Fredrika to shoot the perfect images. Thomas Nordanstad's groovy Marais apartment became our HQ, the rendezvous point for all photographic sorties. With the arrival of Sasha Stjärne, who dropped in one weekend from Berlin, we were a remarkably merry band.

Ever since I let my foreign-resident permit lapse, cousins Joshua Sigal and Howard Haskin have fed me, given me a bed, and made me feel Paris is still home. Over some three decades, Michael Saklad has cooked for me, introduced me to his favorite farmers and musicians, allowed me to take over his space, provided technical support, and plied me with reading material. Laurel Hirsch and Carmella Abramowitz Moreau ate with me, drank with me, and were essential interlocutors. Journalist, author, and mentor Patricia Wells taught me to go see firsthand, ask more questions, and to cut anything I didn't wholeheartedly believe in.

NEW YORK

My longtime Rizzoli editors Christopher Steighner and Sandy Gilbert Freidus came to me with the idea of a bistronomy cookbook, and Charles Miers, the publisher, greenlighted the project. Chris gave me extraordinary sway with the design; I got to pick the photographer, designer, and illustrator. And in the way of the best editors, he smartly, and delicately, shaped the project and the writing. Sales director Jennifer Pierson helped sell the book around the world.

At Fredrika's upstate New York studio, photo assistant Darrell Taunt consistently predicted whatever she needed (and told amusing stories). Food stylist Simon Andrews, who has a how-does-he-do-that flair for knowing what a camera lens sees, prepared the beautiful dishes for the studio shots. In the mornings, Tom Behrens sustained us with superb egg sandwiches and then, after-hours, with Pantagruelian cookouts and late-night bonfires. Max Behrens gave up his bed for me and amiably consented to having a perfectly nice August weekend hijacked by a food shoot.

Food & Wine style editor Suzie Myers graciously pulled together props, including the exquisite handmade plates and bowls from Humble Ceramics, vitrifiedstudio, Irving Place Studio, and Studio & Clam Lab. Also at *Food & Wine*, Dana Cowin, the editor in chief, is a supreme talent scout (Fredrika Stjärne! Courtney Eckersley!); executive food editor Tina Ujlaki first hired me in 1996; restaurant editor Kate Krader enthusiastically assigns me France stories; and executive editor Pamela Kaufman saves me from utter embarrassment as a writer.

Over the course of multiple cookbook projects, Karl Willers has submitted to my recipe tests and always arrives with a bottle of wine. Bill Lee is an unwavering friend and hiking confederate. Barbara Sigal was airport chauffeur and extremely patient.

JAMESTOWN, RHODE ISLAND, AND BEYOND

Designer Courtney Eckersley completely immersed herself in the content and seamlessly and imaginatively stitched together images and text. Cut-paper artist and BFF Jessica Palmer's silhouettes of herbs and root vegetables seem to defy their paper origins and come alive. Phenomenal baker Jane Carey did a final test on the tarts for me. Lee Rosenbaum guided me so I could move smoothly from one book project to the next. Jake Wien's questions about bistros inspired the two charts in the introductory chapter. Hank Sigal and Kerry Abbott are staunch supporters. Ken Newman is a dining companion of surpassing perspicaciousness.

index

(Page references in italics refer to illustrations.)

First published in the United States of America in 2015 by
Rizzoli International Publications, Inc.
300 Park Avenue South
New York, NY 10010
www.rizzoliusa.com

Photographs © 2015 Fredrika Stjärne

Illustrations © 2015 Jessica Palmer
www.jessicapalmerart.com

Project editor: Christopher Steighner

Designer: Courtney Eckersley

Food stylist: Simon Andrews

Photo assistants: Romain Diani, Darrel Taunt

Prop stylist: Suzie Myers

Copy editor: Monica Parcell

Proofreader: Ivy McFadden

Indexer: Cathy Dorsey

—

2015 2016 2017 2018 / 10 9 8 7 6 5 4 3 2 1

Distributed in the U.S. trade by Random House, New York
Printed in China

ISBN: 978-0-8478-4610-8
Library of Congress Control Number: 2015 9 35643

JANE SIGAL (left) lived in Paris for twelve years and earned a Grand Diplôme at L'École de Cuisine La Varenne. She's a contributing writer at *Food & Wine*, and her articles appear in such publications as *The New York Times, Saveur, The Wall Street Journal, Every Day with Rachael Ray,* and *Time Out New York.*

FREDRIKA STJÄRNE grew up in Sweden and began her career as a fine art photographer. She then moved to New York City to complete her Master of Fine Arts degree at the School of Visual Arts. Stjärne is now the creative director of *Food & Wine* magazine, where she formerly served as director of photography for fifteen years.

PATRICIA WELLS, for more than two decades the restaurant critic for the *International Herald Tribune,* is the author of the award-winning *Bistro Cooking,* as well as more than a dozen other books. She also runs a successful cooking school in both Paris and Provence.